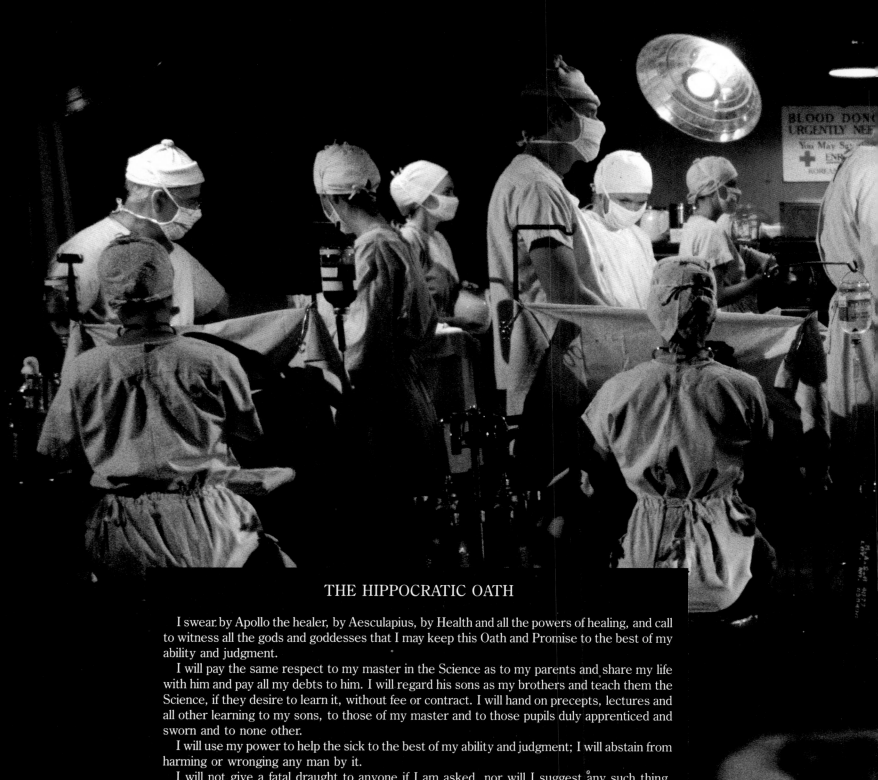

THE HIPPOCRATIC OATH

I swear by Apollo the healer, by Aesculapius, by Health and all the powers of healing, and call to witness all the gods and goddesses that I may keep this Oath and Promise to the best of my ability and judgment.

I will pay the same respect to my master in the Science as to my parents and share my life with him and pay all my debts to him. I will regard his sons as my brothers and teach them the Science, if they desire to learn it, without fee or contract. I will hand on precepts, lectures and all other learning to my sons, to those of my master and to those pupils duly apprenticed and sworn and to none other.

I will use my power to help the sick to the best of my ability and judgment; I will abstain from harming or wronging any man by it.

I will not give a fatal draught to anyone if I am asked, nor will I suggest any such thing. Neither will I give a woman means to procure an abortion.

I will be chaste and religious in my life and in my practice.

I will not cut, even for the stone, but I will leave such procedures to the practitioners of that craft.

Whenever I go into a house, I will go to help the sick and never with the intention of doing harm or injury. I will not abuse my position to indulge in sexual contacts with the bodies of men or of women, whether they be slaves or freemen.

Whatever I see or hear, professionally or privately, which ought not to be divulged, I will keep secret and tell no one.

If, therefore, I observe this Oath and do not violate it, may I prosper both in my life and in my profession earning good repute among all men for all time. If I transgress and forswear this Oath, may my lot be otherwise.

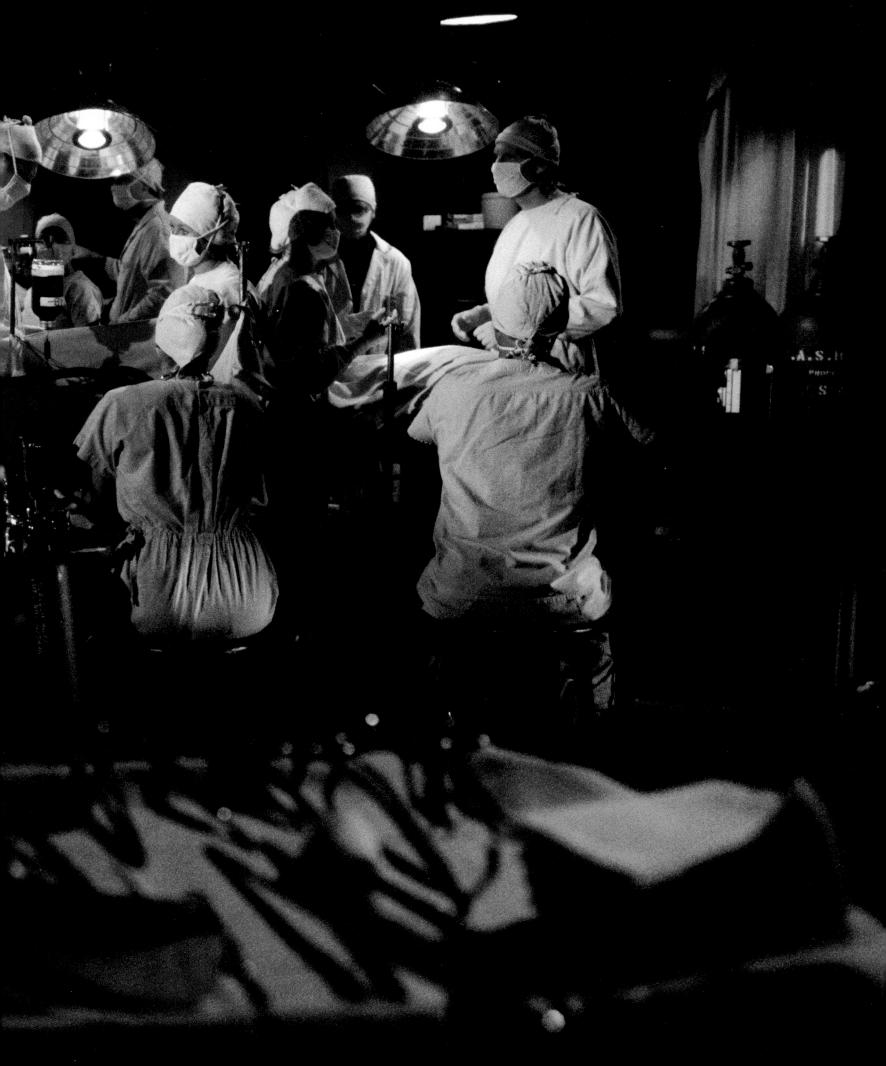

THE COMPLE

M*A*

INTRODUCTION BY
LARRY GELBART

OVER 110 COLOR PHOTOS

COLUMBUS
BOOKS

TE BOOK OF

S*H

BY SUZY KALTER

251 SHOWS DEPICTED

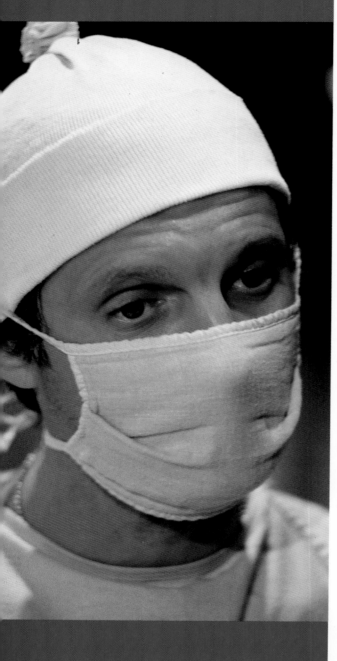

DEDICATION

To Dr. Leon Gray Berman and Dr. Seymour S. Kalter,
the Hawkeye and Hunnicutt of my childhood.

ACKNOWLEDGMENTS

Dear Dad,

You think war is hell? You should try reading 251 scripts and then rewriting them to make sense in only a couple of paragraphs. You've heard of meatball surgery? Well, I guess I've become a meatball author. I have to admit, Dad, that toward the end, a one-way ticket to the Laughing Academy in Tokyo didn't sound half bad.

I guess what really got me through it all were my cohorts—you never met a better bunch of guys. Larry Gelbart not only wrote the introduction but checked out the first four years worth of shows. I guess you could say he "closed" for me and watched over my shoulder. He even knew how to spell surreptitiously. Then there was Burt Metcalfe; I really came to appreciate him as the years whizzed by. He got a little antsy when I spelled his name wrong, but we worked it out. Not only was he *the* expert on Years Five through Eleven, but he diligently went over photographs to help identify them. Any other man would have put out the Do Not Disturb sign and gone to the Officers Club. No offense, Dad, but if a book could have parents, Gelbart would be this book's father and Metcalfe its godfather.

Of course, they're not the only ones who helped out, believe me. Michael Hirsh, the producer of *Making M*A*S*H* for PBS, lent me his transcripts, which proved invaluable; Michael Harris let me go through his files at the Smithsonian Institution; most of the cast members were gracious enough to go through the same old questions and answers one last time so that the material in this book could be a little more fresh (the Alan Alda and David Ogden Stiers material came from previous interviews); and former writers and producers likewise took time away from current projects to delve back into history.

Many other people helped sew this baby together, Dad, so I can't forget them either: Danny Simon, Emily Cole, Suzanne MacAfferty, Chuck Panama, Pat Miller, Dona Nicoloff, and especially Joe Lustig at Fox; and I certainly can't forget Colonel David Wagner from the Army's Public Information Office. Then there's Jim Calio at Time Inc.; Dr. Debra C. Kalter, my sister the doctor, who checked out the medical information; and Yvette Kalter—whose Lamme's pralines got me through the last four chapters of this book.

Well, Dad, I'm sure you think the acknowledgments must be ending now, but acknowledgments being what they are, I still have to thank my editor, Robert Morton; my friend and agent, Joan Stewart; and my wonderful husband, Michael Gershman, who truly fought his own Battle of Pork Chop Hill when I tackled this project. He deserves the Purple Heart, the Bronze Star, and the Red Badge of Courage.

Oh, yeah! There's one other thing, Dad. It's about the mistakes. There are bound to be a few in here, so I hope you won't think any the less of me. I could hold my own in a M*A*S*H trivia contest, I guess, but a few people may catch me on the inevitable slipups that do occur. But, hell, the patient won't die.

Well, I guess that about does it. Or am I supposed to thank you and Mom for sending me to Douglas MacArthur High School?

Goodbye, farewell, and thank you all.

Your loving daughter,
Suzy Kalter
8 March 1984

P.S. Larry—I stole your caduceuses wild joke....

AUTHOR'S NOTE

The stories in the Battle Notes sections of this book come directly from the scripts of the 251 episodes of M*A*S*H. The average script contained three story lines. In the interest of clarity and with the intent of conveying the meaning of each show rather than its total content, some story lines have been eliminated. The small amount of additional material that had to be created for the sake of style, clarification, or continuity was done by or with the permission of Larry Gelbart or Burt Metcalfe.

If you find any mistakes in the book, take two aspirin and call me in the morning.

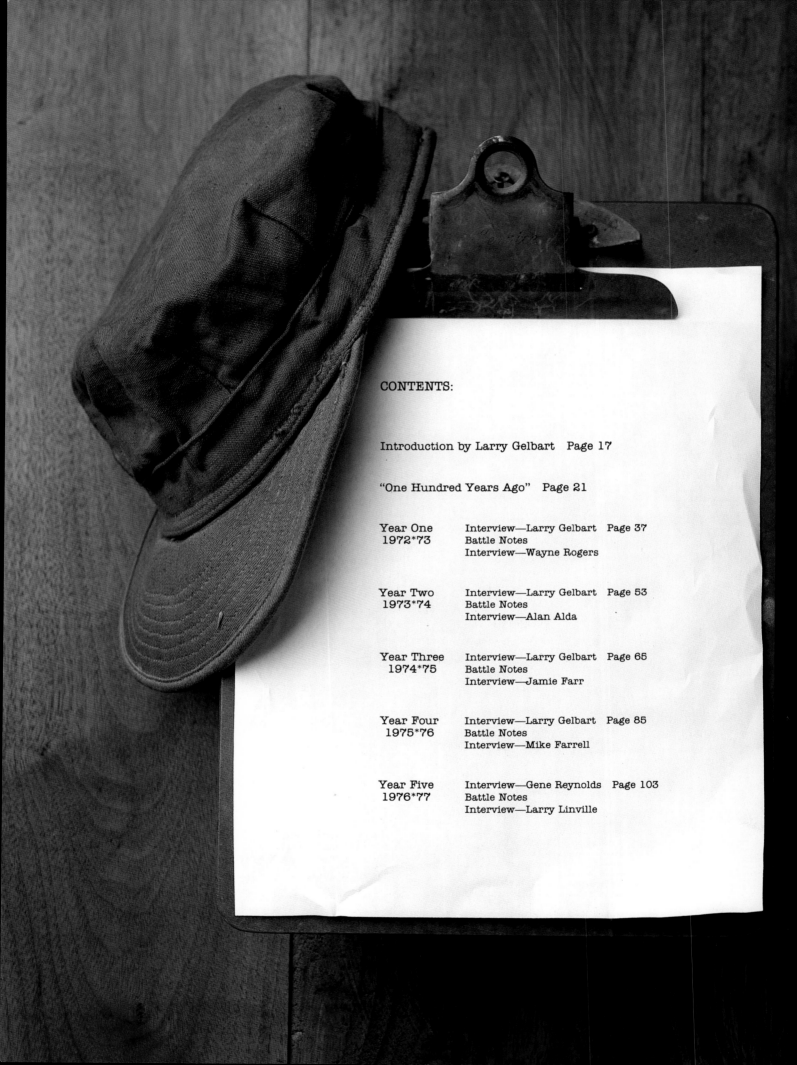

CONTENTS:

Introduction by Larry Gelbart   Page 17

"One Hundred Years Ago"   Page 21

Year One   Interview—Larry Gelbart   Page 37
1972*73   Battle Notes
                  Interview—Wayne Rogers

Year Two   Interview—Larry Gelbart   Page 53
1973*74   Battle Notes
                  Interview—Alan Alda

Year Three   Interview—Larry Gelbart   Page 65
1974*75   Battle Notes
                  Interview—Jamie Farr

Year Four   Interview—Larry Gelbart   Page 85
1975*76   Battle Notes
                  Interview—Mike Farrell

Year Five   Interview—Gene Reynolds   Page 103
1976*77   Battle Notes
                  Interview—Larry Linville

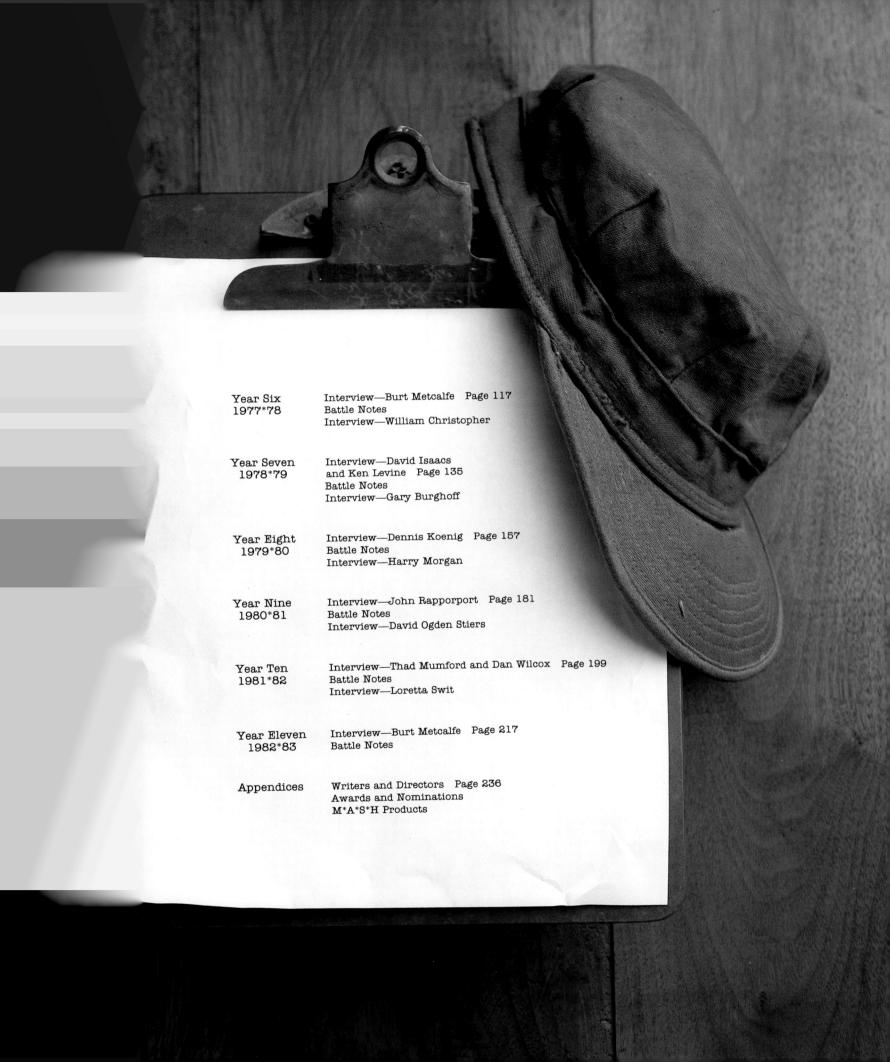

Year Six   Interview—Burt Metcalfe   Page 117
1977*78   Battle Notes
                 Interview—William Christopher

Year Seven   Interview—David Isaacs
1978*79   and Ken Levine   Page 135
                 Battle Notes
                 Interview—Gary Burghoff

Year Eight   Interview—Dennis Koenig   Page 157
1979*80   Battle Notes
                 Interview—Harry Morgan

Year Nine   Interview—John Rapporport   Page 181
1980*81   Battle Notes
                 Interview—David Ogden Stiers

Year Ten   Interview—Thad Mumford and Dan Wilcox   Page 199
1981*82   Battle Notes
                 Interview—Loretta Swit

Year Eleven   Interview—Burt Metcalfe   Page 217
1982*83   Battle Notes

Appendices   Writers and Directors   Page 236
                 Awards and Nominations
                 M*A*S*H Products

INTRODUCTION BY LARRY GELBART

FADE IN:
INTERIOR: A DOCTOR'S OFFICE—DAY
A psychiatrist, SIDNEY FREEDMAN, MD, admits LARRY GELBART on an initial
visit.

                    FREEDMAN
          Please lie down on the couch.

                    GELBART
          I don't usually do this on a first date.
                    (complying, looking up)
          There's a mirror on the ceiling.

                    FREEDMAN
          I treat a lot of actors.

                    GELBART
          I'm a writer.

                    FREEDMAN
          Of comedy?

                    GELBART
          Drama. I can't help it if people laugh at it.

                    FREEDMAN
          And that's your problem?

                    GELBART
          M*A*S*H is my problem.

                    FREEDMAN
          How'd you do that?

                    GELBART
          What?

                    FREEDMAN
          Speak in asterisks.

                    GELBART
          Comes from doing the series too long.

                    FREEDMAN
          "Doing" it?

                    GELBART
          Writing it, mostly. Stories, scripts, creating charac-
          ters. I invented you.

                    FREEDMAN
                    (suppressing a smile)
          Oh, really?

                    GELBART
          Sidney Freedman, the psychiatrist. You're a Sigmund
          of my imagination.

                    FREEDMAN
          You actually believe that?

                    GELBART
          All I have to do is backspace and you're out of this
          scene.

                    FREEDMAN
          Please continue.

GELBART

I've been away from the series for eight years. It's
been off the network for two seasons. And I'm still
working on it! Still rewriting it in my head; sharpen-
ing speeches; cutting dialogue; making fixes no one
knows and not anyone needs.

FREEDMAN

Why are you doing it?

GELBART

I was always compulsive about the series. Wanted it
just right, just so. When I was on the set, I'd bite loose
threads off the actors' costumes. Sometimes I'd bite
loose actors. I was rabid on the subject.

FREEDMAN

But, surely, now that the series has finished...

GELBART

Finished? With reruns? Now that it's off, it's on more
than ever! It's everywhere! On film, on tape, on T-
shirts. It's a beer. It's a vodka. Who knew we were doing a show that people would see and hear and wear
and drink?

FREEDMAN

Shouldn't that be a source of pride instead of pain?

GELBART

The pride is in what we did. The pain comes from no
longer being who we were when we did it. Maybe
that's why I keep doing my phantom rewrites so that
I can keep alive some part of the past that we—Gene,
Burt, the cast, and crew—shared together. That wonderful time when we were innocents, not an institution; when we were blissfully ignorant, yet to become
icons.

FREEDMAN

Very perceptive. And alliterative, as always.

GELBART

You try to give pain a certain style.
            (pause)
Maybe that's what the series was all about...

FREEDMAN

You're smiling.

GELBART

I've been searching for a definition of what M*A*S*H,
excuse me, MASH, was all about for a long time. I may
have just stumbled on it! Makes me happy.

FREEDMAN

A psychiatrist doesn't see a lot of happy people.

GELBART

Happy people don't pay the rent.

FREEDMAN
            (surprised)
I always say that.

GELBART

I gave myself the speech instead of you.

                         FREEDMAN
                         (amused)
You still think you're in charge here?

                         GELBART
Except for the book that follows this introduction.

                         FREEDMAN
What are you talking about?

                         GELBART
The part that follows us. It starts on the next page.

                         FREEDMAN
My dear fellow, we're in an office, not a book.

                         GELBART
Really? Watch this...

                                                    DISSOLVE TO:

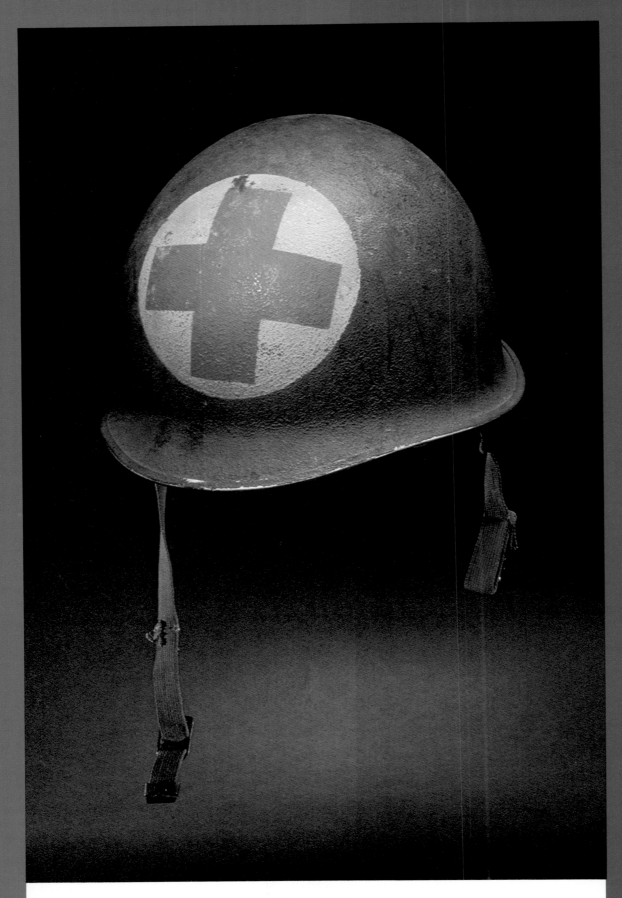

Korea, 1950

Photographer David Douglas Duncan to soldier: "If I were God and could give you anything you wanted, what would you ask for?"

Soldier: "Gimme tomorrow."

A film frame from the show's title credits

It was not even a war. The Korean "police action" began in June, 1950, and ended almost exactly three years later. It cost the United States 142,091 casualties, created three million Korean refugees, and spawned one of the most popular television series in American history, M*A*S*H — the tragi-comic story of doctors at war in a Mobile Army Surgical Hospital three miles from the front lines.

Hawkeye—I happen to be an officer only because I foolishly opened an invitation from President Truman to come to this costume party. As for my ability as a doctor, if you honestly question that, I'm afraid I'll have to challenge you to a duel...specimen bottles at 20 paces.

Based on the best-selling novel of the same title by Richard Hooker and the subsequent Twentieth Century–Fox movie (Hollywood added the asterisks), M*A*S*H played down the high jinks and hilarity of the original vehicles and strode into the minefields of commercial television, dealing with topics rarely seen on television at all and less frequently mentioned on what was supposed to be a situational comedy. While *All in the Family* and even *The Mary Tyler Moore Show* had pioneered the move on TV away from brainless comedy and dealt occasionally with fairly controversial issues, M*A*S*H became famous for its ability to deliver a laugh and a cry in the same show, all the while convincing its audience that General William Tecumseh Sherman was right all along: "War is hell."

"M*A*S*H was about people under stress, people standing around in other people's blood and guts, hating being there. We had a seriousness of purpose but we enjoyed the craziness," said Alan Alda, who played the lead crazy, Dr. Benjamin Franklin ("Hawkeye") Pierce.

"M*A*S*H was about helping people," said Harry Morgan, who played Colonel Sherman Potter, the second commanding officer to head up the fictional 4077 Mobile Army Surgical Hospital.

"M*A*S*H was about grace under pressure," said Larry Gelbart, who created the series and wrote the pilot based on the book and movie.

"The villain was senseless violence, and the hero was the resiliency of the human spirit," wrote one television reviewer.

Hawkeye—I don't know why they're shooting at us. All we want to do is bring them democracy and white bread, to transplant the American dream: freedom, achievement, hyperacidity, affluence, flatulence, technology, tension, the inalienable right to an early coronary at your desk while plotting to stab your boss in the back.

If they didn't quite know what the show was about—they didn't care. More than thirty million Americans tuned in once a week, many with Kleenex boxes in hand. In their hearts, they, too, were antiwar, anti-Vietnam, antimilitary, antibureaucracy, antispit and polish, and anything but antipathetic.

Hawkeye was their hero.

21

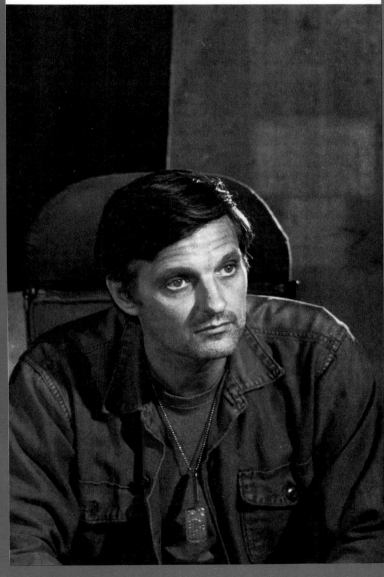

Alan Alda as Hawkeye Pierce

Opposite: A prop helmet now in the Smithsonian Institution

"ONE HUNDRED YEARS AGO"

Originated by a man who happened to be a Republican and who believed in the appropriateness of the Korean War, M*A*S*H became the antithesis of everything Dr. Richard Hornberger (author "Richard Hooker") stood for. "I think we should have been in Korea," he said recently. "If you're going to start a war, you might as well play to win. No one in his right mind would be pro-war—but I operated on a thousand or so wounded kids, and I know more about war than a bunch of undereducated actors who go around blithering those sanctimonious, self-righteous noises."

"I was not part of the Vietnam antiwar movement in the United States because I lived in England," Larry Gelbart explained, "so M*A*S*H was the contribution I know I would have made if I had been able."

"There was no question about it," producer Gene Reynolds ventured. "We were literally in Korea but figuratively in Vietnam."

By 1972, with Vietnam in the news every evening, CBS Television brought viewers back to 1950. A mere twenty-two years old, the Korean War felt like it was a hundred years ago and yet had only just happened yesterday. Americans responded accordingly. They already knew war was hell.

When General Sherman first said those words, there were no Mobile Army Surgical Hospitals (MASH). The ambulance was first used in the Civil War: the wounded were taken to field hospitals—local hospitals that were converted for war use—or to makeshift facilities. Soldiers with anything more serious than superficial wounds often bled to death before they received medical care. Many of those who survived nevertheless lost limbs that might have been saved, even though surgical techniques were far from modern, and miracle drugs were yet to be invented. The boys in blue and gray just didn't get enough help in time for it to matter.

By World War II, more surgeons were operating closer to the front. Battle deaths were cut tremendously. In the war's later years, helicopters—rather newly developed—evacuated some wounded to field hospitals, but the bulk of the work was still done by ambulances made up of Jeeps fitted out with stretchers or reconditioned buses. By the time of the Korean conflict, helicopters were used to evacuate a larger percentage of the wounded; in Vietnam, choppers would provide practically all the short hop transportation. After three years at war in Korea, choppers flew some seventeen thousand wounded into one of five MASH units that were located in the battle zones or to more permanent evacuation hospitals in cities held by American or United Nations troops. Countless other wounded were airlifted in obsolete torpedo bombers (TBMs) that were fitted out to carry six to nine wounded and could land in tight spaces or on the war's flying workhorse, an R–4D transport plane that had limited abilities to pick up wounded because it needed an airstrip on which to land.

Upon arrival at a MASH, a patient's first six hours determined his survival possibilities. If he was stable after twenty-four hours, his chances of survival were greatest. On average, the MASH units saved the lives of more than ninety-five percent of their patients. After sufficient recovery in a mobile hospital, patients were shuttled to an evac hospital, usually by ambulance, and were then sent by bus or train (a regular train for wounded ran from Pusan to Seoul) to an airfield and flown to Tokyo or Okinawa for further treatment.

"I would say that M*A*S*H is about a group of people trying to hold their sanity together while they are doing meatball surgery," said Loretta Swit, who played Major Margaret ("Hot Lips") Houlihan, chief nurse at the 4077. "Meatball surgery is immediate surgery—patch them together and keep them alive as best you can." Psychiatrist Sidney Freedman, a character in the series played by Allan Arbus, defined what the surgeons were doing as "fix 'em up, close 'em up, and holler next!"

There were 910 reserve doctors and 686 dentists stationed in Korea during the "conflict." Most doctors who served in MASH units were young, averaging twenty-five to twenty-eight years. Most were drafted after completing an internship or during a residency or were members of reserve units that were activated or were serving out a prior commitment to Uncle Sam, who had granted them deferments to finish medical school. A few were in private practice; a few were regular Army. Like their television counterparts, most were ordinary guys who merely woke up one day and found themselves on their way to a nightmare.

Hawkeye—Okay, Major, honey. I'm going to have a couple shots of Scotch and go to bed. I'd normally ask you to join me but obviously you're a female version of the regular Army clown. That turns me off.

Hot Lips—I wonder how a degenerated person like that could have reached a position of responsibility in the Army Medical Corps.

Father Mulcahy—He was drafted.

While some World War II surgeons also served in Korea or Japan, most of the doctors in Korean aid stations on the front lines or in the MASH units were too young to have served in the earlier war. Likewise, few Korean War veterans became "cutters" (surgeons) in Vietnam, leaving that job to another generation of doctors who never knew that Korea had just been the dress rehearsal.

A real MASH unit consisted of a group of tents and Quonset huts connected by canvas-covered walkways that protected the patients and the personnel from weather and flying debris. The 8055, on which the fictional 4077 was based, housed two hundred beds, ten doctors, and twelve nurses; the 8076 had a total staff of

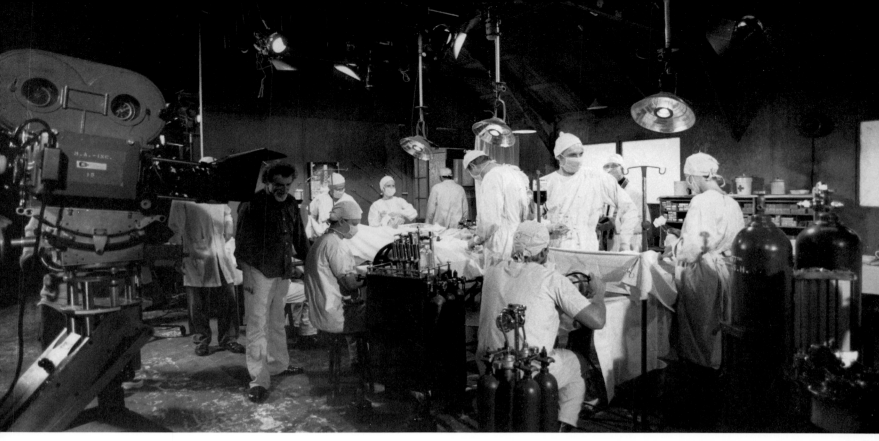

The OR set on Stage 9 at Twentieth Century-Fox

248. (The television version was comprised of forty people, including background actors—extras.) Created as a hospital on wheels, hence the name, a real MASH unit was constantly on the move; one unit in Korea "bugged out" (decamped) a total of thirty-three times.

Doctors regularly worked on eight-hour to twelve-hour shifts in the operating room (OR); during a "deluge," a period of heavy casualties, eighteen-hour to twenty-four-hour stints were not unusual; and sometimes more was required. As interns and residents, these young doctors were used to long hours, but doctors in Vietnam reported working sixty hours straight during the Tet Offensive, with only occasional one-hour breaks. During a deluge, doctors were fed orange juice and coffee while they operated; nurses were often required to help with more personal functions while surgery continued nonstop. It was not unusual for a doctor to show signs of extreme stress from the demands of a MASH unit and be rotated out after only three months of active duty.

Because of medical advances after World War II, technology changed rapidly during the early 1950s. Lecturers made the rounds of the five MASH units to demonstrate new methodology; medical conclaves were held frequently in Tokyo and Seoul; and the 38th Parallel Medical Society organized itself to meet regularly to exchange notes and play poker. Not everyone could join this elite group—you had to earn your way in through intellectual, surgical, or alcoholic prowess.

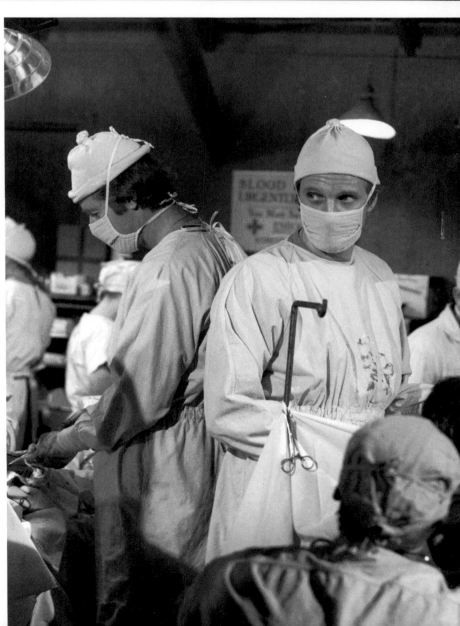

BEST CARE ANYWHERE/
MEDICINE ON TELEVISION:
WAR ON TELEVISION

Before it aired, M*A*S*H was considered by some to be just another gimmick to pair up two already popular television features—doctors and wars. Neither the public nor the network was prepared for high quality entertainment that also dealt with serious subjects.

Medicine came to television early on and has remained a fixture in both comedy and drama. *Ben Casey* and *Dr. Kildare* highlighted the trend in the early 1960s, followed by *Marcus Welby, M.D.* and *Medical Center* in the 1970s. Later, Danny Thomas played a pediatrician in a short-lived comedy, *Doc*, while Bob Newhart became America's best loved shrink. While *Quincy*, the medical examiner with a nose for controversy who probably owed his existence to the success of M*A*S*H, offered up a slightly new character twist on the doctors-as-gods theory, it was M*A*S*H that first presented the notion that doctors were real human beings.

War also had been a regular feature on television. When M*A*S*H aired, war was available in sitcoms (*McHale's Navy* and *F-Troop*), on old movies, and in the evening news with reportage from Vietnam. M*A*S*H was the only medical/war television show that merged these two dramatic elements with comedy in a thoughtful formula. Americans had seen soldiers at work and at war on *Sgt. Bilko, Hogan's Heroes,* and *McHale's Navy*, where the object seemed to be to take the military for all it was worth, to gain privilege for oneself and one's friends through sneaky means, or to pull pranks on the enemy or superior officers. Only after M*A*S*H became successful did television executives think that serious might be combined with funny.

PAGING DR. HOOKER

Dr. Richard Hornberger wrote his fictional account of his years at the 8055 MASH in Korea under the pseudonym Richard Hooker. The book was rejected by seventeen publishers before William Morrow Publishers Inc. took it on. They paid a small advance for the book and were as surprised as anyone when it became a big-time movie success, which spawned more book sales. Dr. Hornberger wrote MASH and two sequels while waiting for patients at his Bremen, Maine, offices, where he specialized in thoracic surgery. (He has since retired from the Mid–Maine Medical Centre in Waterville, Maine.) His manuscript was polished by W. C. Heinz, a sportswriter turned novelist who became Dr. Hornberger's equal partner. Each man has since realized approximately $250,000 in additional revenues from the success of the television series or, as Dr. Hornberger puts it, "one gallbladder a week." While he

Opposite (above and below) and above:
Props and equipment from the M*A*S*H sets,
as displayed in the National Museum of American History
at the Smithsonian Institution in Washington, D.C.

never became rich from M*A*S*H-mania, Dr. Hornberger was not ungrateful for the $500 he received each time an original episode aired. When M*A*S*H went off the air, he wryly remarked that he wouldn't miss the show, but he would miss the money. (He receives less for reruns.)

Dr. Hornberger considered himself the real Benjamin Franklin Pierce. He was 26 when he was drafted during a surgical internship and really was from Crabapple Cove. He did not like Alan Alda's interpretation of himself and maintained that he was a shy kind of guy, not a big womanizer. His book revolved around the antics of three surgeons, "Hawkeye" Pierce, "Trapper" John McIntyre, and a Southern gentleman doctor named Duke Forrest from Forrest City, Georgia. The plot of the book and the subsequent movie (which "Horny" liked so much that he saw it seven times) lacked the depth that M*A*S*H later became famous for. Instead, they played it for laughs. The high jinks included a fake suicide by the camp's dentist; emergency surgery performed on a congressman's son by doctors who really wanted to be playing golf; and a $5,000 football game between the 4077's Red Raiders and the 325th Evac's Rams. Only the movie blood in the OR showed the serious side of things.

One subplot of the book was Hawkeye's decision to try to get his Korean houseboy admitted into his former medical school. This story line became the basis of the TV episode pilot. Gelbart then created sufficient original material to make the pilot totally fresh while still continuing a strong memory of its ancestors.

Trapper—Look, lady. I want to go to work in one hour...and we figure to crack that kid's chest and get out on the golf course before it's dark. So find the gas passer and tell him to premedicate the patient...and give me at least one nurse who knows how to work in close without getting her tits in my way.

M*A*S*H THE MOVIE

The movie rights to Dr. Hornberger's book were bought for about $100,000 by Ingo Preminger, director Otto Preminger's brother, and a screenplay was written by the formerly blacklisted Ring Lardner Jr., who had every reason in the world to be antigovernment and antiestablishment. Fifteen directors turned the script down, although it later received an Oscar as Best Screenplay of the year. (The film was also nominated for Best Movie.) Robert Altman finally directed for the relatively small sum of $25,000; it was a low budget film.

"The television version of M*A*S*H is the most insidious kind of propaganda," said Altman. "I think it's terrible. It says—no matter what platitudes they use—that the guys with the slanted eyes are the bad guys. They don't show the blood, the horror. They don't make you pay for the laugh. It's only done for commercial reasons.

That isn't the reason I did the movie; it isn't the reason the artists involved did it. There was a point to be made, and we made it."

The movie was made and released within two years of the book's publication—a short interval in moviedom—with the hills of southern California serving as the ridges of South Korea. It was released in the fall of 1970 when anti-Vietnam sentiment was high, and it was one of the first 1970s-style blockbusters that attracted repeat viewers. The film earned $36 million at the box office and was seen by approximately fourteen million people.

M*A*S*H FOR TELEVISION

It was William Self, then president of Twentieth Century–Fox Studios, who wanted to turn the movie into a television series even while those around him were skeptical. Because the movie set was still standing, Self knew that the cost of a series would be relatively inexpensive. Fox already owned the rights; there was little to lose. Both ABC and CBS were interested in the concept but wanted to be convinced. Said Self, "Fred Silverman (then head of programming at CBS) had a lot of reservations about a project based on a movie that dealt almost entirely in nudity, profanity, blood, and sex. I thought it would be a good television show because the characters, the story, and the basic situation were all strong." CBS committed to a pilot show before the script was ordered, an unusual step in series making, and as a result beat out ABC for the millions that were to come. The pressure was put on Self to make his dream come true.

Father Mulcahy—Everyone shows their anxieties in different ways, Colonel. But to refuse to eat, to shun the necessities of life...

Potter—It's not the anxiety, Father. It's the pimento loaf.

Self hired Fox contract producer Gene Reynolds to produce M*A*S*H. Reynolds, whose credits included *The Ghost and Mrs. Muir* and who subsequently created *Lou Grant,* had just been fired by ABC as producer of *Room 222* because "the recent episodes hadn't been funny enough," according to Reynolds. He and Self flew to London to meet with Larry Gelbart, a friend and former colleague of Reynolds', who had said he would like to work with Reynolds on the right project.

Gelbart was a hotshot comedy writer who began his career writing gags for Danny Thomas while still in high school. He had been a joke writer for Bob Hope—he actually visited Korea with the star in 1951—and was one of the writers of the famed *Caesar's Hour.* He won a Tony Award for co-writing the Broadway musical hit *A Funny Thing Happened on the Way to the Forum* and then moved to London. He was producing a comedy television show with the British actor Marty Feldman and had already seen, and enjoyed, the movie version of M*A*S*H. He was sent the book and the Lardner screenplay and then spent a week or two working nights with Reynolds and Self to create the basic characters and story line for the pilot. They decided immediately to eliminate one of the three leads—thus, Duke Forrest bit the dust—and to expand the role of Frank Burns. Six weeks later, Reynolds called Gelbart from California to see how the pilot script was coming along.

"I just mailed it," Gelbart assured Reynolds. Then he sat down to write it. He dictated for two days—he normally writes in longhand—then shipped the script to Hollywood. He was paid $25,000, the going rate in those days for a pilot by a top-notch writer like Gelbart. (Today's price is $50,000 to $100,000 for a top writer, though Gelbart earns more.) His pilot script, delivered in November, 1971, was slightly different from the one that aired in the fall of 1972. In it, Hawkeye was portrayed as married but having a girlfriend at the MASH unit named Lieutenant Dish, a character from the movie who was also married. But Frank Burns, also a married man, and Hot Lips Houlihan were having an affair, as they had in the movie, so the network nixed Hawkeye's situation with a note that it was a show about doctors, not adultery. Thus, while Lieutenant Dish appears in the pilot, though as a single woman, she soon disappeared.

With the pilot script in hand, Reynolds hired his friend, Burt Metcalfe, as associate producer and casting director. A former actor, Metcalfe was a casting director at another studio but was unhappy enough to take the gamble of leaving a steady job. The basic characters had been decided in London and were cast in Los Angeles by Metcalfe. During the first year, there were several character and casting changes as Reynolds and Gelbart shook down the show. (For example, the actor who played Father Mulcahy, George Morgan, was replaced after the pilot; several other characters had to be eliminated because there were too many people in the OR; and Corporal Klinger was invented as a one-shot character and became a regular.)

The first actor cast was Gary Burghoff, who had played "Radar" O'Reilly in the movie. No other actors from the movie were approached; Reynolds thought they were too well known even to consider his invitation seriously. So Metcalfe put out the word around town that he was looking for two leading men to play Hawkeye and Trapper—what's known in the industry as an "extensive search." Approximately seventy-five actors read for the parts, which were considered of equal importance at that time, almost interchangeable.

Metcalfe tested six men for the part of Trapper and ultimately cast Wayne Rogers with CBS's approval. It was then thought that Trapper would be the lead character, as he had been in the film. Rogers was then a fairly well-known actor who had been a star of the soap opera *The Edge of Night.* McLean Stevenson was suggested for the role of Colonel Henry Braymore Blake by CBS. Stevenson actually wanted the Hawkeye role but was

eventually persuaded to play Henry. Larry Linville and Loretta Swit were quickly cast in their roles because Metcalfe remembered them from other performances on stage and television.

About four weeks before the pilot was to be shot, Alan Alda's agent, Mickey Freiberg, approached Reynolds and Metcalfe on behalf of Alda, whom he felt might be interested in a series although he lived in New Jersey and would have to commute. Alda was a well-known New York stage actor who had done several made-for-television movies. Alda's friends suggested that he not do the show since there was much discussion around the business that there was no way to make a TV version of M*A*S*H successful and that, therefore, anyone involved in it would be hurt. Additionally, Alda was reluctant to commit to a show that, in his opinion, could run as long as five years, but his wife asked him to give it careful consideration. He loved the pilot script and agreed to meet with Gelbart and Reynolds to discuss the show but only after he finished work on a movie-for-television, *The Glass House,* which happened to be the day before M*A*S*H rehearsals were to begin. The producers had a dilemma.

Had Alda not agreed to do the show, the part would have to be cast in less than twenty-four hours. Though they had seen many actors in the search, there was not a list of names ready because they were optimistic about bagging Alda. Burt Metcalfe remained confident that if he had needed another actor the next day to play Hawkeye, he would have found one. "Those things have a way of getting cast, God knows," he said. "But it might have been a very ordinary show with another actor. We'll never know."

Soldier—I hear you guys are terrific doctors but you don't exactly go by the book.

B. J.—Sure we do.

Hawkeye—But our book has pictures of naked people playing volleyball.

Gelbart moved back to the United States a week before production began and was on hand for final rewrites of the pilot script. He rode his bicycle back and forth between Stage 9, where much filming took place, and his office in the old Writers Building—a few hundred yards away—as he polished and refined lines. The pilot was shot partially on the same outdoor set as the movie and at the Fox studios in Beverly Hills, where it remained all eleven years. It cost approximately $250,000—about one-third the cost of a half-hour pilot today. The actors were relatively inexpensive; the bigger names received about $10,000 for the pilot appearance, and the others earned half that. By the last years of production, a typical half-hour episode cost about $600,000 to produce, and Alan Alda's salary (approximately $235,000 per show) soared to more than five million dollars a year—paid partially by CBS.

The original cast. *From left:* Loretta Swit, Alan Alda, Wayne Rogers, McLean Stevenson, Larry Linville, Gary Burghoff

THE MAKING OF M*A*S*H

The pilot went on the air as the first show in the series in September, 1972. (Pilots are often broadcast separately in the spring; ratings and viewer reaction determine if the show will become a series in the fall.) *Time* magazine labeled it one of the biggest disappointments of the 1972–73 television season. The Nielsen ratings ranked it forty-sixth out of eighty-four shows; it was not what you'd call a smash hit. The rumor around Stage 9 was that as long as the show broke above 50, Silverman would keep it on the air. Originally, thirteen half-hour episodes were created, then nine more. At the end of the year, the CBS network asked for an additional two shows, and everyone breathed a sigh of relief—the extra order made them believe they would be "picked up" the following year.

From its inception, M*A*S*H was meant to be different. It was the only filmed television show with a rehearsal day. (Traditional sitcoms are done on a soundstage; the cast and crew have four days to prepare and then shoot the episode on videotape in one long day, often in front of an audience.) Reynolds wanted the show to "look classy," so he insisted on film rather than tape and the use of outdoor as well as indoor locations. He also wanted helicopters, trucks, ambulances, and other equipment that were difficult to manage on a soundstage; hence, the cast and crew had to use the old Fox Ranch for exteriors. Even before Alan Alda joined the show, making his now-famous remark that the show must not become *Abbott & Costello Go to War*, Reynolds and Gelbart were working to make it something quite out of the ordinary. They never considered *Abbott & Costello* in the first place.

PA announcement—Hear ye, hear ye. It's oh-seven-hundred and all is hell. Incoming wounded, folks.

As on most series television shows, the shooting schedule for M*A*S*H was a grueling twelve hours to fourteen hours a day; a half-hour show was meant to be completed in three or four days. Working conditions were difficult, with bad weather at the Fox Ranch, inadequate dressing rooms, insufficient toilets, and bad coffee. Fatigue was one of the biggest enemies of cast and crew; Loretta Swit took to wearing support hose for extra strength and, in later years of the show, stopped wearing her heavy combat boots when they wouldn't show in a take. (She wore sneakers.) Complete shows and parts of episodes had to be filmed out of sequence for scheduling reasons based on the availability of Fox Ranch because Twentieth Century–Fox had given the property to the State of California, which renamed it Malibu Canyon Creek State Park. The site was not, therefore, completely at the producers' disposal.

All the while, the network censors were watching.

"The network was not anti about our being antiwar. They were antiheavy and antiserious," Larry Gelbart says. "Most of our battles with them stemmed from the fact that we wanted to veer so far from what was considered half-hour comedy. They called us up periodically to have it out with us. While the cast and crew were out at the Fox Ranch fighting the elements, Gene and I fought two of the most unnatural forces in the world—the network and the studio—for the right to deal with bolder and more serious subjects than they were inclined to allow, like the effects of violence, adultery, amputation, derangement, impotence, homosexuality, transvestism, and interracial marriage. Most of the battles with Army brass on the screen came out of our battles with the network."

Reynolds remembers specifically that censors refused to allow Radar to use the word "breasts." Gelbart was told to take the word "virgin" out of dialogue. "I got it back the next week," a triumphant Gelbart reports. "I introduced a soldier who was from the Virgin Islands." Reynolds also tells about the only story rejected by the CBS network. It was written by Stanley Ralph Ross and dealt with Hawkeye having two love affairs with two different nurses, each on a different shift. They discover his duplicity and then set him up by simultaneously announcing that they are pregnant. "The network said that it implied dalliance and we couldn't do that. What were Frank and Hot Lips doing?" he asks facetiously. "Chewing on each other's epaulets?"

Gelbart often made good use of the real news for story ideas. The show *Cease-Fire* aired the week of the Vietnam cease-fire. A show about "friendly fire" (*For the Good of the Outfit*) brought tremendous network criticism but was proved a bitter reality on the evening news and later was explored in a best-selling book entitled *Friendly Fire*. The breakthrough show for M*A*S*H aired midway in the first season. It was *Sometimes You Hear the Bullet*, in which a friend of Hawkeye's dies on the operating table, and it was criticized for being too serious. Before it ran, the average M*A*S*H episode dealt with minor, humorous matters—Frank panning for gold (*Major Fred C. Dobbs*) or Hawkeye sharing a pair of his long johns (*The Long John Flap*). The network not only told Reynolds that he would lose viewers if he continued with programming like *Sometimes You Hear the Bullet* but sent a henchman to talk to him over lunch, who said, "Someday I'll tell you guys how you screwed up M*A*S*H."

CBS was a stickler for correct medical information, so a medical adviser was used; Dr. Walter Dishell was consulted before a script was written, he checked dialogue and medical procedures, and he kept tabs on OR scenes. (Dr. Dishell and Alda even wrote one episode together.) Before M*A*S*H aired, the network made it clear that they did not want any gory operating room scenes, lest they offend viewers. "It didn't turn off fourteen million people who saw the movie," marvels Reynolds, who advised Gelbart that the OR was OK in moderation.

Hawkeye—I always feel very patriotic after OR. My whites are covered with red and it gives me the blues.

At the Fox Ranch during the filming of *The Sniper*

A sound engineer at work

Opposite: A view of the Stage 9 sets from the catwalk

PAGING DR. SMITH

About sixty percent of the M*A*S*H story lines came directly from research; the stories that were fictional usually grew out of the writing team's explorations of how the characters would react emotionally in certain situations. The first year's shows were created from general research done by Larry Gelbart. He worked with photocopies of pages of the 1950 editions of *Time* magazine and filled four black notebooks with notes of story ideas. A show like *Major Fred C. Dobbs*, one of the worst ever, grew from a tidbit Gelbart found in his *World Almanac* that named Korea as the fifth-largest gold-producing country in the world. Hardly earth-shattering news or relevant to the war.

Since the network didn't want anything very serious, Gelbart was under reverse pressure. He was forced to tone down his own ideas about what would make a good story in order to offer up what would be acceptable to the network for a first year show that did not have very good ratings. While there were some important shows in the first-season, there was a lot more skirt chasing, drinking, and old-fashioned sitcom antics than are generally associated with the program. Mostly, Trapper played Ethel to Hawkeye's Lucy.

Gelbart began to interview a few real MASH doctors during the first season but did not know that doctors could provide so much usable information until after he and Reynolds actually went to Korea in 1974. The resulting improved story lines reflect both the research and his own growing sophistication. In addition, of course, once it became a hit show—which it did almost immediately in its second season—M*A*S*H carried enough clout to keep the network shopkeepers at bay.

After Gelbart left the show—he claimed he was wrung out of story ideas after having written 97 episodes, the equivalent of twenty-five full-length feature films— Reynolds carried the story banner and continued the research with Korean and then Vietnam veterans. Along the way, Metcalfe moved up to co-producer and then full producer when Reynolds left after the fifth season. One of Metcalfe's tasks was to give approval on story lines, since he was the only person who had been with the show since its inception and could remember what had and had not been done. There was never any written record of story lines. Nevertheless, there were very few mistakes. In 251 episodes—almost 750 stories—a joke was only repeated once. In both *War Co-Respondent* and *That's Show Biz, Part 1*, a woman arrives at the 4077 and is greeted with the remark, "When did this line start using stewardesses?" The same story was repeat-

Above and below: Filming at the Fox Ranch

ed once (*Preventative Medicine* and *White Gold*) but was unwittingly changed by Mike Farrell so that the later version bears little resemblance to its ancestor. There were some minor errors with names: Father John Francis Patrick Mulcahy gets postcards from his sister addressed to Francis but admits that his mother calls him Johnny; Dr. Sidney Freedman began life as Robert Freedman and had a name change in his next appearance. Errors in history happened a little more frequently, but not often, since there was no definite time period to the show. (Throughout the eleven years of M*A*S*H, General Douglas MacArthur was never replaced.) But small details escaped Metcalfe or Dr. Dishell: a drug called Levophed is used casually in a story in Year Eight but its first use in medicine forms the major story line of a show in Year Ten (*Birthday Girls*); Hawkeye signs off one letter sending love to Mom but in a later show (*Sons and Bowlers*) gives a poignant speech about how she died when he was ten.

Hawkeye—I can take umbrage, I can take the cake, I can take the A-train. I can take two and call me in the morning, but I cannot take this sitting down.

Metcalfe estimates that he spoke to some two hundred and fifty different doctors, nurses, chopper pilots, and orderlies in his never-ending quest for good material. He knew he was coming to the end of the series when a new interviewee would tell him a story he had heard before. Fans often sent in their own tales, both real and imagined. Some story ideas were actually purchased (for $250) from physicians who had served in Korea: Dr. John Vester of Cincinnati sold three stories to M*A*S*H and heard his name and a medical paper he had written mentioned in one of them.

Gelbart kept a master list of names of Korean men, a map of Korea, and some pages of an Army handbook on his desk. Metcalfe got so chummy with his veteran informants that he was invited to a reunion of former MASH surgeons. He went, tape recorder in hand.

Many stories surfaced that were not usable. Latrine jokes were popular at all MASH units but are considered in poor taste on network television; in their spare time and during lulls, medical officers in Korea sometimes gave physical exams to prostitutes and performed tests for venereal diseases—subjects considered not for family viewing. Producers-writers David Isaacs and Ken Levine, who also did extensive research with Metcalfe, found many stories that they couldn't use either for reasons of good taste or simply because viewers would not believe them. Even a perfectly true story, like the time everyone at the 8063 MASH had a party and dyed his or her hair and clothes red, was reduced to the third story line of an episode because it was just too hard to believe. Writer-producer Dan Wilcox found a fabulous story about an entire outfit that wanted to go home so badly that they stood outside in freezing weather until each man got frostbite. Although true, the story was considered too unpatriotic to use on TV.

Almost everything used on the air was true, but many Korean vets called the show good entertainment but bad history. (Vietnam veterans more identified with its spirit.) Said Charles E. Hannan, MD, a former MASH surgeon in Korea, "You get a feeling of empathy for some of the conditions but there wasn't near the frivolity in a real MASH as on the show. In our spare time, we would read a book or play bridge around the potbellied stove."

Dr. William Enos agreed, "We fooled around some but there was not quite as much boozing. Liquor was kind of hard to get, and there was little romantic activity."

Dr. Eugene McCarthy of Harlingen, Texas, was a former World War II surgeon who wrote to ask that if the 4077 was only three miles from the front, why were the wounded brought out in helicopters instead of ambulances.

Dr. Dave Fitchett of Albany, New York, added the information that in his MASH OR, which was in a Quonset hut, there were no gurneys—metal hospital beds on wheels—so patients were brought in on litters and placed on sawhorses for surgery.

Potter—We're low on surgical gowns, Klinger. Get three cartons.

Klinger—Those gowns are as good as got. How about matching pumps?

While most of the stories were true and all the medical information was accurate, only some of the military information was precise. The writers did have a consultant at the Army, but they felt free to use a little poetic license. When McLean Stevenson decided to leave the show, the writers needed a way to send Colonel Blake home. In his final episode, *Abyssinia, Henry*, Blake is told he has enough "points" to go home. In actuality, the Army had given up its point system after World War II and, in any case, it had never rotated doctors based on points, according to Colonel David Wagner.

Perhaps the most ironic mistake of all aired in Year Nine when Corporal Klinger's serial number was broadcast—RA19571782. But in the Army's code for serial numbers, RA (Regular Army) was given only to volunteers for service—US was used for draftees.

Occasional players Christopher and Farr join the original troupe.

SUICIDE IS PAINLESS;
IT BRINGS ON MANY CHANGES

"There are two schools of thought," explains Burt Metcalfe, "on what happened to M*A*S*H over the years. Some people say that Years One through Five are similar and that Six through Eleven are of a different ilk, and they tend to call those later shows more sentimental. Others, myself among them, see Years One through Four being similar, Year Five separate, and then Six through Eleven different yet again. When Larry Gelbart left after Year Four, the show naturally had to change. Then Gene left after Year Five. I couldn't be what Gene and Larry were, so Alan and I forged our own way in our own manner."

Even within that overall picture, there are variations from year to year and even script to script. Not every script was a piece of perfection. Some were actually dreadful. No one is more painfully aware of that than Gelbart. "I wince when I see some of those reruns." Gelbart admits that he once rewrote a scene that had already been shot and still finds himself mentally rewriting the reruns.

"There are a lot of shows in there we'd like to forget," said Isaacs and Levine, who created many of the more memorable stories.

Despite its unevenness, M*A*S*H remained one of the best shows on television and, no matter who wrote it, one of the most honored. Nominated for nearly a hundred Emmys over its eleven-year history, the show's quality was so consistently high that few outsiders were able to detect the nuances of change that were apparent to serious observers.

When the show finally went off the air, a few critics pointed out that it had become too sentimental and was bogged down in Alan Alda's personal philosophy, especially his ardent feminism. Other critics thought that Alan's appeal to women viewers was useful for counter-programming by CBS, which finally placed the show against *Monday Night Football* and saw it hold its own.

Regardless of their reasons, and despite having seventeen different writers and numerous cast changes, M*A*S*H kept Americans glued to their sets for ten full years. Year Eleven ran as a partial season (fifteen episodes and a final two-and-a-half-hour movie). When the last show was scheduled for February 28, 1983, the hype was on. Newspapers ran contests asking readers to write in how they thought the show should end. A reader of the *Chicago Sun Times* suggested that Hawkeye be exposed as Gregor Yoshenko, a KGB mole planted by the Soviets to ridicule the U.S. government.

Another thought that Bob Hope should come out and sing *Thanks for the Memories*. Newspapers even began running interviews with war veterans to compare the real MASH to TV's M*A*S*H.

On the big night, celebrities were polled to ask if they were staying home to watch. M*A*S*H–BASHs were held in almost every major city to watch the final show; fans gathered in bars in their old Army fatigues; numerous cities ran blood bank drives concurrent with the last show. The city council of Fairfield, Ohio, postponed its regular meeting so the mayor and council members could stay home and watch the final show; four hundred Yeshiva College students turned up in the school's auditorium wearing fatigues, surgical gowns, and yarmulkes; Fordham students in Alan Alda's old dorm room set up a still and opened shop as the show aired.

The final episode, *Goodbye, Farewell and Amen*, was devised as a two-hour movie but ran two-and-a-half hours because enough good footage existed and Alda (who directed) was reluctant to cut it. The actors were never sufficiently compensated for the extra half hour, but, as always, they cared more for the quality of the show. The network was glad to give the show extra time—it was busy selling commercial time at $450,000 per thirty-second spot, $50,000 more than a Super Bowl spot. About one hundred and twenty-five million Americans watched the last show, and CBS garnered $13.6 million in gross revenues. The show earned a 60.3 rating and a 77 share, which means that seventy-seven percent of the people watching television in America on that night, at that time, were tuned to M*A*S*H. (By comparison, the 1982 Super Bowl had one hundred and ten million viewers and *Roots* had ninety-nine million.)

Throughout most of the commotion, the actors remained surprised that the show was being taken so seriously. Toward the end, they worked to protect their privacy and prohibited press access to the set. Mostly, they worked from dawn until dark on a dirty, olive drab, flea-ridden set that held them captives from the real world, much like the people they portrayed.

"You have to remember," says Loretta Swit, "we were just doing our jobs and having a good time."

Hawkeye—This is war. War is hell. It stinks. It's filthy. Beej, can I borrow your cologne?"

B.J.—Yeah, I'll trade you for some clothespins.

M*A*S*H's final cast, with Executive Producer Burt Metcalfe seen between Alda and Farrell

Gary Burghoff clowns with Gene Reynolds *(left)* and Larry Gelbart *(right)*.

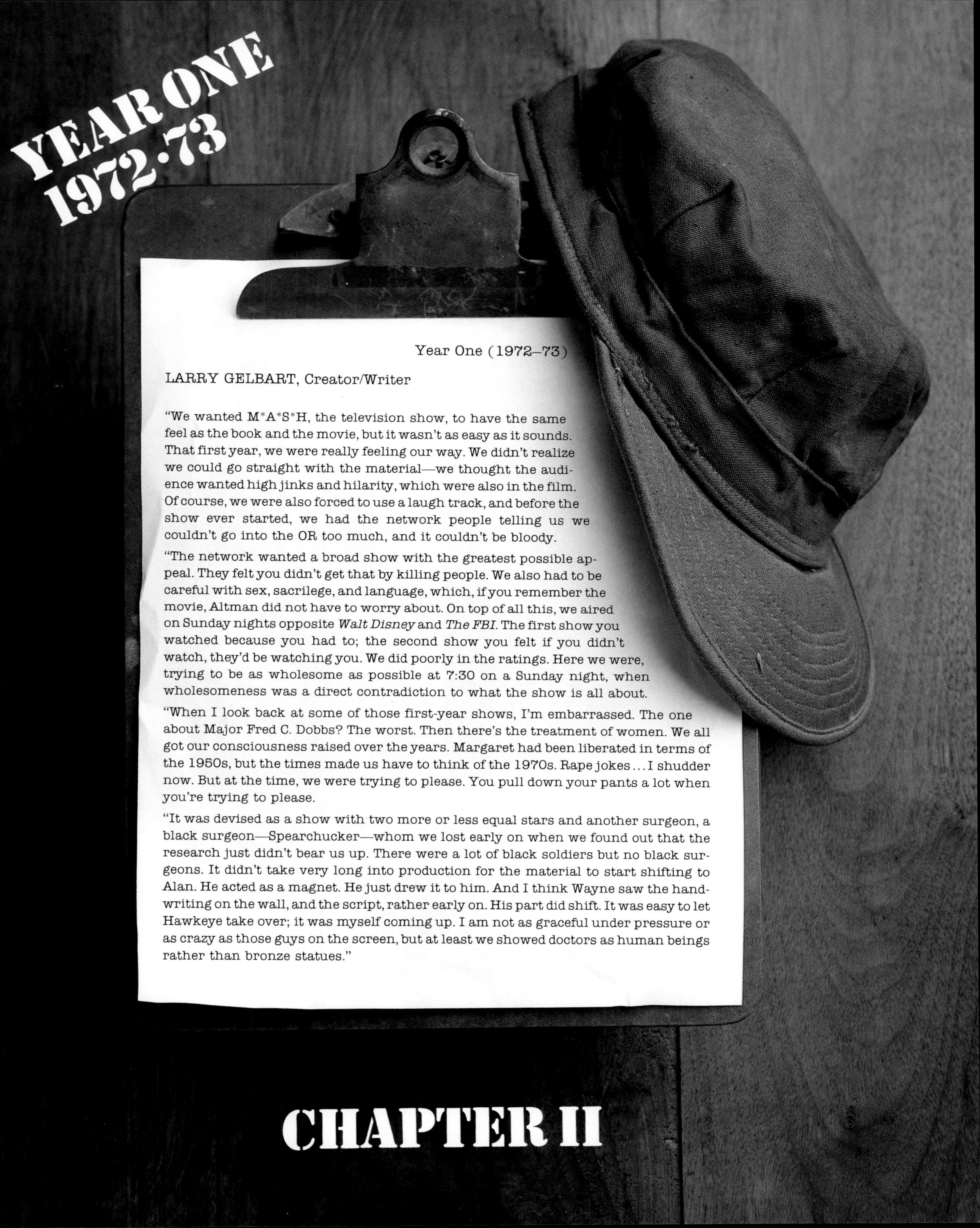

Year One (1972–73)

LARRY GELBART, Creator/Writer

"We wanted M*A*S*H, the television show, to have the same feel as the book and the movie, but it wasn't as easy as it sounds. That first year, we were really feeling our way. We didn't realize we could go straight with the material—we thought the audience wanted high jinks and hilarity, which were also in the film. Of course, we were also forced to use a laugh track, and before the show ever started, we had the network people telling us we couldn't go into the OR too much, and it couldn't be bloody.

"The network wanted a broad show with the greatest possible appeal. They felt you didn't get that by killing people. We also had to be careful with sex, sacrilege, and language, which, if you remember the movie, Altman did not have to worry about. On top of all this, we aired on Sunday nights opposite *Walt Disney* and *The FBI*. The first show you watched because you had to; the second show you felt if you didn't watch, they'd be watching you. We did poorly in the ratings. Here we were, trying to be as wholesome as possible at 7:30 on a Sunday night, when wholesomeness was a direct contradiction to what the show is all about.

"When I look back at some of those first-year shows, I'm embarrassed. The one about Major Fred C. Dobbs? The worst. Then there's the treatment of women. We all got our consciousness raised over the years. Margaret had been liberated in terms of the 1950s, but the times made us have to think of the 1970s. Rape jokes ... I shudder now. But at the time, we were trying to please. You pull down your pants a lot when you're trying to please.

"It was devised as a show with two more or less equal stars and another surgeon, a black surgeon—Spearchucker—whom we lost early on when we found out that the research just didn't bear us up. There were a lot of black soldiers but no black surgeons. It didn't take very long into production for the material to start shifting to Alan. He acted as a magnet. He just drew it to him. And I think Wayne saw the handwriting on the wall, and the script, rather early on. His part did shift. It was easy to let Hawkeye take over; it was myself coming up. I am not as graceful under pressure or as crazy as those guys on the screen, but at least we showed doctors as human beings rather than bronze statues."

CHAPTER II

YEAR ONE—BATTLE NOTES

The M*A*S*H cast during the filming of *Iron Guts Kelly*

M*A*S*H—THE PILOT

The men in the gaudy Hawaiian hula shirts were doctors, all right. Doctors at war, in fact. They just didn't like to think about it too often. When they weren't elbows deep in guts, they tried to get away from it all or as far away as the confines of the war would allow.

In the beginning, they played a lot of golf, stroking golf balls into the wild blue yonder safely behind the river valley in which the 4077 Mobile Army Surgical Hospital was located. The course lacked the refinement of, say, Pebble Beach, but it had its own panache. Posted near the tee was a simple cautionary phrase: DANGER MINEFIELD.

The golfers were Doctors John Francis Xavier McIntyre and Benjamin Franklin Pierce, known as Trapper John and Hawkeye, respectively—not that you had to have a nickname to get drafted. Hell, by the fall of 1950, they were drafting every MD under the age of thirty anyway. Trapper was from Boston. They took him right from a surgical internship at a fashionable New England hospital. He was a tall man, about six-feet-three, with thick, curly hair the color of summer sand and a choirboy grin that undoubtedly helped earn him his *nom de joie* after he trapped a young Wellesley coed in the john of a train and had his way with her. Or so she claimed.

Pierce was a Yankee doctor also, but from the small town of Crabapple Cove, Maine. He didn't even play with guns as a child and wasn't quite certain how the draft board got his name and address. He, too, was tall, with dark hair, an Abraham Lincoln jaw, and big, brown, cocker spaniel eyes.

"Fore!" shouted Trapper as he teed off. The din of incoming helicopters drowned out further conversation as the doctors joined the stampede of corpsmen, nurses, and surgeons who ran to greet the helicopters and gather the wounded into their competent arms. After all, a doctor who shot 127 in Korea when it wasn't even a Wednesday couldn't be all bad.

> You said I sounded a bit callous in my last letter, Dad. Let me see if I can put things in a better way. At this particular Mobile Army Hospital, we are not concerned with the ultimate reconstruction of the patient. We care only about getting the kid out of here alive enough for someone else to put on the fine touches. We work fast and we're not dainty. We try to play par surgeon on this course. Par is a live patient.

Hawkeye wrote his Dad a lot. Mail was one of the most sacred of celebrations, followed only by drinking, sex, and Sunday services with Father Mulcahy. Every now and then in the tent he shared with Trapper—not inaccurately known as The Swamp—he got an interesting piece of mail. Now, he had a letter from Dr. James Lodge, Dean, Androscoggin College, which accepted his recommendation to admit Ho-Jon, his Korean houseboy, into the school. Overjoyed at first, Hawkeye quickly realized he'd have to ante up two thousand bucks. This called for one of his famous schemes.

"What's on the mind of every man on this base?" he asked Trapper.

"Sex," the man replied easily. He was a doctor. "Except for the baseball perverts. Then home or Tokyo, whichever comes first."

"Right. So let's have a raffle."

The plan was to host an "all-you-can-drink" bash for $10 per head and then raffle off a weekend for two with the lush and luscious Nurse Dish. Colonel Henry Blake, the CO, was a pretty easy touch and agreed to the scheme.

"Dis–gusting!" announced Major Margaret Houlihan, the chief nurse, who was supported in her furor by Major Frank Burns, a Regular Army clown who was probably drafted merely as a Communist plot to teach humility to the rest of the poor sons of bitches at the 4077.

Anyway, Frank outranked Captain Pierce, so when Hawkeye slugged him, Burns wanted to press charges. Henry dismissed the charges but had to cancel the party to show just a little respect for rules and regs.

Thinking everything was well under control, Henry then flew off to Tokyo for a staff meeting with General Hamilton Hammond. Radar O'Reilly, the company clerk, had Blake sign a batch of papers before he took off, even though the colonel was not scheduled to be gone long and Tokyo was only an hour from Seoul by plane. But among the signed papers was the key to Ho-Jon's future: Radar presented the two "cutters" with the kingpins to their raffle, the forbidden weekend passes.

"When did he sign these?" asked an incredulous Hawkeye.

"He thought he was ordering a ton of ice cream," O'Reilly replied. "Fudge ripple."

The resulting party would have been a S*M*A*S*H if Major Houlihan hadn't insisted on calling Colonel Blake and General Hammond in Tokyo. She suggested they fly back and catch the party-givers red-handed. Hammond crashed the party and angrily ordered a court-martial. But his command was drowned out by the whir of incoming choppers. The first casualties from the landing at Inchon were arriving, and even Hammond had to scrub up and join the battle to save lives.

After ten hours, Hammond emerged from the OR, tired but elated. Trapper and Hawkeye also emerged, tired—and handcuffed. Blake ordered their manacles removed with a grin. "Forget it, boys," he announced. "Hammond was too impressed to arrest you."

HENRY, PLEASE COME HOME

No wonder Hawkeye and Trapper were sick with worry when they discovered that Henry Blake had been transferred to Tokyo—Frank Burns was the next in command and was about to become their boss.

"That *doctor*? I use the term only because it gets a laugh when I refer to Frank," lamented Hawkeye.

As one of his first commands, Frank ordered the still that Trapper used to make "gin" shut down. The Swampmen turned to action. They were willing to do anything to get Henry back, and Hawkeye knew how to get his man—through Radar.

Radar reported in sick, so sick that Henry rushed right back to camp to be at the young man's bedside. Once back, Henry pushed the noncooperative Frank out of his way with fury. "I'll have you busted down to male nurse!" threatened Blake.

"But it's my outfit!" Frank protested.

"Not any more," Henry sighed.

Mission accomplished.

Henry, Please Come Home

TO MARKET, TO MARKET

Henry's antique desk was his pride and joy. "I had to bump four privates and two second lieutenants off the plane to get it here," he stated with pride. But when hijackers took off with most of the 4077's medical supplies, the desk became a pawn in a life-or-death barter.

Furious that vitally needed supplies has been swiped, Hawkeye and Trapper went to Tokyo to out-black-market the black marketeers.

"What about a swap?" Trapper asked.

"Yeah," echoed Hawkeye. "Free hospitalization for you and your friends, appendix operations, nose jobs. . ."

The black marketeers did not come cheap. They already had a health plan. In fact, the only thing that really interested them was that desk of Henry's. So Charlie Lee, the mild-mannered marketeer, came calling at the 4077 disguised as a South Korean general on an inspection tour. While Blake served drinks and prattled on about the desk, Lee gave the antique his seal of approval. Later that night, the Swampmen negotiated the finer details of the transfer of goods with Lee.

Next morning, the Korean dawn chattered with a chopper's rotors.

"My desk! My beautiful hundred-year-old desk!" Henry shouted in despair. He looked to heaven, where he saw a "Huey" helicopter with a grappling hook, holding the desk secure as it surged for altitude.

Two hundred vials of hydrocortisone magically found their way to Hawkeye a few hours later.

GERM WARFARE

For Frank Burns, it was easy to hate North Korean soldiers. They were the enemy. Trapper and Hawkeye weren't so sure. So they were reluctant to ship out a wounded soldier who needed blood and rest. Henry saw it Frank's way—bed space was at a premium, and the man needed AB negative, which was rare.

Hawkeye transferred the man to The Swamp and checked the camp donor cards. The only person who matched was Frank Burns. Surreptitiously at night, the doctors relieved their bunkmate of a pint of blood, planning never to mention the loan—no "thank yous" to be written or spoken.

Then the North Korean developed hepatitis. To Hawkeye and Trapper, Frank became a natural suspect, though *he* couldn't imagine why. From a urine specimen they collected after plying Frank with beer, the doctors were able to get a report back from a Tokyo lab. Major Frank Burns did not have hepatitis, but he was seriously anemic and needed rest.

THE MOOSE

The Japanese word for woman is *musame,* which led to the slang term, "moose," a term Americans in Korea used to refer to the women they took up with as girlfriends and mistresses—or slaves.

Opposite and above right: Henry, Please Come Home

Right: Larry Linville as Major Frank Burns

After Hawkeye met Sergeant Leonard Baker's seventeen-year-old "moose," his sense of civil liberties was outraged. He offered to purchase the girl to set her free, but Baker wanted $2,000. He had trained her well, he claimed. To raise the dough, Hawkeye dreamed up Operation Poker, wherein Radar used a telescope to spy on Baker's cards and mouthed cues into an earpiece Hawkeye was wearing. The surgeon soon won both the game and the girl.

But if Hawkeye simply set the girl free, she might be sold again, even by her own family. He certainly didn't want a "moose," so he began to teach her about self-respecting work. When her brother came to collect her for another sale, she was able to defy Korean family tradition and stand up to him. "I tell brother most important words I learn from you," she explained to Hawkeye. "Shove off!"

I HATE A MYSTERY

It was an epidemic of sorts. Everyone at the 4077 suffered a loss. Small but nice items were being stolen: Frank's silver picture frame; Margaret's antique hairbrushes; Trapper's watch; Henry's fishing reel. The "missing in action" items then turned up in Hawkeye's footlocker. Everyone thought he was the thief.

Henry promptly filled out court-martial papers neatly provided by Margaret and Frank; a lawyer arrived from Seoul to represent Hawkeye. But Hawkeye wanted to catch the burglar himself, so he set a trap. He announced on the PA system that fingerprinting equipment was being flown in to the 4077. Then he sat back to watch. Agatha Christie would have been proud of him. Sure enough, the thief returned to retrieve all the evidence, and Hawkeye knew he could nab his man.

Dressed dramatically in a Sam Spade getup, he gathered the group around him and stylishly sprang his trap: "I made it publicly known that there were fingerprints to be found on the stolen articles in order to tempt the thief to repeat his crime and retrieve his ill-gotten booty. In doing so, he has exposed himself! The stolen articles were treated with hydrochloric alpha terracin, a chemical that even now is turning the criminal's fingernails green."

The officers and enlisted men looked at their fingernails, all except for Ho-Jon, who automatically placed his hands behind his back.

"I did it for the money," he explained, "to bring my mother and sister from our village up north. To bribe border guards. I didn't think anyone would miss their bits and pieces. Everyone here is so rich. I didn't think you'd give me bribery money. Bribery is dishonest."

CHIEF SURGEON WHO?

"Let's go, baby, or this boy's kidney's never going to dance again," said Hawkeye, as he gently goaded those around him to quicker and cleaner efficiency. He was a remarkable surgeon, in all the right ways—good hands, good heart, not full of himself, like those who thought they were in the God business. Everyone was impressed with his technique. Except Frank.

So when Hawkeye was appointed Chief Surgeon, Frank was really miffed.

Not one to leave things alone, Margaret convinced Frank to help her call General Wilson Spaudling Barker in Seoul so he could check out the new Chief Surgeon—by "accidentally" stumbling on him at a party. Arriving at 2 A.M., Barker was in time to see an unflappable Hawkeye playing poker.

"You haven't heard the last of this," an incensed Barker harrumphed.

Hawkeye claimed he wasn't listening to the first of it as Barker stomped off to find Henry. Instead, the general stumbled into one love nest after another, first Frank and Hot Lips, then Henry and his chief nurse, Leslie.

Disgusted, he went to the VIP tent but was roused by incoming choppers. So he scrubbed, went to the OR, and was shocked to observe a totally professional Dr. Pierce take control. "And may I make a suggestion about your Major Burns?" the general asked Blake after he'd discovered who had talent and who didn't.

"Give him a high colonic and send him on a ten-mile hike."

REQUIEM FOR A LIGHTWEIGHT

It was a deal, pure and simple. Henry needed a boxer to take on General Barker's pugilist in an intercamp boxing match. The surgeons wanted Henry to countermand a transfer for one of the staff's best-looking nurses. So Trapper volunteered to fight, and Hawkeye signed on as coach.

To little avail. After watching a training session, Henry wanted to write Trapper's mother a condolence note; Father Mulcahy suggested that only prayer could help and set to the task. But it was Ugly John, the Australian gas passer, who had the best punch line.

"I pulled this gag in college," he explained as he used an eyedropper to saturate a boxing glove with ether.

Outraged at the deception, Frank—that famous moralist—and his henchwoman, Hot Lips Houlihan, exchanged the ether bottle for plain old H_2O, sending poor Trapper into the ring against a behemoth. He didn't stand a chance.

Hawkeye discovered the switcheroo halfway through the first round and returned with a second bottle of ether. Weakly, Trapper waved the now-saturated glove in front of his opponent—and not only KO'd him but the referee as well.

COWBOY

"Shell shock," a psychological but quite real wound, was recognized as early as the Civil War. Over the course of time, it was called by several different names; by the Korean War, it was known as battle fatigue or combat exhaustion and affected even the strongest of men.

Cowboy was a helicopter pilot who had been hit in the shoulder and sent to the 4077 for a stitch in time. While his behavior was erratic, there seemed no reason to connect him with the strange set of events that suddenly befell the camp. In fact, members of the staff were busy blaming each other for the calamities that surrounded them and didn't recognize the symptoms of battle fatigue in one of their patients until it was almost too late.

Henry was up in a chopper with the seemingly recovered pilot when he noticed that Cowboy was wearing a parachute and he wasn't.

"Don't I need a parachute, too?"

"You don't need one, sir. It'll only break your fall."

Then, as the man began to shove the colonel from the cockpit, Trapper came on the chopper's radio and announced that Cowboy had a letter from his wife. "It says, 'I love you more than ever,' " Trapper revealed, having realized that mental strain had almost broken the man.

"Let's go home, Cowboy," said Henry. "Let's go on home." The Cowboy began to cry—slow, large tears of pain and confusion. Henry simply nodded.

War is hell.

YANKEE DOODLE DOCTOR

By World War II, films were a big part of military life. They taught soldiers how to build latrines, avoid trench foot, and so forth. And they were used for propaganda. By the Korean War, the Army had no problem in locating professionals to run their little motion picture factory.

Lieutenant Duane William Bricker was one of those pros. Bricker was working for Brigadier General Cyrus Clayton, who wanted a documentary made about "saints in surgical garb" at the 4077.

There was to be a lead role, naturally, that called for a doctor as the film's spokesman. Both Trapper and Frank thought they were perfect for the part, but Hawkeye got the nod. "Oh, jeepers," cursed Burns.

Stardom wasn't all it was cracked up to be. It didn't take long for Hawkeye and Trapper to realize that Bricker's *Yankee Doodle Doctor* movie was a corny, unrealistic, soppy piece of pure propaganda. So they did the only patriotic thing left to them—they broke into his footlocker and exposed the undeveloped film.

"He was a liar on film. He was making a documentary fairy tale."

Fairy tale or no, Henry felt pretty grim about it. He *wanted* the film made to show off his unit. So Hawkeye made his own film. Frank narrated, Radar was the patient, and the camp mutt barked on cue when the *Yankee Doodle Doctor* berated the dogs of war. Beneath the jokes, Hawkeye laid bare his gritty integrity. The last shot showed him standing next to a young, bandaged GI in postop.

"Three hours ago, this man was in a battle. Two hours ago, we operated on him. He's got a fifty-fifty chance. We win some, we lose some. That's what it's all about...no promises, no guaranteed survival...no

saints in surgical garb. Our willingness, our experience, our technique are not enough. Guns have more power to take life than we have to preserve it."

BANANAS, CRACKERS AND NUTS

Twelve-hour operating shifts were common at the 4077. Eighteen-hour shifts were not unusual. During big battles, doctors worked around the clock, drinking coffee held for them by nurses while they cut and sewed. After one such siege, Hawkeye and Trapper thought a week of R&R was their due, but Henry was leaving for Seoul and Frank, as CO, would have none of it.

So Hawkeye quietly went bananas. He placed the camp dog under an oxygen tent in intensive care; he turned down a date with a nurse he had the hots for; he even went to the mess hall dressed in full surgical kit and dissected his food before eating it.

Perplexed, Frank and Hot Lips called in Dr. Mandel Sherman, a shrink from Tokyo, who confirmed Hawkeye's condition. Then Henry returned and knew immediately it was another prank, despite protestations from Sherman, Burns, and Houlihan that the cutter was sick, sick, sick.

Radar got the good doctor off the guest list at the "Laughing Academy." He convinced Dr. Sherman that Margaret's hot lips were meant for him and sent the shrink to the tent of an unsuspecting Major Houlihan. Her outcries aroused the camp. Henry ousted the psychiatrist and turned over two passes to Tokyo to the boys from The Swamp.

They were triumphant for only a moment. Then Radar perked up those famous ears and announced apprehensively, "Here they come."

"Don't stop the meter," Trapper shouted at the chopper pilot. Then he loosened his tie and went to scrub up.

EDWINA

It was a form of *Lysistrata* all over again. The women banded together and decided they wouldn't put out until one of the doctors got real cozy with Nurse Eddie, who was getting no attention and whom Hawkeye had quite accurately dubbed "a land mine in bloomers."

But the strike against their manhood was unbearable so the doctors drew straws, and Hawkeye was forced to woo the lovely Edwina. When they ate together, she stepped on Hawkeye's ankle; when they toasted each other, she spilled her martini on him; when they danced, she backed him into a hot stove.

"Hey," said Hawkeye, who was ready with a diagnosis. "You don't have to hurt someone to make sure you don't get hurt first."

Two weeks later, when Nurse Eddie shipped out—her hitch over—she said a fond farewell to her friends at MASH. "Thank you, Hawkeye. I'm grateful to know I can be myself with a man, to know I don't have to beat him to the hurt."

DEAR DAD

Dear Dad,

A lull, at last, after almost three straight days of meatball surgery, seventy hours of sewing kids together. If this keeps up, I was thinking of asking the Army for a raise; either that or putting on some lipstick and earrings and getting a discharge. If war was hell in Sherman's day, you can imagine what it is now. If jokes seem sacrilegious in an operating room, I promise you they are a necessary defense against what we get down here at this end of the draft board.

Henry Blake is a good doctor and a pretty good Joe. As a commanding officer, well, it's a bit like being on a sinking liner running to the bridge and finding out that the captain is Daffy Duck.

Christmas here in Korea, as with you in Maine, is soon upon us. There is *some* effort to celebrate the idea of Peace on Earth even though there's shooting in them thar hills.

How far had Radar gotten in Project Jeep in my last letter? I think he had mailed the back seats by then. This week he is smuggling out the front seats. It took Trapper and me a while to figure out what he was up to until we X-rayed one of his packages and found out he was mailing a Jeep home, piece by piece.

To bring you up to date on my copilot, Trapper, as I wrote you earlier, he has developed a thriving, very lucrative practice on the side over here. He gives smallpox vaccinations to the local kids and on a good day he collects fifty or sixty smiles...the kind you never forget.

Father Mulcahy is stringing popcorn all over the place in an attempt to give this cesspool a Yuletide look. Being so far from home at Christmas is kind of hard on all of us, though I've done my best to keep up the nurses' morale, but I've only got two hands.

'Tis the day before Christmas, Dad, and I'd much rather be in the house; just too many creatures stirring around here for my comfort. Frankly, the last thing I ever figured when I went to med school was that I would be dressed up like Kris Kringle to entertain war orphans and end up flying into battle to save a man's life. But I guess all those kids down there are in the last place they ever figured, too.

Merry Christmas, Dad. Peace on Earth.

Love,
Hawkeye

Above: Love Story

Opposite, above and below: Dear Dad

LOVE STORY

Many a girl back home grew tired of waiting for her man to return. Radar got his "Dear John" letter in record form, made in one of those newfangled recording booths that catered to chatter for soldiers. Hearing it was no easier than reading that Linda Sue had decided to marry Elroy.

Radar took it hard. So hard that Hawkeye and Trapper decided to find him a new girl. Their choice was Lieutenant Louise Anderson, a nurse who outranked Radar in every way. To get their boy through the preliminaries, the doctors had to train him to say, "Ahhh, Bach," every time Nurse Anderson mentioned music. But the gig was up when Radar fell asleep during one of Anderson's nonstop monologues about the composer and had to be nudged back to reality.

"Ahhhh, Bach," said Radar, waking with a start.

TUTTLE

Sister Theresa's orphanage, ten miles east of the 4077, was the pet concern of many of the doctors, as well as Father Mulcahy. It was Hawkeye, in fact, who set up one of the first endowments for the care of these homeless Korean children. If Maimonides, philosopher and physician, was right in saying that the most important charitable deeds were done anonymously, he would have applauded Hawkeye's decision to sign requisition slips for supplies for the orphanage with Captain Leroy Tuttle's signature.

Tuttle was Hawkeye's imaginary childhood playmate, the one who broke windows and wet the bed.

"And when you got drafted?" asked Trapper.

"He got drafted, too... in case I wet my cot."

As Tuttle's good works became more and more renowned, other members of the team wanted to meet him. Radar quickly assured Henry that the colonel had already had breakfast with Tuttle, and Frank sulked because he had been ignored. Hot Lips wanted to appraise his style and even called one of her friends at HQ to check him out.

When Hawkeye discovered that Tuttle was about to receive fourteen months of back pay that could be donated to the orphanage, he contrived to have the "man" sign for his check. But when his good deed put him in line for decoration, Hawkeye had to bring in the news that while Tuttle was on a surgery call in the field, he had unfortunately left the chopper without benefit of chute. Of course, he left his GI life insurance to the orphanage.

THE RINGBANGER

Colonel Buzz Maxwell was a ring banger. He liked to pepper his conversations by banging his big West Point ring on any hard surface he could find. And he did a good bit of ring banging when he stayed in The Swamp on a visit to the 4077 as he harangued Hawkeye and Trapper about the need to get his boys back to the front.

The doctors were on to him fast. Ring bangers were invariably gung ho Army types whose enthusiasm always spelled death and disaster for the soldier. So to make life more of a possibility for a few more men, Hawkeye and Trapper set about convincing Maxwell that he suffered from such serious battle fatigue that he had to go stateside for a complete rest.

DEAR DAD... AGAIN

Dear Dad,

Sorry I haven't written sooner, but you know how the work piles up here. Korea's pretty much the same story. The fighting goes on—the hatred, the violence, the senseless brutality, men behaving like animals—then, of course, there's the war. Business, unfortunately, remains very brisk. I think you know by now I'm not being flip, but doing meatball surgery you either develop a thick skin or you wind up in the Tokyo Giggling Academy.

Luckily, we've got an extra pair of hands these days ...Captain Adam Casey. He's a really fine cutter, every bit as good as I am. And I'll get him for it. The work may be hard and ugly, but we can always count on the North Koreans to hand us a couple of laughs. I don't want you to get the idea that this is a madhouse. We're nowhere near that organized. What we are is bored out of our skulls, we're down to games like mouse-a-thons. Back home, we would have been arrested for some of the stuff we've pulled, but then, you can kill people over here and get a medal for it, so no one's very sane.

This is the longest letter I've written since the one I sent the draft board telling them why I shouldn't be sent to Korea—that I felt it was unpatriotic to leave my country during the time of war.

Remember the fellow Casey I just wrote you about? Well, it turns out we got a message from the provost's office that he's not a doctor at all and his name is Schwartz. Maybe pretty soon they'll tell us the war's not a war.

I forgot to thank you for sending me your old tuxedo. It really added a touch of class to our no-talent night here last week. I'd like to write more but it is Saturday night, the one night we all look forward to. I'm going to the shower now, shave, put on a clean uniform, and cry myself to sleep.

Your son,
Hawkeye

SOMETIMES YOU HEAR THE BULLET

Doctors dealt with death on an hourly basis. They never got used to it, just tried to remain as untouched as possible, counting the lives saved rather than lost. It was the only way to keep some sanity in the midst of insanity. Of course, sometimes it didn't work.

Hawkeye experienced the great joy of an unexpected reunion with an old friend—especially in such a godforsaken place as Korea—and the unspeakable pain a doctor feels when he cannot save a life.

It all began when Tommy Gillis stopped by the 4077 to visit Hawkeye, whom he'd known since fifth grade. Gillis was writing a book called *You Never Hear the Bullet*—life in the infantry as observed firsthand.

"There was a young blond kid in my outfit. I looked over at him one day and half of him was gone, and you know what he said? He said, 'I never heard no bullet.'"

They had a drunken night in The Swamp, then Gillis returned to his outfit. They flew him back twelve hours later. "I'd give you a kiss, Hawk, but I can't lift my head."

A shaken Hawkeye tried to cover. "You'd just get my mask icky."

"I heard the bullet," said Gillis, then he was gone.

Tears streamed down Hawkeye's face as he fought for control. "This is the first time I've cried since I'm in this crummy place," he told Henry.

"All I know is what they taught us in command school. Rule Number One is that young men die and Rule Number Two is that doctors can't change Rule Number One."

THE LONG JOHN FLAP

It was cold in Korea in the winter, so cold that guns and vehicles froze. Soldiers had to chip the ice off mortars to fire them; carbines jammed in mid-action; and wounded were sometimes strapped to Jeep radiators to keep them from freezing to death before they could get shipped to an aid station.

So Hawkeye, son of Maine, kept warm in long johns while the rest of the 4077 wondered why the Army couldn't send enough parkas or mittens to Ouijongbu. It was, therefore, a supreme act of charity when Hawkeye gave his long johns to Trapper because his friend had the flu. But Trapper lost them in a poker game to Radar, and Radar traded them for a leg of lamb. The cook gave them to Frank, who had busted him for keeping an unsanitary kitchen. Hot Lips asked Frank to leave his wife for her but was rewarded instead with the long johns, a true token of esteem. When she washed them and hung them on the line, Corporal Klinger, who got no warmth from those little black dresses he was wearing, stole them on bayonet point. After an attack of guilt, he went to the padre for absolution. Father Mulcahy took the long johns to Henry, who was rushed into surgery with appendicitis. He paid Hawkeye with the long johns.

Delighted to be warm again, Hawkeye was just curling up for a good night's sleep when he noticed that Trapper was coughing and wheezing again.

"Oh, no," he groaned, "No...no...no...no..."

MAJOR FRED C. DOBBS

It was just like a scene from *The Treasure of the Sierra Madre*—everyone at the 4077 had gold fever, which, unfortunately, was nothing they had been taught to treat in med school.

It was Radar who touched it off, with his announcement that Korea was the fifth-largest gold-producing nation in the world. Then Hawkeye and Trapper stepped in, preying on the greed that was the basis of Frank Burns' soul.

Burns had finally secured the transfer he had been talking about for several months and was about to ship out. But HQ was unable to secure a replacement for the major, which would have put even more work on the burdened shoulders of the Swampmen. They *had* to come up with some way to convince Frank to stay. Greed was the answer. "He even became a doctor out of greed," Hawkeye had been known to sniff. "He married for money; if there was money in dying, he'd lie down in front of a truck."

So his prank-loving comrades borrowed some real gold from the Painless Pole's dental offices, mixed it with the

fool's gold that Radar had been mining, and made Frank wild with money lust. He had the transfer rescinded in order to seek his fortune with pick, pan, and shovel.

At least the Korean government could never sue him for malpractice.

STICKY WICKET

"You're inconsiderate, bloody arrogant, insulting with your nurses, demanding, distracting, and dumb! And furthermore, you're surgically incompetent!" Sooner or later, the words had been bound to escape Hawkeye's lips, and when the day arrived, Frank—the recipient of the honesty—marched right into Henry's office and filed a TD 603—in triplicate, of course.

"I'd like to file a countercomplaint against Burns for masquerading as a surgeon and a human being!" Hawkeye shouted at Colonel Blake.

While the war of words went back and forth, one of Hawkeye's patients—a boy he had saved from certain paralysis—began to run a fever. His condition deteriorated rapidly. Frank couldn't have been more delighted.

Though Hawkeye slept at the boy's bedside for two nights, he still couldn't put his finger on the problem. Medically, there was no reason he could think of for the turnaround. Then, in the middle of the night, it came to him. Rousing a team, he ordered surgery, opened the boy, found a small perforation in the sigmoid colon—and saved the patient.

One more American was going to enjoy the Eisenhower years.

THE ARMY-NAVY GAME

Army and Navy had been playing their traditional Thanksgiving football game for generations. It was usually a good game, but to servicemen, it was something of a religious experience. So you can imagine how annoyed everyone at the 4077 was when heavy bombing kept interrupting the broadcast of the game.

It wasn't even halftime when a live bomb landed right in the compound and sat there ticking. Wounded could not be evacuated because of the land mines nearby; HQ was reluctant to help out because everyone there wanted to listen to the ball game. Tension was thick. Klinger even changed into a navy blue suit.

"This is the suit I was drafted in. I wasn't going to wear it again until I got a discharge, but with that bomb out there, I figure I'll be going home in a million pieces."

HQ eventually called back to say that they had traced the bomb to the CIA, and the only thing they knew about it was that it would detonate two minutes after it *stopped* ticking. The surgeons drew straws on who would perform the bombectomy. Frank lost but fainted, so Hawkeye stood in for him. Padded with mattresses, with Trapper to assist, he opened her up for a look-see.

That's when they realized the ticking had stopped.

"I'm all for getting out of here," Trapper hissed.

Then the bomb exploded. It was a tinny, hollow noise. Leaflets spewed all over the compound:

GIVE YOURSELF UP. YOU CAN'T WIN.
DOUGLAS MACARTHUR

CEASE-FIRE

The black taffeta party dress with the bow on the shoulder was marked down to $5 at Klinger's Cease-fire Sale, and he said he'd throw in the matching earrings for free.

"After all, with the cease-fire coming, we'll all be going home, and I won't need this stuff any more. Everything half price; all sales final."

Rumors of the cease-fire had actually begun after the triumph at Inchon in September, 1950. Everyone was sure the war would be over in weeks. Except Trapper. He kept saying he'd believe it when it happened. Hawkeye was much more optimistic. He bet Trapper $50 that

it would happen, and in the spirit of the whole thing, even cancelled all back poker debts. Then he had to wriggle out of marriage plans with all three of the nurses who had read between his lines.

Henry, Radar, Frank, and Hot Lips all packed and prepared for home, while Ho-Jon and his numerous relatives dismantled the camp, carting off a few "souvenirs." They had all but stripped the camp and were just taking down the PA system when the announcement burst forth like gunfire:

"Attention, all personnel! There is no cease-fire! Repeat. No cease-fire! All personnel report to surgery. Incoming wounded! Incoming wounded!"

SHOWTIME

"Short-timers fever" is an ailment with no medical cure. Just before discharge, a perfectly healthy soldier grows paranoid that as he is about to leave something will happen that will prevent him from returning home or returning home intact.

Above and opposite: Cease-Fire

Captain George Kaplan, one of the dentists, suffered from "short-timers fever." He even refused to play football lest he injure himself.

The USO had sent over Jackie Flash to entertain the troops with his song, dance, and skit routines that served to relieve anxiety for at least a couple of hours. Most of the surgeons couldn't make the show since they were busy in another theater—the operating room—but Kaplan joined the enlisted men and watched the show. Radar was having such a good time he even joined the band for a drum solo.

Then Kaplan's driver arrived to take him to the airfield at Kimpo, but the dentist thought the boy looked too young to drive safely. So he took the wheel and crashed the Jeep in less than five minutes. He was rushed to preop and bound in plaster, the last casualty of the day.

He'd go home stiff, but not as a stiff.

YEAR ONE (1972–73)

NAME: ROGERS, WAYNE
CHARACTER: MCINTYRE, JOHN FRANCIS XAVIER ("TRAPPER"), MD
RANK: CAPTAIN, USAMC (UNITED STATES
ARMY MEDICAL CORPS) SERIAL NUMBER: ER60304734

"I read the M*A*S*H pilot, and I liked it. I was one of a couple of guys who tested for the part. I don't even know who the others were. I don't remember that I had any previous understanding of what M*A*S*H was supposed to be before we went on the air or that I thought about it. I never thought of Trapper as the starring part. There was none of that kind of stuff going on there anyway. There was no jealousy among the actors. There was no one trying to grab all the lines. It was the concept we all cared about.

"I used to say to Alan how lucky we all were, how lucky Fox was—and no one even knew it. What if we were two people who were not compatible? What if we hated each other? We just all showed up on the set one day to start rehearsal. Maybe we met in Gene's office first, I don't remember. Alan and I had never met. As it turned out, we were interested in the same things— the work, primarily. Neither one of us was the kind of guy who cared where his parking space was or what the work conditions were or how big his dressing room was. *He* loved to rehearse. *I* loved to rehearse. It was serendipitous.

"When M*A*S*H was first conceived, it was not on the cutting edge of any great TV ideas. It was really *All in the Family* that was the breakthrough show. That's what really allowed a show like M*A*S*H to be done. Personally, I think *All in the Family* is the one that should be celebrated.

"I have some wonderful memories of that first year. Alan and I used to drive on location together. He liked to drive; he knew I hated to drive. He picked me up, or I drove to his house, I don't remember. Anyway, the whole ride out to the Ranch, we'd discuss our dreams. They were interrelated dreams, and we talked about them and what they meant, and it was wonderful.

"And McLean, off camera, was the funniest man I ever met. Apropos of nothing, he would entertain us. One day, he had a flyswatter in his hand, and one moment he was cooking eggs, the next it was a butterfly net, then he was an Indian paddling a canoe with it, the next moment he was waving a baseball glove.

"I loved the people and I loved the work, but very early on, it was obvious my time wasn't being used well. If you read the book or saw the movie, you know that Trapper John was the thoracic surgeon, the chest cutter. Then one day, they made Hawkeye a thoracic surgeon. They took away Trapper's credentials, his identity! It didn't bother me that they chose to make Hawkeye more important, but don't emasculate my character. Keep him in reality, give him his validity. My beef wasn't with how I was treated but with the integrity of the character.

"The first year they were very much trying to find their way. The show had to find itself. When we had scripts like *Major Fred C. Dobbs*, we all talked about it. We didn't think it was great and, in the light of time, discovered it wasn't. We knew it was dumb, we talked it over and were told that the network said we had to do a certain number of these lighter shows. We were always working on what the show was and where it was going. I think Larry Gelbart was the key. In the beginning, he wrote mostly sketches—that was his background—and he was the best. When Mel Brooks, Neil Simon, Carl Reiner, and those guys all sit down together, they all listen when Larry talks. There is no one quicker. As time went on, he began writing real scenes instead of just jokes. That's one of the big differences after the first year. I was happy to see it change. The key to longevity and the key to ratings is to take a serious idea and look at the other side. Audiences get hooked by a strong idea, and they love to laugh. I'm convinced that's the secret.

"I liked the relationship between Hawkeye and Trapper. Alan and I talked about the difference in the characters a lot. Hawkeye was more cerebral. Trapper was more impulsive, seemingly more fun loving. But they took that character and manipulated him rather than integrating him into the story.

"After the third or fourth script of the season, I went to the producers and said something like, 'It appears this part is getting smaller.' I'm paranoid anyway—all actors are—and maybe they were trying to kill me off. You get the feeling they're trying to write you out, little by little. I said, 'Listen, what are the plans here?' I remember Larry Gelbart saying, 'You're kicking the lines around a little.' I said, 'Yeah, I was upset about this thing and my mind wasn't on the script as much as usual.' Larry wrote rhythm jokes, and you had to get the timing just perfect or they wouldn't be funny. You had to adhere very closely to the line. I was conscious of that, and I tried very much to make his jokes work.

"I went back and it got a bit better, but by the last ten shows, it was the same thing again. At the end of the year, I said, 'What are your plans?' and the guys just waffled me. I said, 'I came here with the understanding that this was a show with primarily two characters and their relationship with the McLean Stevenson character, and if that's not so, I have a solution to your problems. I can do less shows and be more involved in those, that saves you money and I won't feel like I'm wasting my time and I won't feel like I'm being treated in some half-assed manner.

"But they assured me that this was not acceptable and that it would go back the way they originally said it would in the second year. So I stayed, but it was not emotionally rewarding in the sense of something that totally fills. I did a play recently. I did not play the lead, I played an ancillary part, but I loved doing this little part. It's not the size of the part but what and how much you can give it. My time means a lot to me, and I have to get the most I can for it.

"Despite the change in scripts, the character of Trapper didn't grow with the material. He started to be manipulated, like he was an ancillary character plastered onto the script. It didn't matter who was playing him, me or 'Chaim Kanipganop'—it could have been anyone. My creative talents weren't being used.

"I hated to leave. I loved the people. I gotta tell you, I never look back. Life must be lived forward."

Wayne Rogers

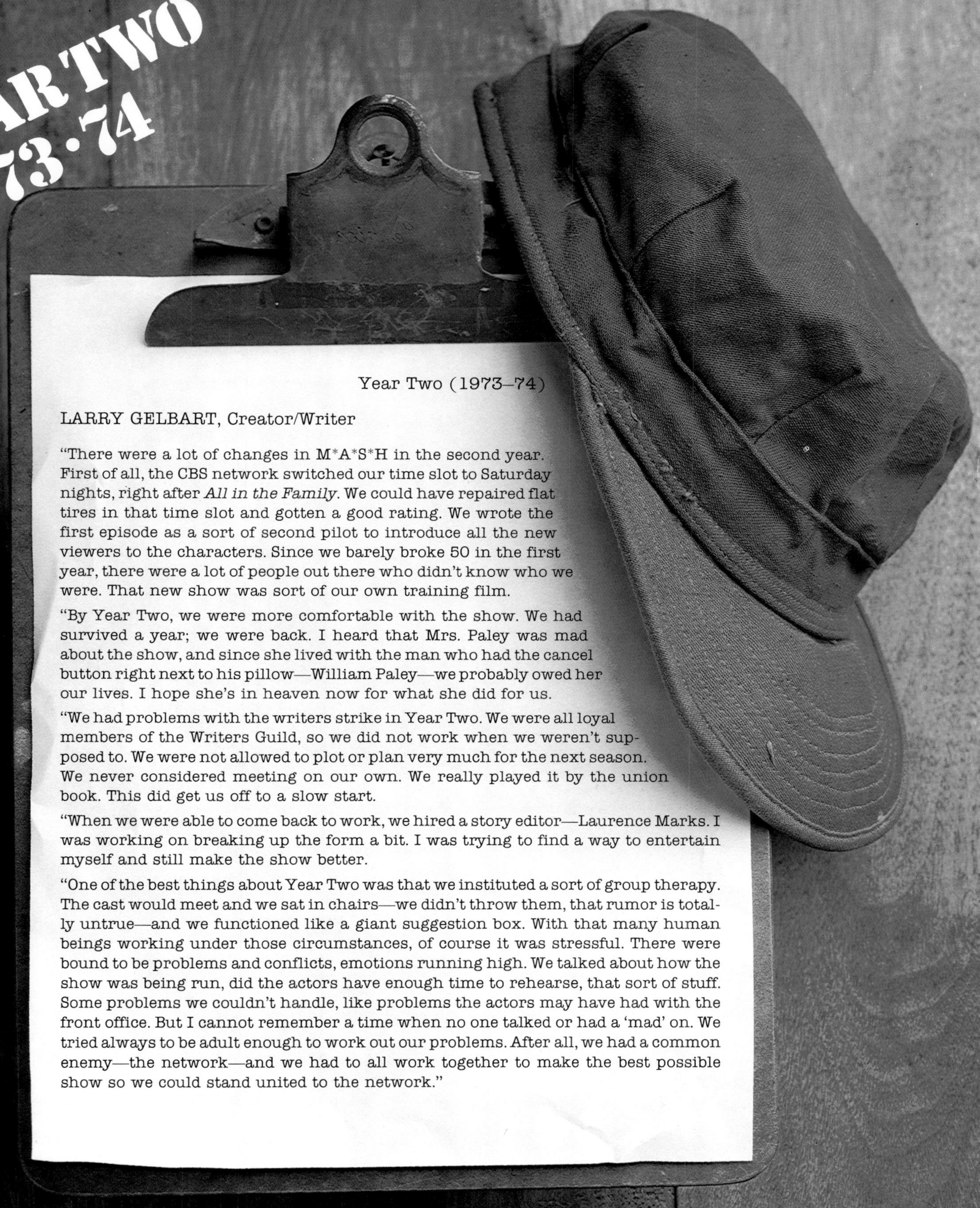

Year Two (1973–74)

LARRY GELBART, Creator/Writer

"There were a lot of changes in M*A*S*H in the second year. First of all, the CBS network switched our time slot to Saturday nights, right after *All in the Family*. We could have repaired flat tires in that time slot and gotten a good rating. We wrote the first episode as a sort of second pilot to introduce all the new viewers to the characters. Since we barely broke 50 in the first year, there were a lot of people out there who didn't know who we were. That new show was sort of our own training film.

"By Year Two, we were more comfortable with the show. We had survived a year; we were back. I heard that Mrs. Paley was mad about the show, and since she lived with the man who had the cancel button right next to his pillow—William Paley—we probably owed her our lives. I hope she's in heaven now for what she did for us.

"We had problems with the writers strike in Year Two. We were all loyal members of the Writers Guild, so we did not work when we weren't supposed to. We were not allowed to plot or plan very much for the next season. We never considered meeting on our own. We really played it by the union book. This did get us off to a slow start.

"When we were able to come back to work, we hired a story editor—Laurence Marks. I was working on breaking up the form a bit. I was trying to find a way to entertain myself and still make the show better.

"One of the best things about Year Two was that we instituted a sort of group therapy. The cast would meet and we sat in chairs—we didn't throw them, that rumor is totally untrue—and we functioned like a giant suggestion box. With that many human beings working under those circumstances, of course it was stressful. There were bound to be problems and conflicts, emotions running high. We talked about how the show was being run, did the actors have enough time to rehearse, that sort of stuff. Some problems we couldn't handle, like problems the actors may have had with the front office. But I cannot remember a time when no one talked or had a 'mad' on. We tried always to be adult enough to work out our problems. After all, we had a common enemy—the network—and we had to all work together to make the best possible show so we could stand united to the network."

CHAPTER III

DIVIDED WE STAND

It was Frank's bitching and moaning that did it. General Cyrus Clayton just couldn't overlook the complaints any longer. He sent down a Captain Philip Hildebrand, MD, US Army, to check out the 4077. "Treating casualties so close to the front," explained the General, "has taken its toll. Maybe that group should be disbanded and shipped to separate units."

Worried that his team would be split, Henry told the staff of Hildebrand's mission and suggested that they cool off whatever personal animosities they had. Hildebrand was not fooled. He overheard Radar's report to Henry: "I've hidden every golf club in the camp, sewed up the hole in the nurses' shower tent, and burned all of Klinger's brassieres."

Hildebrand pretended he had dropped in to observe surgical technique, but Hawkeye wasn't good at pretending anything. Even his friendly overtures about Frank were comic. "The three of us are thinking of going into practice together after we get home—Frank would park cars."

Still, it was hard to fool the man. He had eyes. He saw Hot Lips and Frank meet for a quick one. He spotted Frank stealing someone's clothes from the shower tent. "Childish is what it is," pronounced Hildebrand, "not child-like. You behave in a manner ill-befitting officers of the United States Army, as well as members of the medical profession. You are only a few miles from the front, I'll give you that, and you won't be the first people to crack under the stress of war."

Ten hours later, Hildebrand sang a different song. He had scrubbed and observed in the OR.

"In my short stay here, I've seen textbook examples of neuroses, psychoses, voyeurism, fetishism, and a few 'isms' I've never even heard of. The people here are mad, quite mad, all of them. They are impossible people in an impossible place doing impossible work. The only act I can think of that would be madder would be to break them up."

RADAR'S REPORT

To: Headquarters, Seoul, Commanding General

From: Lieutenant Colonel Henry Blake, Commanding Officer

Subject: Weekly Activity Report and Personnel Record. Period: 17 October to 22 October, inclusive.

17 October: Incoming wounded unusually heavy. All surgical personnel on full alert, working 24 hours. Among incoming surgical cases one enemy prisoner, subheading Infantry, sub-subheading Chinese Communist. Description of prisoner wound attached, see schedule under Wounds comma Chinese comma Communist.

18 October: Lieutenant Erika Johnson reported to duty with Major Margaret Houlihan, Chief of Nurses. Small incident in OR led to wounding of Lieutenant Johnson by berserk Chinese prisoner. Description of wound attached, see schedule under Wounds, comma, Nurses. Father Mulcahy tried to calm prisoner by yelling "Bungchow," thinking it was Chinese for peace and friendship. Unfortunately, it really means, "Your daughter's pregnancy brings much joy to our village." PW contaminated Captain McIntyre's patient in the melee he created before his surgery. PW surgery completed by Captain Pierce. Prisoner recaptured by Corporal Max Klinger, who sustained personal loss of property. See Requisition Form S427J-9, requesting replacement of one brassiere—brand name, "Miss High Rise," 36-B. Acting on complaint of Majors Burns and Houlihan, Colonel Blake has requested psychiatrist from Headquarters to determine if Corporal Klinger can be discharged on Section Eight.

19 October: Number incoming wounded decreased. Captain McIntyre's patient critical. Chinese PW making postop recovery. Lieutenant Erika Johnson recuperating under personal supervision of Captain Pierce. Major Sidney Freedman, divisional staff psychiatrist, arrives tomorrow.

21 October: Doctor Freedman agreed to grant Corporal Klinger a Section Eight. Klinger refused to sign the papers when he discovered it would go on his record for life, not just wartime. Lieutenant Johnson requested transfer.

22 October: Dr. McIntyre lost patient due to complications in OR incident. See deaths, comma, US. Wounded Chinese prisoner recovering.

FIVE O'CLOCK CHARLIE

They called him Five O'clock Charlie, a lone North Korean pilot in a beat-up, single-wing civilian crate that had seen its best years before World War II. He was some kind of hero, Five O'clock Charlie, who felt obliged to fire on a dummy ammunition dump on the far side of the camp at exactly 5 P.M. every night. He was as regular as Ex-Lax, dropped only one mortar and consistently missed. It got so that the staff took to placing bets on just how far he would miss.

Frank was the only one who was not amused. While everyone else turned out for Charlie Spotting as if it were the Queen's Cup Polo Match, Frank requested antiaircraft guns to secure the compound. When General Clayton's Jeep was destroyed by one of Charlie's misplaced bombs, the general decided Frank was right—he sent down a howitzer.

Appalled to have guns at a hospital, Trapper and Hawkeye quickly trained the ROK gunners to blow the dump. Thinking he had finally hit his target, Charlie flew off in glee, never to return again. His departure was announced on the PA:

"And so as he flies the Blue Lady of the Skies into the sunset, we bid aloha to Five O'clock Charlie. With a fond farewell, we return to our duties."

FOR THE GOOD OF THE OUTFIT

They called it "friendly fire" when your own team "accidentally" fired on your men. It killed just the same.

When most of the wounded brought into the 4077 after a shelling turned out to be South Korean civilians, it didn't take long for Hawkeye and Trapper to realize the villagers had been strafed by mistake. Outraged, they forced Henry to get an Army investigator to collect evidence and depositions.

Stars & Stripes reported that the village of Tai-Dong had been fired on by the enemy. The 4077 was pressured to hush up what they knew—for the good of the outfit. Major Ralph Stoner, the investigator, was suddenly transferred to Honolulu. A cover-up was brewing. Trapper and Hawkeye were about to be shipped to the Army's version of Siberia—a little aid station just on the other side of the 38th Parallel.

Then, to everyone's delight, Frank and Margaret turned up with some signed affidavits they had squirreled away. That really put Clayton on the spot.

"We'll be looking for a new story in *Stars & Stripes*, General," Hawkeye said.

"Page one," said Trapper.

"Write it up yourself," the General ordered. "I'll see it gets printed."

DR. PIERCE AND MR. HYDE

Hawkeye walked the fine line more delicately than most. He felt that it was his duty to question the war and its insanity, to push the Army and its insanities to the limit. He was always probing for the boundary that ended just before court-martial. He did so because he had to. He was incapable of turning his eyes, his heart, and his mind away from what he saw. And what he saw drove him to a state of agitation that most would call madness. He was, of course, neither mad nor insane, simply angry and heartsick and, sometimes, totally exhausted.

Once he was so tired after three days of continuous meatball surgery that he slipped into a slaphappy condition that rendered him wackier than ever. He decided to wage a one-man campaign to end the war.

"Just why are we here? What's this war about? Who started it? Was it something we said? Why should the Koreans want to take over America?"

Burns had all the answers. "Let me tell you something, Pierce. Those godless Commies have run their own countries into the toilet while half the people over here haven't even seen a bathroom. And believe you me, they want one. If they can't get bathrooms by subversion, they'll get them by war."

If it was toilets the war was being fought over, Hawkeye was willing to donate the Army's latrines to stop the fighting. First he photographed one so he could mail a snapshot to the North Koreans, then he actually put a latrine on a truck to drive it to Pyongyang, the North Korean capital. Obviously, he didn't know that General Clayton was inside at the time.

"McIntyre," Henry asked, "why does he do these things?"

"I guess he's just unstable," Trapper replied in a patronizing kind of voice. "You see, he took this weird oath as a young man never to just stand there and watch people die."

L.I.P.
(LOCAL INDIGENOUS PERSONNEL)

It was impossible not to be involved with the locals. Hell, the Army had taken over their country, was training their men, mending their wounded, and often marrying their women. Many more women weren't offered the benefits of marriage.

But Corporal Philip Walker wanted to marry Kim, the mother of his child, and he wanted the wedding held before he was shipped home in two weeks. It wasn't as easy as it sounded once the CID (Criminal Investigations Division) officer heard his case and revealed his own opinion of the local women. He thought they were only out for what they could get from US servicemen.

Trapper and Hawkeye to the rescue. They got Lieutenant Willis, their new best friend from CID, drunk on martinis and then moved him to the nurses' tent. When he came to, he thought he'd had a very wild night.

"Yeah," Hawkeye agreed, "and we've got some pictures, too."

"A setup so I'd okay the Walker application? Forget it. I framed more guys in my time than you'll ever operate on. You're bluffing."

The pictures called the bluff. And Willis signed the papers.

"What the hell do I care if Walker marries some bimbo! Let's see him try and get an apartment back home with a Korean wife!"

KIM

"Don't tell me they're drafting five-year-olds?" asked Hawkeye when he took the shrapnel from the leg of a South Korean boy. It didn't take long for Kim to become the camp favorite. Margaret read to him; Hawkeye let him bunk in The Swamp; Radar shared his teddy bear. Trapper wrote his wife to see if Cathy and Becky would like a brother.

When Louise wrote back saying "yes" to the adoption, Trapper ran to tell Kim the good news. He soon discovered that Margaret and Frank had taken the boy on a picnic but had become so engrossed in each other that they did not see him wander off—into a minefield.

Frantic to save the boy, Trapper ran in after him and then he, too, became trapped. As a helicopter hovered to pick them up, Kim dropped his ball and set off a mine. But Trapper and the boy were unhurt and landed safely back at camp. There, they got another shock—Kim's mother had been found.

"Sir," Radar asked, "would you still like to adopt a son? I've been checking and there are possibilities..."

"You got something around five-feet-five? Wears dirty glasses? Never shaves? Two stripes?"

"Well, I am a little old, but could we try it for a week?"

THE TRIAL OF HENRY BLAKE

You had to feel a little sorry for General Clayton. There was a war going on, but all he got was guff from Margaret Houlihan and Frank Burns. Pushing, those two were always pushing to have everything at the 4077 run by the book. Sometimes Clayton found he just couldn't ignore them.

One day he called Henry Blake to Seoul for an official hearing to determine whether Blake was fit to continue his command. Frank Burns had evidently made the charge, listing numerous offenses:

—Conduct unbecoming to an officer in allowing gurney races on Kentucky Derby Day.

—Engaging in private enterprise by allowing Radar to sell wing-tipped shoes.

—Aiding and abetting Klinger in desertion by allowing him to build a hang glider and shove off for freedom.

—Consorting with the enemy by giving medical supplies to a nun who was working a mile north of the 38th Parallel.

Frank was certain Henry would be demoted so he could inherit the command; Hawkeye and Trapper had ideas to the contrary. Threatening to tell Burns's wife about Hot Lips, they forced Frank to drop charges.

Henry was welcomed back like a king. The happy crowd turned out to greet him, each one wearing black-and-white wing-tipped shoes and a great big smile.

DEAR DAD ... THREE

Dear Dad,

The war goes on. And on and on. Our biggest enemy is boredom. You know it's boring here when Trapper and Frank Burns do anything together...today they are playing—and drinking—gin.

Occasionally, we get a kid who comes in with an unexploded grenade that's been shot into his body. Something they neglected to tell us about in medical school. There must be an easier way for a surgeon to make $413.50 a month. After all this time here, I'm still amazed at how young they are when they come in and how old they are when they go home.

Love,
Hawkeye

THE SNIPER

The North Korean sniper must have thought he was firing on General MacArthur's camp, which is why he was so damned persistent. He really meant to become a hero.

Instead, he just made life a little more difficult for the 4077 by firing down on the camp from one of the nearby ridges. He had Henry and Radar trapped in the shower tent. An ambulance driver was wounded trying to unload casualties. Men who thought they had escaped the front with their lives and had a good chance of being patched up at the Mobile Hospital were now being shot at—again.

"It's obvious what we have to do, Henry. Surrender. If we surrender, we can keep working," said Hawkeye.

So they raised the white flag. The ploy worked long enough to get the wounded into the hospital and call HQ for some outside help. A chopper dutifully appeared, pelted fire into the hills, and left. Shortly thereafter, the sniper raised his own white flag—bloodstained.

"It's a trick," cautioned Margaret.

"I'll get your bag," Radar said to Hawkeye.

Unarmed, Hawkeye strode off up the hill, not looking back. The flag had gone down, so he had to poke around the brush looking for his patient. He soon found him—a 17-year-old boy, badly wounded—lying next to a shattered rifle, eyes wide with fear and helplessness.

"If you knew how lucky you are to be getting this house call..."

CARRY ON, HAWKEYE

Asian flu was a virulent form of the grippe that attacked the intestinal tract, rendering the patient unable to eat, stand, or concentrate on anything more than the desire for his mommy to take care of him. It ran through military camps in epidemic proportions, sending hundreds of soldiers to bed and bathroom for forty-eight miserable hours.

Trapper John was one of the first victims. Henry followed, then Frank. Hawkeye and Hot Lips assumed joint command, with Margaret making it clear that she outranked him.

"I want you to know I'm CO," she fumed.

"Funny, you don't look like carbon dioxide."

Together they beat the clock, handled the paper work, and the incoming wounded—until Hawkeye caught the bug. By that time, the others had recovered. They rewarded their hero with a commemorative roll of toilet paper in recognition of his service and dedication while they were ill.

"Thanks," said Hawkeye. "This really gets me where I live."

THE INCUBATOR

"You mean I've got to wait seventy-two hours to ship blood to Tokyo and get results back before I treat this kid?" Hawkeye was incensed. "His white count is higher than a kite. His head's so hot you can fry an egg on it! Why don't we have our own incubator?"

Because the Army hadn't shipped any to Ouijongbu. But three went to Pusan, so Trapper and Hawkeye went to get one, only to discover a lot of Army doubletalk and black market shenanigans. They had only one

Scenes from *The Sniper*,
with guest actress Teri Garr
at upper left

choice of action; they decided to crash a press conference held by General Maynard M. Mitchell, who didn't know what the hell they were talking about when they questioned him about an incubator. Mitchell had them cited for insubordination, conduct unbecoming to an officer, and a few other violations.

Henry got them off the hook, but they still had no incubator. Then Radar went to work. Within twenty-four hours, he had a gift for the Swampmen.

"Ta-dah! Happy Germs, sirs!"

He didn't say he had traded it for Henry's golf bag.

DEAL ME OUT

Major Sidney Freedman stopped by the 4077 every now and then, ostensibly to play poker but also to keep tabs on everyone's mental health. Freedman was stationed with the 325th Evac in Seoul, but he considered Ouijongbu commuting distance.

Poker was an important part of every fighting man's survival skills—even Harry Truman was known to deal a few hands while holed up on an aircraft carrier for strategic conferences. The game in The Swamp changed personnel frequently, with players dealing themselves in and out.

One night, Henry had to get up when Radar reported he had run over a local; Frank had to be dealt in when he found that he couldn't operate on his next patient, who happened to be an Army counterintelligence officer. Frank knew that regulations said intelligence officers could not be operated on unless another intelligence officer was on the scene. Afraid Frank's patient would croak while his doctor played it by the book, Trapper and Hawkeye dealt themselves out in order to disobey orders and save the man's life.

They were arrested for the violation later, but not before Sidney dealt himself out to take care of a psycho who was holding Frank as a hostage. By the time reveille was sounded, all the players were back at the table, and it was caduceuses wild.

HOT LIPS AND EMPTY ARMS

Major Margaret Houlihan had tantrums every now and then, usually brought on by a letter from someone back home. The letter usually triggered an envy response and caused the good major to reevaluate her life and her circumstances. During these periods of angst, she felt old, ugly, unmarried—which she was—and childless—which she also was—and frustrated—which she was without doubt. Invariably at such times, she requested a transfer.

This time her transfer was granted. She got really sloshed at her good-bye party and, in fact, was so drunk that she called Frank "Ferret Face" and astonished everyone.

The sound of incoming choppers forced Trapper and

Hawkeye to take her to the shower for a sobering discussion.

"New surgical procedure," announced Hawkeye. "You have to scrub up from head to toe. In your clothes."

Once she was sober enough to work, Margaret realized that it would be hard to find such loyal friends at another hospital and changed her mind about the transfer.

"Doctors," she whispered in her mask so only they could hear her, "I'm grateful for your helping me."

"Don't mention it," said Hawkeye.

"To anyone!" Trapper added.

OFFICERS ONLY

To Trapper and Hawkeye, all men were created equal. Some, however, had more equal fathers. Take the case of Private Gary Mitchell, for example. His father, General Maynard Mitchell, was so pleased with the medical attention given his boy that the entire 4077 benefited.

Trapper and Hawkeye got three-day passes to Tokyo, which they used to their best advantage. When they returned, they discovered that an Officers Club had been built for the 4077. Unfortunately, however, only officers were allowed to use it—leaving some of their friends out in the cold.

To make their point, they waited until General Mitchell arrived for the club's opening and tried to take his son inside.

"General," said Hawkeye, "perhaps you never realized it, but your wife gave birth to an enlisted man. Don't you think we should stretch the point and make an exception here for relatives, sir?"

The general readily agreed, and Hawkeye waved in his family—his son, Radar; his sister, Klinger; his cousin, Archie; his nephew; his. . .

HENRY IN LOVE

While at a medical conference in Tokyo, Henry met a cute young thing named Nancy Sue Parker and fell head over size-12 Army boots in love with the twenty-year-old chickadee. A civilian clerk, Nancy Sue got herself a pass to the war zone and came calling on Henry one weekend.

Henry spent the week preparing for her arrival. He dyed his hair, did push-ups, and began to jog himself into a lean, mean machine. On her arrival, Nancy Sue impressed no one but Henry. The others found her not only juvenile but an outrageous flirt. When Nancy Sue made a blatant pass at Hawkeye, there was obvious panic in the surgeon's heart.

"Thanks from the bottom of my mouth, but we're not in the parking lot at the prom. One of us loves Henry Blake—and I think it's me. So it's been nice meeting you and your pom-poms, but no thanks."

Radar, well tuned to the tension caused by Nancy Sue, patched through a well-timed call to Henry's wife. Within seconds, Henry came back to earth, remembering the real girl back home.

Nancy Sue left the next day.

FOR WANT OF A BOOT...

It was the Army way of life. If you wanted it, you couldn't get it. If you didn't need it, you had a lifetime supply. So when Hawkeye's right boot wore out and all he could get from the supply officer were diapers or rubber pants, he decided to put together his own barter deal.

The supply officer hinted that he could be more helpful if he could only get a dental appointment; the dentist wanted a pass to Tokyo; Hot Lips got involved in the deal because she wanted to give Frank a sincere little birthday party; Radar wanted a date with Nurse Murphy, who wanted a hair dryer and, naturally, Klinger had the only hair dryer in the war—which he was willing to part with only for a discharge.

When the discharge fell through, the whole pyramid collapsed, and each person reneged on his part of the deal. In the end, Hawkeye, undaunted, started wearing a golf bag on his right leg.

OPERATION NOSELIFT

It was against Army regulations for cosmetic medical work to be performed on GIs at mobile hospitals. The plastic surgeons that were on loan to Uncle Sam, therefore, worked out of Tokyo General Hospital, fondly called "Tokyo Gen" by those who knew it well, where they worked their magic on burn victims and did facial reconstruction for those unlucky souls who had seen the inside of a mortar from close range.

When Private Danny Baker asked Hawkeye for a nose job, it turned out that the young man had such an obsession with his nose that it was hard for Hawkeye and Trapper to turn him away. Hawkeye decided to call Dr. Stanley Robbins, a friend of his from medical school who was serving his war duty at Tokyo Gen. Robbins finally agreed to come in to Ouijongbu for the weekend if he could be provided with the favors of a nurse—and not at the operating table. Hawkeye agreed to make the arrangements.

Next came the tricky part—the paperwork. Baker had to be "officially" sent to Tokyo, and Radar had to "injure" his nose while playing baseball and require rhinoplasty. All went well. Baker got his new nose, and Robbins got his nurse.

Except that Hawkeye had forgotten to find a nurse and never knew which one Robbins hooked on his own.

THE CHOSON PEOPLE

One of the most painful aspects of the Korean War was its effect on the local population, most of whom had very little idea why UN troops were fighting in a civil war.

When the family that had owned the farmland on which the 4077 then stood came back to reclaim its land, it was not easy to explain the situation. Public relations became even more strained when a young South Korean woman arrived with an infant and insisted that Radar was the child's father.

Radar rather liked the idea. "I'd had two beers, and I was looking for trouble," he explained. "I was coming back home in the Jeep when I saw her hitching a ride. I stopped. I'd rather not say any more in front of the baby."

A blood test proved that Radar was in no way related to the child. The woman and her baby would have become another tragic pair of displaced persons, but the farm family took them into their hearts. They all headed south to a refugee camp and a new life.

The war made strange families every day.

AS YOU WERE

In one of the many lulls between fighting, and with boredom at a peak, Frank asked Hawkeye and Trapper to operate on his hernia. The cutters were happy enough to comply—things in camp were so slow that they had taken to wearing gorilla suits for a few laughs.

Frank was being prepped when incoming wounded forced him off the gurney and onto his feet. Serious shelling and a lack of whole blood made conditions in the OR worse than usual. And when it rains, it pours. Frank's hernia became so bad that he had to be sent to preop while at the same time the doctors had to admit a Korean woman who was ready to give birth.

Frank came out of anesthesia to the cries of a baby.

"Congratulations," Hawkeye said. "You and Hot Lips are the proud parents of a five-pound hernia."

Their surgical duties finished, Hawkeye and Trapper moved on to the Officers Club—gorilla suits and all.

"Two martinis, please," ordered Trapper.

"And don't spare the bananas."

CRISIS

Heavy bombing knocked out the supply lines just south of Seoul, cutting off the 4077 without sufficient food, fuel, bandages, or shuttlecocks for badminton.

"How do they expect us to fight the war without shuttlecocks?" Hawkeye deadpanned.

To make do, each officer had an assigned emergency job—heating, power, rationing, morale, etc. To save on fuel, the heating officer moved three more men into The Swamp, including Klinger, whose nightly beauty routine kept everyone awake. Klinger was soon dispatched to the nurses' tent.

With lack of sleep, lack of heat, and grueling hours in the OR, tension ran high. Then the men discovered that Frank had been wearing electric booties all along.

"They're hunting socks," Klinger explained. "They run on a battery. I got a bra just like 'em."

Fortunately, the crisis ended before Frank could be lynched. HQ sent through the needed supplies and everyone settled back to normal except for Henry, whose office furniture had been burned for firewood.

Where there's smoke, there's fire.

GEORGE

In 1950, homosexuals were called "queers," and the world's treatment of them was, indeed, queer. The wounds that brought Private George Weston to the 4077 were unique.

"You don't get bruises like that in combat, Trapper. Looks like someone used him for batting practice."

George explained it himself. "Two guys got beaten up in my outfit. One colored, the other homosexual. As you can see, Doc, I'm not colored."

No one at the 4077 could have been more homophobic than Frank Burns, who, as soon as he discovered Weston's disadvantage, began to arrange for the man's dishonorable discharge. Henry signed the papers.

The only thing to do was to make Frank realize that every man has a secret that would be better left out of his records. Sure enough, they got old Ferret Face to confess that he had paid for the answers to an exam for his board certification, a little secret that would certainly tarnish his standing in the medical community if it went on his record.

Private Weston was returned to his unit shortly thereafter. He served out his hitch and later returned to the States a war hero. Which he was.

MAIL CALL

Mail call brought no excitement to Hawkeye's life, so he felt compelled to cook up a little trouble with someone else's mail. When he discovered that Frank's entire portfolio of Wall Street stocks had arrived, and the man was going all over camp boasting to everyone how much money he had made in the market, Hawkeye decided to get to work. To his credit, he told Radar not to put through any phone calls that Frank might be requesting.

Then he got to work convincing Frank to sell off everything he owned in order to invest in what sounded like the hottest new corporation around, Pioneer Aviation, a company that Hawkeye had just invented. The tip made greedy Frank desperate to reach his broker.

Hot Lips was most appreciative. If Frank could clean up on a stock deal, he would be rich enough to divorce his wife and marry her.

"Actually," Frank admitted, "I was thinking more of a cute little apartment for you, close to my office, you know, for lunch times? I'll pay the rent and give you $100 a month allowance."

"I get $400 a month now as a major."

When the prank had gone far enough, Hawkeye confessed. "I made it all up to help you look foolish."

"But I don't need any help," said a sheepish Frank.

SMATTERING OF INTELLIGENCE

The CIA had been created shortly after World War II and was still learning real spy stuff at the outbreak of the Korean War. But the Army got its intelligence from G-2, so there was plenty of competition.

Colonel Flagg showed up at the 4077 again, this time with a broken arm. He was the apparent victim of a chopper crash, but he soon proved to be in the compound on a snooping mission. The Swampmen only discovered this when Vinny Pratt, a boyhood friend of Trapper's, also turned up at the 4077 and explained that not only was Flagg a spook but that he had broken his own arm just to get a few days in the hospital to check everyone out. Pratt was privy to this because he, too, was a spy. Pratt and Flagg had more official identities than the Great Impostor, and they soon began to out-snoop one another.

Disgusted, Trapper and Hawkeye decided to give the spies something to think about. When they learned that each man was checking out Frank Burns, they planted two separate files: one that proved beyond a doubt that Frank was a Communist; the other proving that he was nothing but a Fascist. When the two spies tried to arrest Frank, Hawkeye explained the gag and forced the two agents to team up as friends.

After all, two cameras are better than one.

Opposite, above and below: Mail Call

It Happened One Night

YEAR TWO (1973–74)

NAME: ALDA, ALAN
CHARACTER: PIERCE, BENJAMIN FRANKLIN ("HAWKEYE"), MD
RANK: CAPTAIN, USAMC
SERIAL NUMBER: US12836413

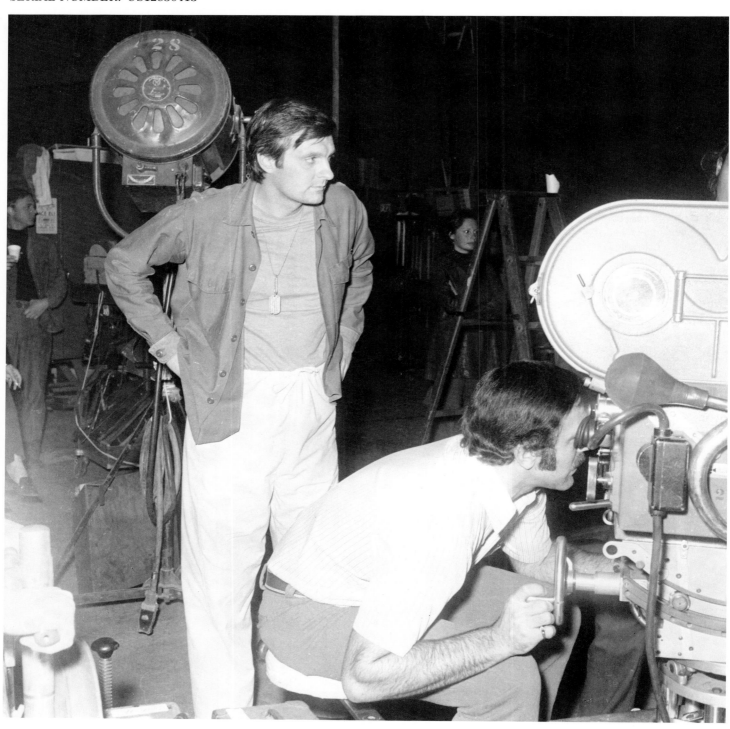

"My first reaction to the part of Hawkeye Pierce was to turn it down. I didn't see how I could juggle the commute and I wasn't going to ask my family to do it. I didn't want our lives controlled by a job contract. The pilot script looked wonderful, but I wanted to make sure it wouldn't be a show in which a lot of silliness was set against the background of war, with the war as just a straight line for the jokes. Larry Gelbart wrote an extremely fine pilot. It was head and shoulders above anything I had read. I had turned down a lot of series, mainly on the basis of quality. I was afraid that Larry would go back to England after the pilot and that the war would be treated by the writers and the production staff as backdrop for lighthearted high jinks. I didn't want any part of that. I wanted to show that the war was a bad place to be...that people got hurt in war and that it was not the occasion of hilarity. The way people reacted to it might be hilarious.

"I had done eight movies and a lot of theater work before M*A*S*H, but I had no problems about going into a television series. It was clear it was going to be a classy project. From the outset, I hoped we could do something of quality. Three or four of the early scripts were done by outside writers and were weak. They were all in the style of light service comedy. It wasn't clear to many people that we wanted to have two levels going on at once. I don't mean two story lines. I mean two levels of intent, with light on top and serious underneath. I remember one week, McLean Stevenson made a very important contribution by saying, 'I really don't think this is the best we can do. I think you should do it, but I wish you would do it without me this week.' He did it in a gentle way. He didn't say, 'I'm walking.' He said he wanted more quality. Gene and Larry responded. Each week, we got a little stronger. The shows Larry wrote were very witty and brilliant and, by the middle of the first season, we had already gotten to show *Sometimes You Hear the Bullet*, where the patient dies on the operating table. We were beginning to mix the dark with the light. The network said, 'What is this? A comedy or a tragedy?' They were afraid the audience wouldn't accept it. The audience has always been ahead of the network.

"By the time I wrote *Dreams*, a story in which exhausted characters lie down at odd moments in a period of heavy casualties and have dreams, the audience sort of had a pact with us. We were allowed to be as imaginative as we wanted because they knew we would never be wanton with them. As the years went by, we found more ways to dig deeper and, instead of doing the same stories, we were looking for different ways to tell different stories. We also found new things to say about the characters. I don't think Hawkeye changed much in the eleven years—I think we just know more about him and see through his behavior more. We see frailties and human flaws and characteristic ways of dealing with people that are not all that heroic but that make him a more rounded person.

"M*A*S*H isn't really a sitcom. We'd do a show without anything funny in it. We'd mix the heavy and the light. We'd be incredibly silly. The brutality of the war combined with the desire to heal—no other comedy on TV has had such a powerful basis. I got a lot of letters from people thanking us for making them laugh and cry at the same time. When you can do that, it's the best kind of drama because it's what life is.

"We never planned the success of M*A*S*H; it just happened. If we had planned it, there would have been enormous disappointments. Our joke in the beginning was that...you know how shows are in the Top Ten? Well, we wanted to be in the Top Fifty. We were at the bottom of the list when we started. We were opposite successful shows, and people didn't know what we were trying to do, and it took a while to get going.

"I had a rough schedule. I was shooting twelve hours a day during the week and writing at night because I was filling in the time I was alone with writing, so I was working fifteen to eighteen hours a day. On weekends, I'd fly out on Friday nights. Arlene was very sweet. She'd meet me at the airport at six in the morning. The hour we had driving from the airport to home was one of the nicest times for us. In the first year, I wrote one show, one or two in the second, and then a little later I was writing four or five. When Larry Gelbart left, Burt turned to me more because Burt and I were the only two people on the writing staff who had been there from the beginning. We were both concerned with keeping a continuity in terms of knowledge of characters.

"I don't know what other people go through with their shows. We were committed from the beginning to doing something as good as it promised to be. It always promised more—it was a bottomless concept; you could always dig deeper into it. We all felt we were dealing with something that was more important than anything we would ever be connected with again. We had a very deep body of water."

Alan Alda

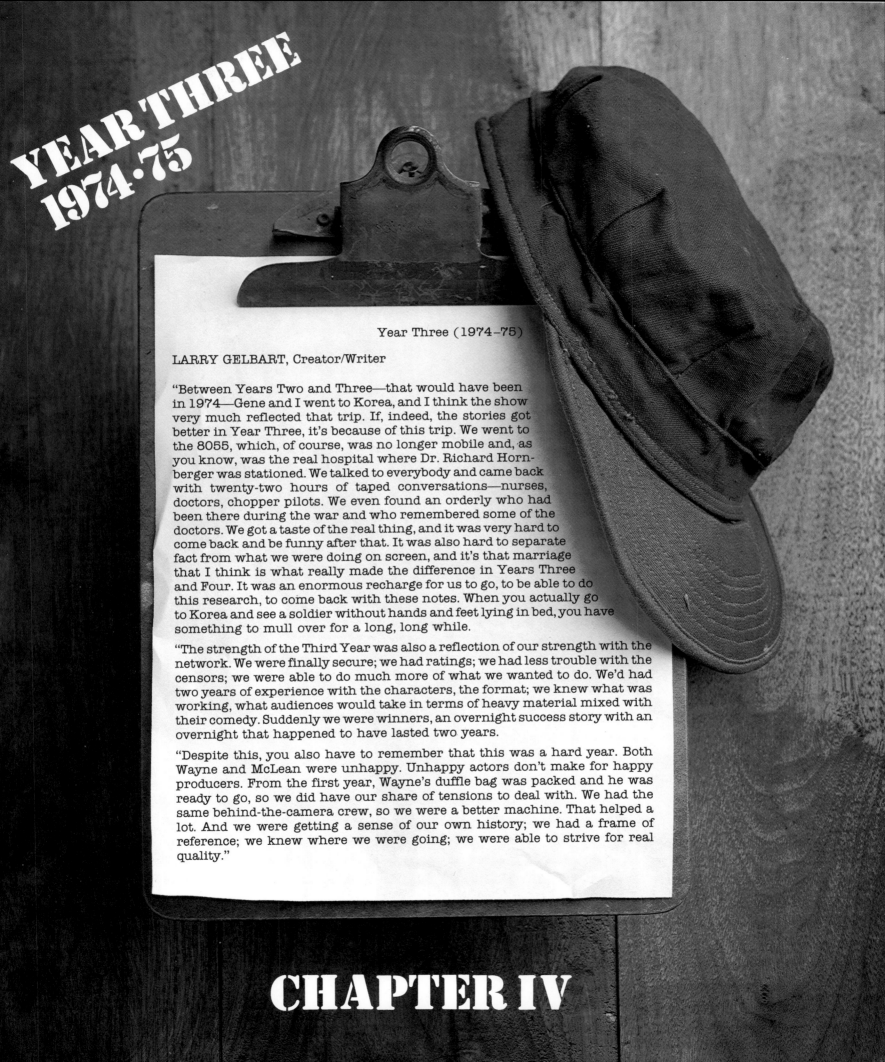

Year Three (1974–75)

LARRY GELBART, Creator/Writer

"Between Years Two and Three—that would have been in 1974—Gene and I went to Korea, and I think the show very much reflected that trip. If, indeed, the stories got better in Year Three, it's because of this trip. We went to the 8055, which, of course, was no longer mobile and, as you know, was the real hospital where Dr. Richard Hornberger was stationed. We talked to everybody and came back with twenty-two hours of taped conversations—nurses, doctors, chopper pilots. We even found an orderly who had been there during the war and who remembered some of the doctors. We got a taste of the real thing, and it was very hard to come back and be funny after that. It was also hard to separate fact from what we were doing on screen, and it's that marriage that I think is what really made the difference in Years Three and Four. It was an enormous recharge for us to go, to be able to do this research, to come back with these notes. When you actually go to Korea and see a soldier without hands and feet lying in bed, you have something to mull over for a long, long while.

"The strength of the Third Year was also a reflection of our strength with the network. We were finally secure; we had ratings; we had less trouble with the censors; we were able to do much more of what we wanted to do. We'd had two years of experience with the characters, the format; we knew what was working, what audiences would take in terms of heavy material mixed with their comedy. Suddenly we were winners, an overnight success story with an overnight that happened to have lasted two years.

"Despite this, you also have to remember that this was a hard year. Both Wayne and McLean were unhappy. Unhappy actors don't make for happy producers. From the first year, Wayne's duffle bag was packed and he was ready to go, so we did have our share of tensions to deal with. We had the same behind-the-camera crew, so we were a better machine. That helped a lot. And we were getting a sense of our own history; we had a frame of reference; we knew where we were going; we were able to strive for real quality."

CHAPTER IV

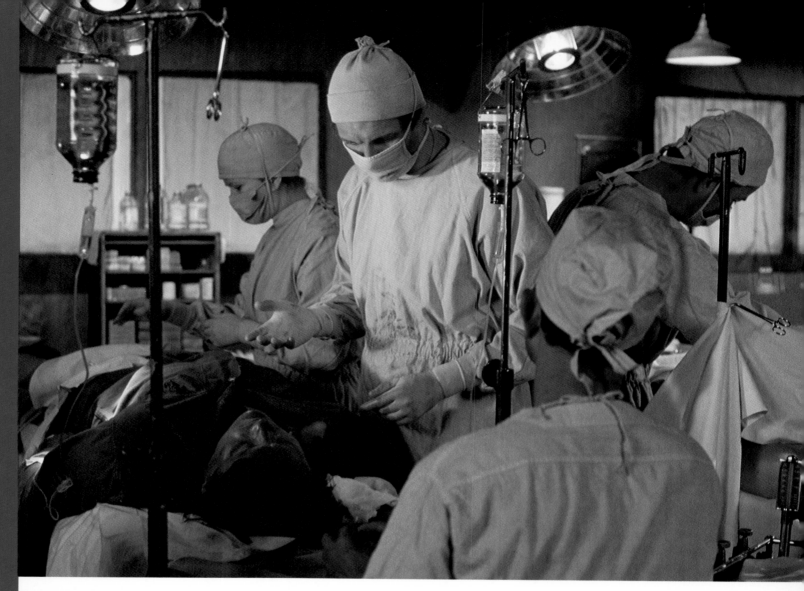

Scenes from *Springtime,* with guest actor Alex Karras

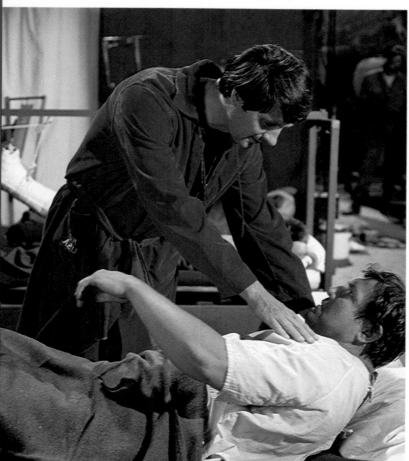

RAINBOW BRIDGE

According to The Book, which is the Army Book of Rules and Regulations and is not to be confused with The Good Book, American wounded were treated first, then Allies, and finally enemies. The enemy was expected to treat wounded in the same manner. But it was well known that many so-called doctors on the other side weren't even MDs. They were male nurses, medics, sons of midwives, maybe even barbers. Like the Dark Ages. After all, not many Korean doctors interned at Mass General. American prisoners' chances of dying from battle wounds were far greater than those of the enemy.

Occasionally, the North Koreans swapped back American wounded. The Chinese did not. So it came as quite a surprise when the Chinese notified HQ that they held nine GIs they were unable to treat and suggested a team from the 4077 drive fifty miles into their territory to pick up the wounded.

"It's an ambush!" shouted Frank, in panic.

"Ambush!" Hot Lips agreed. "You better consider the very real possibility of capture, torture, brainwashing, and even—rape."

Good old Margaret, you could always count on her to put her finger on the pulse of the matter.

The real dangers seemed insignificant to Trapper and Hawkeye. They cared more for patients than their personal safety. They volunteered immediately. Afraid that Frank would look like a coward for not going, Hot Lips convinced him to join the mission and sent him off packing a small pistol that her father had given her mother on their wedding night.

Just as the Swampmen approached the enemy, Frank blabbed that he was carrying a gun despite the Chinese ruling against weapons.

"Are you out of what's left of your brain?" asked Hawkeye, more disgusted than usual.

Naturally, when Captain Lin Tam, the Chinese medical officer in charge of the swap, discovered the breach of faith, he called the whole thing off and stalked away. But Hawkeye and Trapper forced Frank to turn in the gun so the exchange could proceed. Tam had been educated in the States and spoke perfect English, so he understood Pierce's pleas.

"You've started something really decent in the middle of an indecent war, Tam," said Hawkeye; "don't let nine men suffer because one idiot thinks he can play General Custer."

The nine men crossed Rainbow Bridge—to freedom, to the medical care they needed, to home.

LIFE WITH FATHER

It wan't easy on Father Mulcahy, administering to the souls of five religions in the compound, providing for the orphans at Sister Theresa's, and then standing in as a nurse or orderly when the need arose. His busy season, however, was usually late afternoon, after mail call.

There was no telling what the mail could bring and how it would affect the personnel.

One week, Henry got a letter from his wife, Lorraine, that made him suspect she was having an affair with a doctor back home—the one who drove a new Jaguar and was a member of the country club. Father Mulcahy got a letter from his sister, a "sister," saying she was thinking of leaving her order to eventually marry and have a family. Very distressing news to John Francis Patrick Mulcahy. Trapper and Hawkeye also got mail—a contest entry blank suggesting that if they located the ten presidents depicted in the farm-scene-cum-entry blank, they would win a pony. Anxious to win the pony for the orphans, they used a microscope to locate some of the famous faces. Stumped after nine, they had no idea where the tenth presidential face was hiding.

Their pondering was interrupted when they were called to OR to perform a circumcision on a local newborn. As they left the OR, Hawkeye's face brightened with enlightenment.

"I know where to look for the missing president!" he announced to Trapper and rushed back to The Swamp.

SPRINGTIME

It was one of those rare spring days in Korea—blue skies, mild temperatures, wildflowers blooming in the minefields, and no incoming wounded. Frank and Margaret were just warming up the passion machine as they enjoyed a picnic. Klinger was nearby, sitting under a tree in a spring frock, reading a book of poetry. The corporal's skirts were soon flying when Radar brought him a letter from home with the announcement that his girl, Laverne Esposito, had agreed to marry him. Father Mulcahy could perform the ceremony via shortwave radio.

Radar picked up Klinger's discarded poetry book and began his own rites of spring with a nurse named Louise. They disappeared for the afternoon while Klinger donned a wedding gown of white satin and Belgian lace before being patched through to Toledo for the proxy ceremony.

Just as the rice was thrown, a dazed and lipstick-stained Radar stumbled into the ceremony and caught the wedding bouquet. Flustered, he quickly tossed the blossoms to Margaret, who was ecstatic.

"Look, Frank!" she shouted gleefully. "I caught it! I caught it! Do you know what that means?"

Then it started to rain.

IRON GUTS KELLY

When Iron Guts Kelly came to call, all were impressed. A three star general who wore matching pearl-handled guns on his hips and was rumored to fight in purple shorts under his Class A uniform, he came to the 4077 to check out the unit's excellent reputation. But the thing that impressed him most was Hot Lips.

So Hawkeye and Trapper were most surprised when later that night Margaret barged into The Swamp, panic written all over her whisper. Guided to her tent, the doctors found Iron Guts Kelly sprawled across a cot—dead.

"If his last words were 'I shall return'," Hawkeye murmured, "don't wait."

"Get him out of here," hissed Hot Lips. "Frank's coming!"

The general's aide wanted it reported that old Iron Guts Kelly died a fighting man, with his boots on, but the doctors refused to fudge the death certificate. Unable to find a nearby battle so he could relocate the corpse, the aide then drove the body to Sector G and ordered the Navy to bomb the hell out of the area.

Weeks later, *Stars & Stripes* reported a touching story of the general's heroic death.

PAYDAY

Payday came once a month and was traditionally followed by a well-attended poker game in the mess tent.

Hawkeye discovered an overpayment of $10 in his monthly salary and dutifully reported it to Radar. He was deluged with the traditional paperwork that accompanied any Army business. But honesty paid well. He got back a check for $3,000. Not anxious to go through all the paperwork again, Hawkeye decided not to report the mistake and instead donated the money to Father Mulcahy for the orphanage.

The next day he was arrested for failure to repay the missing $3,000. Not wanting to explain the delicate situation to Father Mulcahy, Hawkeye did the only other thing he knew how to do—he sat in on the poker game. And when Trapper cleaned up, Hawkeye commandeered his buddy's winnings and paid off his debt. There wasn't too much Trapper could say—he had staked his way into the game by stealing Hawkeye's watch.

O.R.

It could be like that—shells bursting, guns booming, planes flying so low the gurneys vibrated. Naturally those days brought in the heaviest casualties, many of them barely-breathing mounds. Father Mulcahy was always close by on those days, to lend a hand or a cross.

They were often desperate times; long shifts, enormous pressure, and countless life and death decisions made without the extra seconds a civilian doctor might have for the same medical conclusions.

During one particularly heavy session, Henry's arthritis got so bad he periodically dropped equipment. He worked through spasms with clenched fists. Hawkeye had to manually massage a man's heart, then later lost him in postop. "Maybe he would have made it," Hawkeye shook his head, "if I could have stayed by his bedside. But there were too many other men who needed me more."

Then Henry drew a patient who was so badly wounded

Officer of the Day

that it would have taken two surgeons eight hours to patch him up. The doctors knew that the first six hours after the wound were the critical ones; if the soldier could make it that far and could get to a hospital in time, he had a very good chance of survival. But this was one soldier whose time had run out.

Henry wasn't too good at decisions in the first place, and this was the kind that no doctor liked to make. Should he attempt to save the man's life, tying up vital blood, supplies, time, and employing doctors who could otherwise help several other men? Or should he let the man go? In agony, he consulted Hawkeye.

"You know, Henry," Hawkeye said gently, "he never should have been brought here in the first place."

OFFICER OF THE DAY

When Hawkeye was Officer of the Day, the war went on hold. Unless, of course, there was an emergency. Like the time Colonel Flagg stopped by with a wounded North Korean prisoner he wanted patched up so he could take the man to Seoul to be executed.

Flagg was an intelligence officer whose intelligence was questioned by everyone, especially Trapper and Hawkeye. "You want me to save the kid's life so you can take it away from him?" was all the incredulous OD could ask.

He and Trapper felt compelled to draw out the healing process as long as possible to keep Flagg from fulfilling his mission. In fact, when Flagg forced them to place the man on a stretcher, the Swampmen found a willing ringer. As the bandaged and blanketed man was moved out of the hospital and lifted into the ambulance, Flagg was a happy man—until Klinger's handbag fell off the stretcher and one more escape was foiled.

THE GENERAL FLIPPED AT DAWN

The sane only acted insane, it was their defense against the insanity of it all. The truly insane had it more difficult. So when Major General Bartford Hamilton Steele arrived to inspect the 4077, he was given the respect his rank called for—by those who could muster up respect for Army brass. Frank turned up all spit and polish; Hawkeye turned up out of uniform in the supply room with a nurse; and Klinger wore a big picture hat, a smashing new dress, matching pumps and handbag, and, of course, white gloves.

One way or the other, Steele was impressed but obliged to make his own contribution. Alarmed that it took a full twenty minutes to evacuate wounded from the front to the MASH, the general decided to move the unit closer to the war.

It was not unusual for a MASH unit to move as the war progressed (one MASH unit moved thirty-three times in one year), but moving onto the actual battleground was not traditional. It was then that Pierce and McIntyre began to suspect that the officer was "quackers."

"That man's a nut," diagnosed Dr. Pierce even though he had only done a three-month rotation in psychiatry his third year of med school. "I've seen that look in the eyes in every Hitchcock movie."

Sure enough, Steele was found to be quite mad. He kept bursting into song-and-dance routines. He would have managed to kill most of the life-saving men and women of the MASH as well as their patients had he succeeded in moving the unit forward. Instead, the doctors were able to ship him home. A few weeks later, they read in *Stars & Stripes* that Steele had a new assignment in the Pentagon—in charge of the entire Asian theater.

Typical Army.

There Is Nothing Like a Nurse

THERE IS NOTHING LIKE A NURSE

The nurses had to be evacuated when the threat of an enemy parachute drop was reported to the 4077 by HQ. Tender partings were the order of the day as the men sang their own version of *arirang*, the Korean lament of lovers parting. Then the hands that were normally used to save lives took up shovels and began digging foxholes. Tension ran high; doctors had to double as nurses—even Radar and Father Mulcahy were forced to scrub. Dr. Spalding took to standing on his head in the Officers Club while Frank threatened Hot Lips' life if she spoke to another man while away.

To break the tension while waiting for the invasion, Trapper and Hawkeye stole the home movies of Frank's wedding from under his bed and yawned through the whole joyless affair. "The plot thins," Hawkeye sighed. "Watch the cake sue for malpractice when Frank cuts into it."

When the enemy drop finally happened, there was nothing to it. In fact, Five O'clock Charlie just buzzed by with a parcel of propaganda love letters: "Harry Truman is sleeping with your wife."

The area was declared safe for women; the nurses were brought back.

"This way, ladies," chorused Pierce and McIntyre as they greeted the returning nurses. "Step right into our cozy little tent. We kept it just the way you left it."

PRIVATE CHARLES LAMB

It was well known that you can take the boy out of the country but not the country out of the boy, so no one was surprised when Radar began to keep stray animals in his own little private zoo.

His prize pet was a lamb, compliments of the UN-sponsored Greek troops, whose wounded were treated at the 4077. When he discovered that the lamb was due to be barbecued at a Greek bash, Radar acted quickly, trumping up a set of papers and wangling a medical discharge for a Private Charles Lamb. Radar rescued the critter and had him shipped to his family farm in Iowa.

"Colonel Andropolis had that lamb flown in from Greece and you tell me the damn thing has flown the coop?" Henry squawked, disbelievingly.

"On Bo-Peep Airlines," Hawkeye chimed in.

Not wanting to ruin the Greek feast day or jeopardize Radar's career, Hawkeye and team labored half the night to come up with a work of art—a lamb created from Spam.

A FULL RICH DAY

War casualties went through elaborate tagging procedures at the front—all designed to enhance survival. The dead were separated from the wounded at an aid station, and the wounded were immediately evacuated for further medical help. The dead got toe tags; the wounded were tagged on their chests or dog tags. Once

Above left: There Is Nothing Like a Nurse

Below left: Springtime

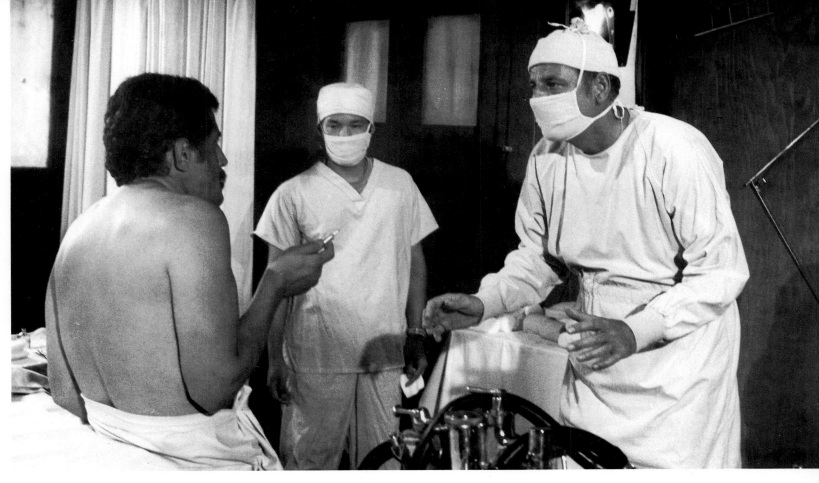

they arrived at a MASH unit, they went through the process of triage—triage is a French word, from the verb *trier*, meaning to separate. During triage, doctors and nurses worked to separate the wounded into three categories: No. 1—those who needed care immediately; No. 2—those who could wait; and No. 3—those who were judged beyond help.

Lieutenant Henri-Batiste LeClerc from Luxembourg arrived at the 4077, proceeded through triage as a No. 2—and then disappeared. It was rather much of a mystery.

"He's kind of dead, sir," Radar reported tentatively, since he couldn't prove that the man was alive.

HQ put pressure on the unit to find a body, but no body was readily available. In desperation, Henry ordered a memorial service for the man, hoping, so to speak, to bury the issue. Just as the PA began to warble the national anthem of Luxembourg, a bandaged figure stumbled from the OR and managed a shaky salute. His aide-de-camp recognized him despite the bandages—the missing man, LeClerc.

"Well, that's how it is," explained Hawkeye, "You lose a few and you lose a few."

CHECKUP

Army regulations prior to 1973 clearly stipulated that all personnel were to have a medical checkup once a year: the enlisted men to be examined by medical officers and the medical officers, in turn, to be examined by each other.

When Trapper resisted his checkup, it was clear to Hawkeye that his favorite tentmate had a problem. Finally Trapper confessed that he had an ulcer but didn't want it treated in a place like the 4077.

"That's not an ulcer, it's a ticket home!" shouted the elated Hawkeye.

The farewell party for Trapper was just underway when the message from HQ arrived announcing that ulcer cases were no longer being sent stateside. Dr. McIntyre had his choice of three weeks at Tokyo Gen or being treated by his own unit.

"The Army, in its infinite insanity, says I cannot go home. Seems my least objectionable option is staying here in this upholstered men's room. So drinks for everyone," ordered Trapper. "The milk's on me."

BIG MAC

It was early in 1951 that General MacArthur made his visit to the 4077. Frank and Hot Lips went berserk with excitement as they prepared for the visit. Hawkeye and Trapper reacted with their typical disdain.

"We should give the general a big treat when he comes to call," Hawkeye suggested. "Why don't we operate on him? For the big finish, how about a postop infection?"

But it was Klinger who was the most excited—after all, he reasoned, if MacArthur saw him in drag, surely the big man would grant the discharge he craved. But Henry would have none of it; in fact, he was so panicked by what Klinger might do that he ordered the corporal to

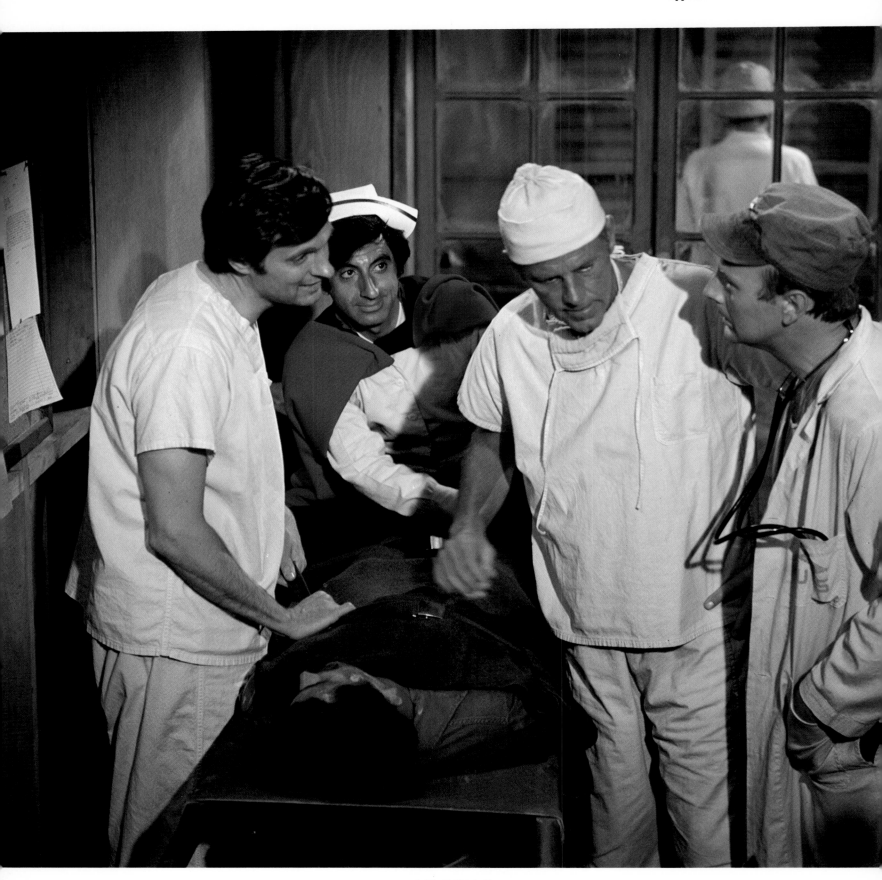

A Full Rich Day

stay out of sight. Klinger was undaunted. First, he showed up in a nurse's uniform, then a kimono, and finally, decked out as the Statue of Liberty, he stood on a tree stump to personally welcome Big Mac. As the general was driven into camp, chomping on his corncob pipe, he looked up from the maps he was studying and saluted Miss Liberty.

Just one more huddled mass yearning to be free.

Above: House Arrest

Left: Alcoholics Unanimous

Top and above: The Consultant

ALCOHOLICS UNANIMOUS

It was drink, not drugs, that got many a man through the Korean War, so when Frank, in charge while Henry attended a medical conclave in Hawaii, ordered prohibition and then personally dismantled the still in the Bachelor Officers' Tent, all hell broke lose.

Hot Lips took to mixing her own brew in the supply room while Pierce and McIntyre hit up Father Mulcahy for a little sacramental grape juice. Frank then ordered the padre to preach a sermon on the evils of drink, which was made required attendance for the entire camp. The large crowd so unnerved Father Mulcahy that he took a slug—or two—of sacramental wine and ended up tipsy. Trapper rushed up to the man's aid but, unfortunately, stepped on Hawkeye's foot and set off a chain reaction that created total melee among officers and enlisted men. As a result of the brawl, Frank ended up in pain on the floor. Margaret rushed to his aid with a swig from her flask and prohibition was instantly repealed.

HOUSE ARREST

The tensions of war often created personal strife among the men, and no one deserved a right hook more than Frank. When Hawkeye actually hit him, Frank filed charges and Hot Lips gave a deposition that reported quite clearly what she had seen. Hawkeye was put under house arrest.

But not everyone agreed that Hawkeye should be court-martialed, including a visiting senior officer who was inspecting the 4077's nursing corps. Colonel Rachel Reese spent a good bit of time with Hot Lips, heard the problem, and then decided to teach the younger nurse an important lesson in the shortness of human memory.

With perfect timing, Colonel Reese made a pass at Frank then stood back and yelled "rape" just as Major Houlihan entered the tent. This made Hot Lips her witness. Frank was then put under house arrest until Margaret decided that she didn't see what she thought she saw and had never seen what she said she saw.

Hawkeye was released. Justice was done.

ADAM'S RIBS

In the field, the men ate C rations. At MASH units, where more or less permanent cooking facilities could be set up, food was shipped from the States and was reconstituted with water or defrosted before serving—not that the men could much care. The frozen chicken from 1939 didn't taste much better when it was defrosted in 1951. After eleven days of liver and fish for lunch, Hawkeye had had enough. "If I eat one more fish, I will develop gills; I've had so much liver, I can only make love if I'm smothered in bacon and onions!"

His dissatisfaction with the food, and the war in general, made him begin to fantasize about the perfect lunch. "There was a place in Chicago, near the Dearborn Street station, can't even think of its name, but the ribs—the best in the world."

By the middle of the night, Hawkeye was obsessed by his vision of the ribs and woke up Radar to patch him through to the Dearborn Street station. They found Adam's Ribs, called in their order, and arranged for Klinger's uncle to run it to the airport. MPs at O'Hare were told that urgent medical supplies were to be routed immediately, and the ribs were overnighted to Korea. Within twenty-four hours, the officers of the 4077 were feasting on thirty pounds of perfect ribs.

Only Henry was annoyed. Hawkeye forgot to order the slaw.

MAD DOGS AND SERVICEMEN

Radar's well-known kindness to animals backfired on him the day the local pooch bit and ran. Concerned that the corporal might contract rabies—a common disease in Korea—the Swampmen asked him to find the dog that bit him so the animal could be tested and he could be treated. The dog was nowhere to be found.

"It's possible, sirs, that the dog was somebody's dinner last night, sirs."

Meanwhile, Hawkeye and Frank squabbled about the treatment of another young corporal who had been in a tank raid and was suffering from hysterical paralysis. Frank wanted to send the little faker to Tokyo. But Hawkeye had consulted with Dr. Freedman, the shrink, and discovered that if the boy could not break through his hysterical reaction quickly, he might, indeed, be paralyzed for life. To avoid that, Hawkeye ordered strict measures to make the boy snap out of it. He was not to

be babied, catered to, brought meals, or bathed. If he wanted anything, he had to get up and walk.

Radar began the long series of painful rabies shots and became quite ill before the good news could be brought in—the dog was found and did not have rabies. Meanwhile, the other patient was crawling. Each corporal would live to see his 19th birthday after all.

THE CONSULTANT

Pierce and McIntyre met Dr. Anthony Borelli at one of the many surgical seminars they were periodically sent to by the Army—designed to keep the field doctors abreast of up-to-date medical technology that had advanced so dramatically after World War II. In Tokyo for a conference, the boys from the 4077 got in a few rounds of golf and girls and managed to miss the lectures entirely. They did, however, convince Dr. Borelli to look them up at the 38th Parallel.

Borelli took them up on the invitation and scrubbed to observe in the OR. Just as Frank was about to amputate a crushed leg, the older doctor interrupted and explained he knew a technique that could save the leg—an arterial transplant that was just being done in the States. Although none of the doctors at the 4077 had seen or read of the surgery, Borelli agreed to do it himself the next day. He sent Hawkeye and Trapper in search of an artery and waited out their excursion with martinis in The Swamp.

When it was time to perform the surgery, Borelli was too drunk to operate. Hawkeye was forced to do an operation he had never even seen before. Although it was successful and the soldier would return home with two legs instead of one, Hawkeye was angry. He decided to have a showdown with Borelli.

"I didn't drink at all in the First World War," the older man explained. "I never drank when I was working in the second war. This place just got to me. I'd forgotten how rough the game can be. You have many good gifts, Hawkeye. It's a pity you can't number compassion among them. I wish you better luck in *your* third war."

WHITE GOLD

As in all wars, barter was a fact of survival. Money could prove worthless but goods were valuable. Medical supplies were even more valuable.

When thieves raided the 4077's penicillin stash, they were mysteriously set free by none other than Colonel Flagg, that bozo from the CIA who just happened to stop by the unit at the exact time of the robbery. Caught red-handed helping the thieves, Flagg explained that he needed the drugs to trade with North Koreans for information.

"Why don't you just torture people for information?" asked Trapper, who'd probably seen one too many war movies.

"Yeah," Hawkeye seconded, "we kind of like to use penicillin for saving lives."

But Flagg was adamant and was carrying orders that allowed him to carry out his heist legally. This left the cutters with just one choice—creative medicine. They doctored Flagg's coffee—"It's vitamins," explained Hawkeye—with a chemical that created stomach cramps, then announced that the colonel was having an appendicitis attack and operated, removing his "ruptured" appendix. As he went under the anesthesia, the last groggy words Flagg uttered were, "Remember, boys, if there's any infection, I've got plenty of penicillin."

Trapper just smiled cherubically. "We've got plenty of penicillin . . . you got plenty of nothing."

BOMBED

"Friendly fire" turned the 4077 into chaos. The latrine was bombed. The phone lines were cut. Trapper and Hot Lips got stuck in the supply room when heavy shelling jammed the door.

When they were finally released, many hours later, both were found asleep under the same blanket—a very respectable distance apart. But Frank thought the worst, as only Frank could do. He was so beside himself with jealousy that he blurted out his love for Margaret and asked her to marry him. Unable to believe her ears, Margaret asked him to repeat the words she had been longing to hear. But the bombing made it impossible for her to hear him.

Once life was restored to normal, Frank forgot he had ever mentioned his love, devotion, or intentions, and Hot Lips was left begging him to say the three little words she longed to take seriously.

LOVE AND MARRIAGE

During the three-year war in Korea, numerous American servicemen took local women as wives, and countless others engaged in affairs of the heart. Army regulations stipulated that a soldier could not marry until the government approved and the bride passed a medical checkup. When Danny McShane requested permission to marry Song Hi, a not-so-young business girl at Rosie's Bar, the match struck a sour note to Hawkeye and Trapper. Song Hi had served behind the counter for two wars and was a good deal older than her husband-to-be. So the Swampmen did their best to talk young McShane out of the wedding.

Shortly thereafter, they were visited by a local medico, Pak, who offered each man $250 to approve Song Hi's medical papers so she could marry McShane. When the doctors hesitated because they were trying to size up the situation, Pak thought they were angling for more dough and explained that he had no more cash to offer because McShane insisted on getting $1,000 for his part

of the deal. It didn't take long for Pierce and McIntyre to realize that a scam was being run out of Rosie's Bar, in which GIs were being paid to marry Korean girls and take them to the States, where they would later be divorced.

Outraged, the doctors busted up the ring and showed Song Hi's X-rays to everyone. She was suffering from tuberculosis and would have never been approved as an Army wife.

AID STATION

I–Corps, located in heavy fire near Seoul, had only an aid station and shuttled wounded from the field to the 4077 or their nearest MASH unit. When they lost their surgeon after a mortar attack, HQ requested relief from the 4077. Hawkeye, Hot Lips, and Klinger took the job.

"The first time I make a house call and the house isn't even there," Hawkeye shrugged on viewing the roofless, bombed-out shelter that had once been an aid station. Two exhausted corpsmen tried to attend the wounded amid constant shelling, dust, and debris.

The new team took over with their typical efficiency. Klinger followed Hawkeye's orders and did everything; Hot Lips calmly took control of patients and still managed to assist once Hawkeye cleared off a table and began emergency surgery. Ironically, back at the 4077, where conditions were cleaner, safer, and easier, Frank was forced to struggle with his own inadequacies while he complained about his working conditions, the work load, the equipment, and the war.

"Frank, if you don't cut that bellyaching out, I'll write in my report that you do not play well with others," Henry threatened.

A day later, replacements made it to the aid station, and the three lifesavers were sent back to their unit, each soldier proud to be alive and proud of a job well done.

"Major," whispered an appreciative Hawkeye as they neared the safety of camp, "if you repeat this to anyone, I'll deny that I said it, but you are my favorite officer in the whole US Army."

And he kissed her cheek.

BULLETIN BOARD

Dear Becky,

I hope you had a nice birthday party. I'd have given anything to be there. In your last letter, you asked what I am doing here, so I will try to describe what it is like. I live in a tent with two other doctors, Hawkeye and Frank. One is a good egg. The other is a lot like the substitute teacher who came for a day and stayed all year.

Most of the time we try to keep the wounded from dying—which is not easy, especially at this time of year. The nurses have to check the patients for frostbite three times a day. Once we got a patient who did not bleed to death because the freezing temperatures here kept his body temperature low. We were able to take this guy who would have died on the field and get him all better in a few days. Now he's healthy and he'll be able to go back and have people shoot at him again.

Love,
Daddy

ABYSSINIA, HENRY

During World War II, the Army developed a system by which men could accumulate a specified number of points—based on length and type of service—to gain an honorable discharge. Henry Blake's number was up in the summer of 1951. He had enough points! He was notified that he would be going home within 24 hours.

Everyone was thrilled for him, especially Frank, who, as second in command, would become the ranking officer. Hot Lips was just as anxious for Frank to take over. Needless to say, Trapper and Hawkeye were not overjoyed.

"If Frank's going to be CO," said Trapper disgustedly, "I'm hanging up my caduceus!"

The leave-taking was difficult, especially for Radar, who was like a son to Henry. Hawkeye and Trapper were pleased for their friend yet envious as well, but they gave him a proper send-off.

"We're giving this party for you not because you're going home but because you're one helluva human being."

"I just wish we could all go home together," said Henry.

The Huey helicopter that arrived to take him to Kimpo first deposited its wounded. A reluctant Henry thought that he should stay and help. He had to be forced on board by the gathered staff.

"Listen, I can save this kid's leg with a vein transplant," he said.

"Henry," chided Hawkeye, "you're fired. Go home to your wife and kids."

So Henry Blake, Colonel, US Army Medical Corps, boarded the chopper and took off as ordered. From Kimpo he would fly to Tokyo, San Francisco, and then home to his beloved Bloomington, Illinois.

At 1900 hours, Radar O'Reilly entered the OR where the doctors were doing their jobs.

"I just got a message. The colonel's plane was shot down over the Sea of Japan. Spun in. No survivors."

Year Three (1974-75)

NAME: FARR, JAMIE
CHARACTER: KLINGER, MAXWELL Q.
RANK: CORPORAL, USA
SERIAL NUMBER: RA19571782

"The third year was a big one for me because it was my first year on contract. Before that, I was what is known as a 'day player'—booked on a per day rate and with no future commitment to the studio or the show. The first year, I did six shows; the second year, I did twelve shows; then they finally got me a contract, and I was really a regular like everybody thought I was all along.

"I had been in partnership with Eddie Caro writing game shows, and things weren't going too well. We weren't selling much, and the unemployment checks were running out, and I was thinking real seriously of getting out of the business entirely. I was just going to quit as an actor. They called me for the sixth show, I think it was. The series hadn't even aired yet. It was called *Chief Surgeon Who?* I knew Gene [Reynolds] from *F-Troop* and I knew the director, so they brought me in for a day's work. Hey, I was happy to get a day's work, $250. They put me in this WAC uniform and high heels and put me on the set. Everyone was in an uproar, laughing. They loved it. I played it the way the director said to — swish, and that was that. When Gene and Larry ran the dailies the next day and decided the part didn't work that way, they called me back. I was just grateful for the next day's work. I never thought of it as anything more than that. I could pay some of my bills, which I hadn't been doing too well up to then.

"The next day, I reshot the scene and played it like a normal guy who was just wearing a dress, and that was the birth of Klinger—absolutely straight.

"They called me back a few weeks later for another show. This one I didn't wear a dress. It was a very straight, serious part. I think they were using Klinger back then for all their research on psychos. But after that, they put me in the dress. Pretty soon, I began getting a lot of notoriety. I did the grocery shopping for my family while my wife went out and worked—my parents had a grocery store when I was a kid, and I was real good at getting healthy food that wasn't expensive and making it go a long way. So in the grocery store, people suddenly started to recognize me and ask for my autograph. After two years of this, it got kind of silly. I wanted to be what people thought I was, a regular. I told my agent that they should make me a member of the family or let me go, and that's when I got my contract. I don't think they changed the billing for another year or two, though—they were trying to save the money.

"I really had very little to do with the development of the character—it was Gene and Larry who did it. I think they took the escape schemes as far as they could go, and the dresses as far as they could go, and when they ran out of that, then they let the character grow, you know, after Radar left.

"I didn't have very much clout that third year. I didn't even have a dressing room. I had this trailer that was a sweat box. I felt like Alec Guinness in *The Bridge on the River Kwai*. It was terrible. One summer after lunch, Gene saw me and couldn't believe it. He's the one who got me a dressing room. It was on the second floor of the A-Building. Actually, it was an upstairs tenement—all you needed was a blinking light and some honky-tonk jukebox music and Gene Tierney to walk in wearing a slinky dress. Then I would have borrowed the dress. There was no furniture. They wouldn't give me any. I raided office supply and adopted a few things. I found a sofa that looked like a letter of the alphabet—the letter U. You could not lie down on this thing. I took Wayne's refrigerator at the end of the year, or maybe it was the next year. I took my lunch to work every day because I couldn't afford to eat in the commissary, and I needed the refrigerator. Then one day some guys came and wheeled it away. I just told the director that if my refrigerator didn't come back, he'd have to call me at home for the next scene.

"It was like that for four years, then I got tough on them. I asked for a new sofa. And I got it. It was sturdy; it was modern; it was too short to lie down on.

"The third year was exciting because finally I did have my contract and the show had really come together. We were very much a hit. I used to love to go to wardrobe in those days. You'd look in there and see Alan's things, maybe a Hawaiian shirt and a bathrobe; Loretta had a few more things; and I had racks and racks of these clothes. The clothes were never chosen as any old thing— each outfit was carefully put together. They all had labels in them, so I knew which stars wore them. Once I saw Ginger Rogers here on the lot, she was doing a *Love Boat* or something, and she called me over and thanked me for wearing one of her outfits. Sometimes Burt and I would meet in wardrobe and we'd have these discussions about purses and high heels. It was ridiculous for two grown men to be having these conversations. After I got enough wardrobe going, I could make suggestions and, if I didn't like an outfit, I could say so. I always wanted to fit into one of Jennifer Jones's outfits, but I never did. I hated the Dame May Whitty. It was so heavy, and it made me look like Maria Ouspenskaya. I think one of my favorite outfits was the little Scotch plaid with the saddle shoes. I could run around all day in that and be comfortable. Wearing earrings all day could be real uncomfortable; I don't have pierced ears, you know. And heels weren't meant for running around in. Once, in the third year, I was doing this scene at the Ranch where I have to run across a field because Radar brings me a letter that my girl is going to marry me. Well, I was wearing these *peau de soie* pumps that cost $25 a pair and, after I ruined two or three pair, it was getting hysterical. That was a lot of money to be throwing down the drain in those days. Finally, I did it in sneakers, and no one ever knew the difference. Until now.

"The third year was a time when a lot of things were honed and when some of the players changed around. There were people who I thought were regulars, who I envied, who suddenly weren't working as much, like the nurse, Ginger, or Colonel Flagg. I had a lot of empathy for them because I'd come as a day player, too. I had no idea I'd be permanent when I got there. To me, Ugly John (the Australian gas passer) was one of the lucky ones. And the third year, while I did have a contract, I was a bit in awe of Alan and the others, so I didn't know where to fit in. Even the last episode of the third year, when Henry Blake died, I had been there the whole season and when we read the page and found out that Henry died, we were all stunned, and Larry asked for comments and a lot of people had their say. But I didn't say anything because I didn't think they would really care what I had to say. I happened to agree with doing it, but I didn't say a word. I still felt like a tack-on and I wasn't that close to any of them. I only spoke when spoken to.

"The whole thing about Henry's death was very hush-hush. I had already finished my scenes and was at home waiting for a call about the wrap party. Loretta was finished also. Then I got a call from the studio asking me to come in for an added scene, and they said Loretta was coming, too. I asked if I needed the pages ahead of time—if I had to study any lines—and they said no, not to worry, it was a quick scene in the OR and just to come on in. I said fine. I came down and they called all the regulars into a corner and Larry had a big manila envelope and he pulled out these pages. We couldn't believe what we had read. We blocked it without saying a word so the crew wouldn't know anything until we actually did it. The impact on the first take was incredible. You could hear gasps from the crew. It was a blockbuster. We had to do it one more time, but on that first take, you wouldn't believe it.

"I was very conservative that third year. I had struggled for so long. I was so grateful, and I knew that I couldn't take any of it for granted. I'd had plenty of times in my career when I thought, 'Aha, this is it,' and then nothing happened. Like I said, I was thinking of getting out of the business. So I wasn't about to forget where I'd been and all the hard times. It's like a marriage, and you should never forget the first date you had with your spouse and how special it was.

"When Radar left, in a sense, I replaced him. I always said the two characters that couldn't be replaced were Klinger and Radar because they were so unique, so special; they had their own stories going. You could replace command characters but not the two enlisted men. They never considered bringing in another actor—nothing they created could come close to what they had. Of course, it frightened me to get out of the dress and stop the scheming. The audiences loved it. Much to my delight, I gained even more favor when I went straight, and no one resented my being the company clerk.

"It might have been at the end of that year, or maybe it was the next year—I don't remember—but it came time to renegotiate my contract, and my agent wasn't having much luck. I was working five days a week and getting what a day player gets for three days. I wasn't asking for much, I just wanted a fair deal. I wasn't out to rob Fort Knox, you know. Well, the man in charge of the money said, 'No way,' and my agent was afraid they'd write me out or have my character killed if I pushed too hard, so I said, 'Let me handle this.' I went over to the prop department and checked out a .45 gun. Then in a comic-strip gallop, I tore across the lot, hiding behind trees and buildings, like I was on some kind of commando raid. I looked in and saw the guy was in his office. I snuck into the building and tried his door. I sure didn't want his secretary to announce me. It was unlocked. I crouched down low, kicked open the door, and stormed in, waving my gun around and shouted, 'Okay, the deal is going to go like this!'

"The guy jumped up and then hid under his desk. He kept screaming at me asking if I was crazy or something. We made a date to sit down and talk it out; I brought him flowers and some cigars, and it worked out fine.

"But what you have to remember is that we're not supernatural people. Yes, we had some great times, did some crazy things, and made a wonderful show. We're just actors who got lucky. We were not terribly important. We were people doing a job, making a living the same as the postman or the grocer or anyone else. We like our work, and we have a good time doing it. That's the bottom line of the whole thing, really."

Jamie Farr

Year Four (1975—76)

LARRY GELBART, Creator/Writer

"Year Four began with a shock. We discovered that once
again the network had changed our time slot. They were
using us as a battering ram. They put us up against formidable opposition; we were a pawn in their game. We felt
we had earned the right to a time slot we dominated; that
we should not have to go to bat every week. We all went en
masse—even Mike Farrell and Harry Morgan, who were
new that year—and talked to the programming people at
CBS. I don't think they had ever seen anything like that before. We sat down with Bob Wood, and he listened to us. I don't
know that it did any good. I think they just listened to our best
arguments and then did whatever they wanted to do anyway.

"By Year Four, you can see that many elements of the actors as
people are integrated into their roles. As I knew the actors better, I was able to use their own personal characteristics in their
roles, thus sort of blurring the line a bit. I was forever biking back
and forth as the show was being shot. It was the accessibility to the
players and a better knowledge of them as people that led to the most
changes in layering and depth. I started playing the clarinet when I was
eight years old. By the time I was nine, I was getting pretty good at it. By the
time I was ten, I was terrific. It took time and practice with M*A*S*H, just
like with anything else."

CHAPTER V

Three scenes from *It Happened One Night*

YEAR FOUR—BATTLE NOTES

WELCOME TO KOREA

Hawkeye took his R&R solo, with a three-day pass to Tokyo and a nightcap at Rosie's Bar and The Famous Curb Service Whorehouse, the guaranteed "last chance before Peking." He straggled into camp so hung over that he headed straight for the showers—clothes and all. Radar was forced to follow him into the Officers' Shower Tent with the big news. Trapper had just been shipped home.

"While I was resting and recreating? How? When?"

Captain John McIntyre, MD, had, indeed, received orders to pack it up and head back to Boston. Captain Benjamin Franklin Pierce, MD, was incredulous. Trapper was gone! Without even saying good-bye! Grabbing Radar and a hot Jeep, he pushed on the pedal and headed toward Kimpo, hoping to catch his buddy before the plane took off. He had to run a roadblock but managed it easily enough after he explained that he was a doctor and that Corporal O'Reilly, seated next to him, was his patient. He raced onto the airfield, hope pounding in his heart. He was ten minutes too late.

Trapper was gone.

Still pissed off, Hawkeye was forced to greet the new man who had landed on the plane that had liberated McIntyre. Captain B.J. Hunnicutt was caught in the middle of the confusion. He felt the chill of Hawkeye's greeting but had no idea of what had gone on or what he was stepping into.

He was just the new guy on the block. He didn't know the territory. Six-foot-three with light brown hair, B.J. was a twenty-eight-year-old nice guy who had finished his surgical residency and had just joined a practice in Mill Valley, California, when he was drafted. He left behind a wife, Peg, an infant daughter, Erin, and the dream that he was about to face the best years of his life.

Within his first five minutes in Korea, he was welcomed by some people who didn't really want to meet him. Then their Jeep was stolen. The next few hours continued at the same pace: stealing new cars, running more blockades, stopping on the road to aid the wounded, meeting the realities of the war head on. Hunnicutt was shocked, but he took it in his stride, finally forcing Hawkeye to notice that he was a real person.

"Hey," Hawkeye commented, "give that man a lady in the balcony."

Before long, Hawkeye was passing on the wit and wisdom he had accumulated while in Korea. "The first thing you learn here, B.J., is that insanity is no worse than the common cold. You've heard of a military post? Ours is a compost. Only the wounded are new. The tedium is relieved only by the bordeom. So pitch in, muddle through, pip-pip. Never mind the reason why ours is but to do and not let 'em die."

B.J. learned quickly.

"I think I hate it here."

Welcome to Korea.

CHANGE OF COMMAND

It was a shock to Frank Burns to discover that he had lost command of the 4077 when he found out that a senior officer who hadn't even seen the inside of an operating room in two years was coming in from Tokyo to take charge.

"This is outrageous," fumed Hot Lips. "Completely unfair."

Frank naturally agreed with her. In fact, he was out sulking when the new CO arrived—Colonel Sherman T. Potter, Surgeon, Medical Corps, United States Army.

Potter, a sprite of a man with gray hair and green eyes, was a lifer on short time, only eighteen months to go. He was Regular Army, all right, having run away from home when he was seventeen to join the cavalry. After the First World War, he took the Army up on its offer to send him to college and then medical school. He was a paper pusher in Tokyo before being sent to the 4077. He'd seen three wars, four continents, and thousands of wounded soldiers. There wasn't a trick in the book he didn't know or a man or woman he didn't understand.

"Okay, Klinger, I've seen these dodge tricks for forty years. Knew a private once, pretended he was a mare. Carried a colt in his arms for weeks. Another fella said he was a daisy. Insisted we water him every morning. Now get into your uniform and out of that froufrou."

Hawkeye and Hunnicutt had good reason to fear. A Regular Army guy could really put a clamp on their style. Their fears proved ungrounded. Potter established himself as a man who could command with a compassionate heart and a fatherly hand. After a twenty-four-hour stint at surgery, Sherman Potter was accepted and accepting.

"Had a still on Guam in World War II. One night it blew up. That's how I got my Purple Heart. Nice outfit you're wearing there, Klinger. Love the handbag."

IT HAPPENED ONE NIGHT

While it was not uncommon for a mobile hospital to pick up stakes and follow the war, no one liked it very much when the war, whether intentionally or not, came too close to the hospital. Artillery shells knocked out power, mortars shook the tents, and havoc was wreaked on the medical teams.

One night, it was twenty below and the Air Force was giving the NKPA (North Korean People's Army) the old heave-ho. The 4077 was just three miles from the front to begin with, but on that night there was a lot of artillery. Klinger was on guard duty, first trying to get wounded (which would not have been too difficult on that particular night) then trying to catch double pneumonia—anything for a discharge. He did end up in a bed, but only because they ran out of type O blood and B.J. and Hawkeye had a bleeder.

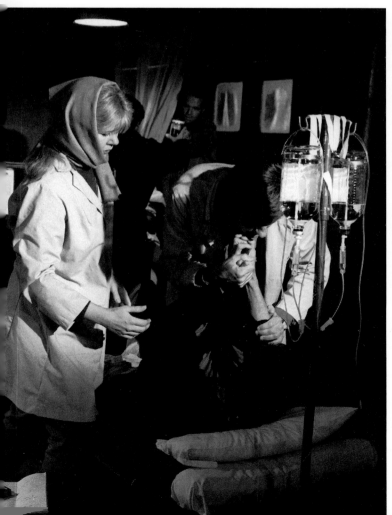

Top and left: It Happened One Night   *Above: Welcome to Korea*

The Late Captain Pierce

"I plugged every hole," said B.J., positive there was no internal bleeding.

"Then he sprang a leak."

"I got an A+ in embroidery."

Despite the desperate conditions, the cutters decided to go back in. Four hours later, their patient was finally home free.

"Listen," B.J. said a little sardonically, "you let me operate on a guy three or four times and I'm finally going to get it right."

"It was good work, doctor," Hawkeye assured him.

"Did you hear that?" he asked Margaret.

"I don't hear anything."

"You know what that noise is? It's silence. They stopped shelling. It's over."

"Thank God."

OF MOOSE AND MEN

Not all the patients at the 4077 had run-ins with the North Koreans. Sergeant Mickey Zale came in with wounds inflicted after he bashed a fist into the side of an ambulance in one of his more painful battles of the Korean War. Zale had suffered a blow to the heart.

A letter from his wife explained it all, admitting to an affair with the man next door but asking for his forgiveness and love. After hearing the story, Hunnicutt began to write a warm, forgiving letter to Mrs. Zale. When he was finished, he went looking for Zale only to discover that the sergeant lived down the road with his "moose" (mistress) in a cozy little case of double standarditis. Hunnicutt was furious. He rushed to the girl's house, letter in hand and righteous indignation firmly in place.

"Carry your own double standard into battle, Zale," he shouted as he handed his letter to the sergeant. "I just took the liberty of writing Mrs. Zale. It just needs your John Hancock. Or Syngman Rhee."

Zale read the letter. "Pretty understanding, ain't I?"

"Well," B.J. said, "you're just that kind of guy."

"Yeah," said Zale, reading from the ghost-written epistle, " 'To err is human, to forgive divine.' Got a pen, doc?"

Statistics keepers don't tally up those kinds of wounds. Perhaps they just can't count that high.

DEAR MILDRED

My Dearest Mildred,

Well, another year has rolled around and we are facing another anniversary away from each other. I'm still trying to get used to this outfit. It's not easy. I'm the new kid on the block.

Did I write you about Radar? The company clerk? Sometimes he acts a little squirrelly. And Father Mulcahy? You'd like him. Major Houlihan is the head nurse, kind of fools around with Major Burns. He's the head twerp. He's married, but I think something's going on between them. Sometimes he has

lip rouge around his mouth and his eyes are all swollen. Seen her with whisker burns. But it's none of my beeswax.

You should see Corporal Klinger, a real pip. Trying to get out on a Section Eight—you know, psycho. My chief cutters are Hawkeye Pierce and B.J. Hunnicutt. Seems that Pierce's dad only read one book—*The Last of the Mohicans.* They're not too big on regulations and are a little weird but good men, nonetheless.

Well, sweetheart, got to make rounds in postop. We're getting around ninety percent survival, which is damn good this close to the ridge. As your cousin Natalie said, and she's been quoted by so many, "War is Hell."

Your ever loving,
Sherm

THE LATE CAPTAIN PIERCE

Graves Registration tagged bodies, recorded the names and ID numbers of the dead, and notified the surviving family members. So when Dr. Daniel J. Pierce was notified of his son's demise, he could only ask Hunnicutt "how and why" before their phone connection was cut. Because President-elect Eisenhower was in the area, all communications were suspended, even between 2 and 4 A.M., which was usually the best time to get a line.

> DEAR DAD. I AM NOT DEAD. STOP. HOPE YOU ARE THE SAME. STOP. THINKING ABOUT SELLING MY CLUBS? STOP. SPENDING MY INSURANCE MONEY? STOP. LOVE, YOUR NOWHERE NEAR LATE SON.

But telegrams were not being sent either. And proving himself undead was no easy matter. Sure, the joke wake that Hunnicutt hosted was a gas, but Hawkeye couldn't get his paycheck, couldn't get his mail, and was unable to contact his father. For all he knew, the old man was having a funeral he wouldn't be attending. It was all very grim and had a sobering effect on his work.

"Wounded keep coming whether I'm dead or not. Trapper went home, and they're still coming. Henry got killed, and they're still coming. Wherever they come from, they'll never run out."

He certainly was taking his death notices seriously. Thank God, Radar was finally able to get a line to Crabapple Cove.

"Quit crying," said a jubilant Hawkeye: "It's all right. I'm alive. I'm well. I just need one little favor, Dad. Could you start giving me an allowance again until they send back my paychecks?"

SMILIN' JACK

The Hueys and Bell helicopters used in Korea could carry two wounded in pods mounted on the landing skids, with the pilot and a medic in the cockpit. When the wounded were unloaded at a MASH unit, the pilot and

The Late Captain Pierce

DEAR PEGGY

medic took off again for the next airlift—angels of mercy. First Lieutenant Jack Mitchell—Smilin' Jack—had flown 839 live ones into the five MASH units scattered around South Korea and was counting as fast as he could, trying to beat 842, the record held by Dangerous Dan Murphy.

But when Potter spied an unhealed bruise on Smilin' Jack's hand, he grabbed the pilot for a checkup. It was what the doctor suspected—diabetes.

"That man's a flying fool," shuddered B.J. "He's got clouds in his blood."

"Yeah," said Hawkeye, "and sugar, too."

Mitchell didn't take the discovery of his secret too well. "Nobody's going to ground me yet! Nobody! I was going to hand in my wings myself. Honest. I've got connections for insulin. I'm OK. I've just gotta tie Dangerous Dan to make Chopper Pilot of the Year."

"Nope," said Hawk, "the sky's off limits now."

He put a not-so-Smilin' Jack on the bus for Seoul to the tune of incoming wounded. It was Dangerous Dan—his two pods loaded—844 and counting.

Dear Peggy,

I know this is my third letter in a day, but it's the only way I can keep my sanity. You can really go out of your skull here sometimes. There's just nothing to do when we're not working. I remember reading that Justice Holmes said, "War is an organized bore." And how!

Which leads me to Frank. Not one of our best doctors. Hawkeye says he became a surgeon after he washed out at embalmers school. This morning he was operating on a kid named Davis, and I was the anesthesiologist. Sometimes you have to double on gas here, ever since Ugly John got shipped home. Anyway, Frank blew it. We lost pulse on the boy and Frank said, "That's that," and walked away. Hawkeye and I had to take over. We bagged him and brought him back.

It's now five in the morning, Peg. I was worried about Davis, so I've been keeping tabs on him. It's still pretty much up for grabs. I've just looked back at this letter and discovered I haven't told you how much I love you. I love you, and when you read this, I'll love you even more.

Better check up on Davis again. I bet he's got family at home waiting for his next letter.

I love you,
B.J.

Above and opposite: The Kids

HEY, DOC

Hawkeye had quite a private practice going—he treated a general for a "private" matter; he operated on a Brit's ingrown toenail; and then he teamed up with Hunnicutt to get Staff Sergeant Terrence Kimble on a slow boat from Pusan with all the supplies he wanted to ship home so he could open a chow joint.

Kimble needed three officers to sign his medical profile so he'd be able to take the boat rather than a plane—the Army didn't want it to be easy to cruise back to the States. Hawkeye appealed to Frank, to little avail.

"But he'll get us a microscope if we sign the papers. We could really help the next wounded kid who needs a blood count!"

"I'm sick of hearing about the wounded," Frank moaned. "What about the thousands of wonderful guys who are fighting this war without any of the credit and the glory that goes to those lucky ones who happen to get shot."

But Hawkeye and Hunnicutt knew that kindness pays. One of their cases paid them with a bottle of Scotch. Another paid them by sending an M–26 tank to the compound to provide a little temporary security. It was that tank that provided the blackmail that was needed to get Frank's signature on Kimble's papers. After Frank made a fool of himself with the tank, Hawkeye and B.J. had to protect the man, didn't they? They just made sure protection paid off.

Kimble's Korean Kafe opened to rave notices in Chatham, New York, ten months later.

THE KIDS

It was fighting over near Kaesong that bombed out Meg Cratty's orphanage and sent forty-three homeless Korean tots over to the 4077 in search of safety and bedtime stories. Colonel Potter read the Army manual to the brood and had them nodding off in no time. Radar ran piggyback relays. Father Mulcahy turned bottoms up for diaper duty. With her kids under safe flaps, Meg was still worried. She had expected to see Sung Lee, a very pregnant woman who was following on foot, but the girl was hours late.

Radar quite literally bumped into her at the edge of camp. Well into her eighth month, Sung Lee had taken a bullet in the lower abdomen and was bleeding extensively. The baby's heartbeat was audible but rapid. Hunnicutt performed a C–section while the OR began to fill with wounded. The newborn wailed, and Father Mulcahy crossed himself. "Another soul among the living," he smiled. "Now I suggest, my friends, that we bow our heads in silent prayer for the mother."

It was either the prayer or B.J.'s nimble fingers—or maybe a combination—but mother and son survived their ordeal. With their vital signs stable, Hawkeye suggested that the baby was more deserving of Frank's Purple Heart than Frank.

"As commanding officer of the 4077," said Potter at

the very informal ceremony, "and as authorized by the President of the United States of America, I hereby award this Purple Heart medal for wounds received in the line of duty to the child of Sung Lee, and it's a privilege to honor the little guy."

THE BUS

Those snobs at the 38th Parallel Medical Society were having another one of their conclaves—spelled p-o-k-e-r. So Frank, Hawkeye, B.J., and Colonel Potter all went to the meeting. It was a slowish time; there was a lull in the fighting.

Radar drove them on the bus and was doing just fine until he got lost on the return trip. Then the bus stalled and died. The boys on the bus might have known their way around a human body with a blindfold, but heaven help them, they knew nothing about the motor of that old bus.

Panicked, Radar spent the night prowling the area on watch for North Koreans while the rest of the gang fretted over his disappearance. An unexpected visitor proved to be a surprised enemy soldier who just limped up to the bus and surrendered.

"His leg's torn up pretty bad," Hawkeye noticed.

"I wouldn't touch him," hissed Frank. "He could be booby-trapped. He could go off in our faces."

"Right, Frank. What he's done is cut a big gash in his leg, inserted a grenade, and disguised it with his own blood."

As the vigil wore on, there seemed less and less chance of Radar being found alive. Frank already spoke of him in the past tense, and everyone else was past being tense.

Dawn brought three happy discoveries: Radar returned safely; Frank finally admitted that he had a stash of candy bars and gave one to each man for breakfast; and the prisoner fixed the bus.

Wars are comprised mostly of very small victories.

Quo Vadis, Captain Chandler

QUO VADIS, CAPTAIN CHANDLER

Name: Chandler, Arnold Lawrence
Rank: Captain
Report from: Sidney Freedman, MD

The man's a victim. As far as he's concerned, he's Christ. Okay, he's not Christ, but he's also not Chandler. Some men lose an arm or a leg. Chandler lost himself. He spent two years dropping bombs on people who never did anything to him, and something inside that kid from Idaho finally said, "Enough. You are Christ. You are not a killer. The next bomb, you drop on yourself."

With the right kind of treatment, maybe we can turn him back into Arnold Chandler. We'll never turn him back into a fighting tool, and it's my professional advice that we don't try.

SOLDIER OF THE MONTH

With conditions what they were at a mobile hospital, the possibility of epidemic was a constant reality. When a mysterious fever hit the compound in the fall of 1951, Colonel Potter decided to appoint a rat-control officer in the belief that the rats were the host factor for mites or fleas carrying whatever disease it was that couldn't even be identified.

Government epidemiologists were all in Shamblee, Georgia, in those days, but Father Mulcahy did a little medical sleuthing on his own while on R&R in Tokyo and brought back the latest news—both Russian and Japanese soldiers had suffered the same symptoms back in the late 1930s. "It was a Nisei who was looking through some old Japanese medical journals and came across the name 'hemorrhagic fever' and realized we were dealing with the same thing. There isn't a cure; it's just common sense medicine except you have to be careful to restrict fluids because a man can drown in his own tissues."

"Thanks for the confirmation, Father," said Hawkeye, who had been seeing a lot of kidney failure in his patients.

"Confirmation is my middle name," Father Mulcahy smiled.

Frank came down with the fever shortly thereafter and begged for water. "I'll give you $10 for a drink of water," he whimpered. Before he passed out again, he wrote his will leaving everything to his wife except his Army uniforms, which he left to Margaret.

When he recovered, she bopped him one on the chin for the insult.

"How'd she even find his chin?" the Swampmen marveled.

DEAR MA

Dear Ma,

This is your boy here still fine with the Army in Korea and hoping you are the same. As usual, I am writing slow cause I know you can't read fast.

I was sorry to hear Uncle Ed went off the wagon on his hunting trip. I sure hope he'll be able to play the pump organ again without those toes. I apologize for not answering sooner, Ma. It's just that I do a heck of a lot of writing in my job. I got about the smallest pencil in the camp.

Monday night Colonel Potter and Major Houlihan went into Kha Doc, which is a native village. We all go once a month to treat the sick, old, and ill. I could've gone, but last time I went, they served grasshoppers and rice. I don't mind that, but the sauce made me sick. I think it was Mexican.

Well, Ma, if they gave me a penny every time I thought about you, I guess I'd be making about a hundred bucks a week.

Hugs and kisses, hugs and kisses.

Love,
Walter

DELUGE

People back home liked to think that what was going on at the 4077 was romantic. They should have been around when the Spam hit the fan on the day the Chinese broke through the UN lines. What a deluge.

Father Mulcahy had his hands full with a soldier who promised God he'd become a priest if he survived his wound, and then changed his mind.

Klinger was drafted out of his Nurse Nancy duds to scrub out a tub so he could dunk a patient in a copper sulfate bath to see if any scraps of phosphorous were left in his leg.

HQ talked about evacuating the nurses, but all hands were needed on deck, especially when supplies ran low and a nervous GI accidentally set fire to the laundry room. Klinger *tried* to put out the flames with a handy basin of water, but it turned out to be a basin of alcohol the surgeons were using as disinfectant. So there was a big explosion and the windows blew, which allowed the rain from the storm to flood through the window.

Some days it just didn't pay to go to war.

THE GUN

Operating across a gurney from Frank Burns on an almost daily basis was enough to convince anyone of the man's very limited capabilities. Out of the OR, he didn't score much higher. But the time he swiped Colonel Robert Joseph Chaffey's gun was the low point of his career.

Chaffey came in as a "head and ankle wound" after a tank ran him and his men into an embankment. A Regular Army type, he wore an 1884 Colt .45 as his sidearm instead of the regular Army issue. Radar checked the piece into the gun bin but discovered it missing the next day.

The colonel was not thrilled to hear the news. In fact, he demanded Radar's head on a silver platter and was pushing for a fifteen-year sentence in the stockade. Potter was the one who solved the case by leaving out the keys so the thief could return the gun. Of course, Frank was so incompetent he couldn't even do that well. While fumbling for the right key, he shot himself in the toe.

"Margaret," he lamented, "I did a terrible thing. I should have known better. When you steal something—don't ever try to return it."

Too bad Chaffey didn't shoot him with their mutual gun.

MAIL CALL AGAIN

No question about it, mail was the highlight of the day.

There were contests for who had the best mail. Hands down, the winner was Burns on the day that Radar let everyone in on the contents of the letter—the lovely Louise wanted a divorce. Radar was more than clairvoyant. He was reading the mail before he delivered it.

Well, Frank rushed to the phone to call the Mrs., who, it seems, had heard quite an earful about a certain Major Houlihan from a returning veteran.

"I don't care what you heard. Houlihan? Looks like an Army mule with bosoms. Not that I ever noticed. Louise, if you divorce me, I'll run right out into the middle of the war. You get rid of that lawyer, and sugar... am I still in your father's will?"

She fell for it—hook, line, and sinker. Don't ask why.

THE PRICE OF TOMATO JUICE

Radar was always anxious to please, so when Colonel Potter took a casual interest in the clerk's tomato juice, the boy interpreted it as a genuine desire and began elaborate negotiations to get tomato juice shipped to the 4077 on a steady basis.

"Morning, sir," said the triumphant O'Reilly when he brought the colonel his newspaper and tomato juice.

"No thanks, Radar."

"But it's tomato juice, sir."

"I know it's tomato juice. Anybody want it?" Potter asked around the Mess Tent.

B.J. and Hawkeye couldn't believe their ears. "Don't you love it?" they asked in unison.

"I do," Potter said, "but it doesn't love me. I forgot I was allergic to it. Last glass you gave me, I woke up in the middle of the night with my nose stuffed to the rafters, looking like I was wearing someone else's face. I can't touch the stuff."

HAWKEYE

Hawkeye overturned the company Jeep to avoid hitting some children who were playing in the road and sustained a concussion. He dragged himself to the hut of a Korean family and was able to send a note for help with their eldest daughter. Terrified that if he lost consciousness he would never wake up, he fell into a state of grace somewhere between consciousness and death.

His hosts spoke no English and did not understand his condition, yet they cared for him patiently while he jabbered nonstop about his life. He traced his family history back to 1680; reminisced about high school and college; rambled on about medical school; thought tenderly of Sol's Deli on Third Avenue; remembered Miss Tomasino, his geometry teacher; and even crooned a few of his favorite tunes.

"I have the feeling that if I fall asleep here I'll wake up in my family plot back in Maine. Why do I have this silly feeling that I may be dying? It's just fear, that's all. What am I worried about? We all have to go sometime. I'd just like to wait around until maybe they come up with a round-trip ticket. But seriously, folks, I've got nine bones in my head and a purple brain and if they don't get here soon and put a Band-Aid on my memory, it's going to all come spilling out. If I can just keep a firm hold on my motor skills, I'll be okay."

And he started to juggle.

Radar arrived shortly thereafter and took him home.

SOME 38TH PARALLELS

War was garbage, so Hawkeye fought garbage with garbage the day he decided to get even with Colonel T.K. Coner. Coner was a real Army clown whose particular peculiarity was to send live men into fire to retrieve dead bodies.

Sickened by such methods, Hawkeye joined the local Koreans in the bidding for the 4077's garbage. For some time, the locals had been fighting for what the Americans threw out, so the Army decided to sell it to the highest bidder. Hawkeye bought a lot, then had a chopper hoist it up.

He then released Colonel Coner from postop and called everyone out for a send-off. At his signal, the chopper pilot let fly one hundred pounds of US Army Grade A Garbage. It fell from heaven on top of Colonel Coner.

"Beautiful," B.J. shouted as he kissed his fingertips in appreciation. "A Tintoretto in barf!"

"I didn't see any of it," Potter lamented, "but I loved it."

DER TAG

It started as a game—Hawkeye and B.J. wanted to see what would happen if they were *nice* to Frank. They invited him to join one of their poker games; they bought him drinks. When he passed out cold, they dutifully carried him back to The Swamp. But B.J. just couldn't shake the old instincts, so he tagged the body with a toe tag that read—"Emotionally Exhausted and Morally Bankrupt."

Burns was still wearing the tag when he stumbled into the latrine and then took a nap in the back of an open ambulance. Not knowing he was there, the driver returned to the front. The aid station called Potter with the news.

"I've got an officer up here, but his dog tags read Frank Burns. Skinny guy, no chin, big pores, no wounds, but a strange tag. But don't send anyone to get him—we've got a big party up here and your people would eat it."

But Hawkeye and Hunnicutt had already left to retrieve Frank. "If we were any closer to the war, we'd be at the Chinese draft board," Hawkeye commented as the shells whizzed overhead.

The doctors worked out of the aid station during the battle since Frank was still out cold. He came to just as they arrived back at the 4077. B.J. and Hawkeye were exhausted and covered in blood and filth; Frank was spanking clean and well rested.

"Another day, another war," he smiled and jogged off to the OR.

THE NOVOCAINE MUTINY

Frank was always filing reports and bringing up charges—against just about anyone. The process seemed to validate his manhood. Once he got Hawkeye into a preliminary hearing for court-martial on a charge of mutiny. Mutiny! Can you imagine?

The way Burns told the story, he was a real hero. The way Hawkeye told the story, Burns was a real jerk. It wasn't hard to tell which man was telling the truth. Still, the verdict wasn't a cinch.

"I have weighed the evidence," announced Colonel Miles Carmichael, the Judge Advocate. "Not merely the testimony but the records of those involved. I have no doubt that Captain Pierce is a prankster who is thoroughly nonmilitary. But the records prove him a top-flight surgeon. Lord knows, I wouldn't want to lead a company of Pierces into battle, but I sure as hell would want him around after the battle. As for Major Burns's surgical skills, if he hadn't been drafted as a doctor, he would have been assigned as a pastry chef! Court adjourned. Case dismissed."

THE MORE I SEE YOU

Hawkeye got the shock of his life the day two new nurses shipped in. One of them turned out to be his old girlfriend from med school, the one who dumped him when she discovered he would always be married to medicine first.

Although she was now married and her husband was a naval officer aboard the USS McKinley, the chemistry in the OR was catalytic. It didn't take long for the love affair to resume its natural course. Then Carlye—that was her name, Carlye Breslin—put in for a transfer.

"I can't stay here with you...the way we are again," she explained. "I love you."

"Oh, now I understand," said Hawkeye sarcastically, trying to hide his pain. "Since we love each other, there's no reason to stay together."

"The only thing I care about is when two people can't live without each other," she said. "Your work's always going to be the most important thing in your life. I don't want to take a back seat again."

So they said good-bye again.

"I love the way she dropped back into my life to give me a little open heart surgery. I guess I don't mind that she's gone again. It's just that she never altogether leaves."

THE INTERVIEW

I think it was Klinger's uncle who sent the wire recording. Everyone sat around one night, listening to the Webcor. Some reporter, Clete Roberts was his name, had come over to interview the 4077, kind of an Edward R. Murrow sort of thing. But it was something else to sit back and listen to his report:

This is Clete Roberts coming to you from Ouijongbu, Korea. This is a room in Korea. A room the fighting men of the war would rather not see. It is an operating room in a MASH, a Mobile Army Surgical Hospital. There are five of these units in South Korea. The concept of treating the wounded close to the front is being tested here for the first time and, if anything can be said to be a success in war, it is this concept. Ninety-seven out of every one hundred wounded men brought here live. Who are the people behind that statistic? That's what we came to the 4077 to find out.

Roberts: What do you feel was the most difficult thing to adjust to over here?

Captain B.F. Pierce: I think it's that everything is painted green. The clothes are green, the food is green—except the vegetables, of course—the only thing that's not green is the blood. The blood is red. That's what you get the most of here.

Roberts: Can you describe what you do?

Captain B.J. Hunnicutt: Essentially, I'm on call for all medical emergencies. But I've never seen a situation that wasn't an emergency. I did three amputations before I had my first breakfast here. When I first came here, I couldn't walk down a corridor full of wounded without being sickened. Now I don't even notice them.

Roberts: Has this whole experience changed you in any way?

Father John Francis Patrick Mulcahy: When the doctors cut into a patient and it's cold, the way it is today, steam rises from the body and the doctor will warm himself over the open wound. Could anyone look at that and not feel changed?

Some 38th Parallels

YEAR FOUR (1975–76)

NAME: FARRELL, MIKE
CHARACTER: HUNNICUTT, B.J., MD
RANK: CAPTAIN, USAMC
SERIAL NUMBER: US94539204

"I was under contract to Universal and had been approached to do a series for Warner's. I read the script; it was a regular television show, I can't even remember the name of it. It was one of those shows with a joke premise. I didn't like it very much, so I turned it down. When the producers asked why, I said, "It's not M*A*S*H." Now, I didn't mean I was waiting for a spot on the real M*A*S*H, but that M*A*S*H had already come to be synonymous with quality. I wanted to be part of a quality show, not just another sitcom.

"A little later, I read in the paper that Wayne was leaving the show and I thought it was interesting because a year or two earlier, my agent had gotten a phone call saying that there were some contract difficulties with Wayne and would I be available to replace him if the need arose. So when I read that he was definitely leaving, I wondered if I would hear from the show again.

"It was a long, slow process with Wayne, so it was months later when I finally did hear from the show and they asked me to come in and talk to them about it. I made it very clear right then that I was not interested in replacing Wayne as Trapper. It had to be clearly a new character. I had no wish to do Trapper at all. Wayne had done it and done it well and was well accepted by the public in that role. The M*A*S*H people said right off that it would be a new role, B.J. Hunnicutt, and that he would be different from Hawkeye the womanizer.

"As things go in this business, it was a pretty good interview. They called me back and asked if I would consider doing a screen test. They were very quick to point out that it wasn't a test for acting ability, they just wanted to see a few people on screen with Alan to test the chemistry. I had no problem with that. Four of us tested, and I got it. Happy me.

"It was a Wednesday or a Thursday that I did the test. They called me on that Friday to say I got the job and to report to work on Monday, so there wasn't a whole lot of time. The second phone call after the studio was from Alan, who asked if we could get together over the weekend. We had Japanese food up at Yamashiro and talked for hours. We went back to Alan's house and talked into the wee hours of the night—about what we thought the characters should be, how they should work together. We were getting to know each other, seeing if we liked each other, feeling out the whole situation. It was terrific. Not too many people would have done that. On any other show, I would have reported to work on Monday morning and met everyone over coffee.

"Alan immediately made me realize how much he cared about the good of the show and was willing to put the show before himself. Although I wasn't in the same league as Alan in terms of public recognition, I was not interested in signing on as a gofer, so I wanted to be sure my character worked. There were to be two equal leads, with Alan being the first among equals, I guess you could say, since it was obvious from the start of the show that it was Hawkeye's show. B.J. was to be a separate, distinct character, not the guy who held the candle for Hawkeye.

"I was full of trepidation that whole weekend. Trapper had been popular, and Wayne was very well liked. I did incredible mental gymnastics on myself. Everyone's going to hate me; I'm an interloper; I'm new to the family; they'll never accept me. I knew a major character had never been changed successfully in a show, so I wasn't sure it would work, and I kept thinking if this show fails in the fourth year, I'll go down in history as the anchor that sank it.

"I got on the set and knew it was going to be fine. It took two years, but I felt more comfortable every day.

"I came from the 'here's the script, you stand over there, now let's do it' experience and, if something was wrong with the lines, you fixed them on the run—every actor knew that was just the way it was. Gene Reynolds was completely different. He kept saying, 'We want to hear from you,' and he meant it! It was astonishing to me. It was revolutionary in television history. Here were actors working together, saying things like, 'God, this line would be much better if so and so said it'—actors giving away lines! They were creating a better show at the cost of their own lines!

"When I was in front of the camera, I'd look out and see the others in little groups working on their lines, honing the script, working out scenes to get them perfect. My Christ, I'd stepped into heaven! Something like that really brings out the best in you. Each person there was driven to reach deep inside and bring out the very best of his ability.

"As for B.J., the first few years were pretty much of a shakedown process. When we started, we had very little. It was agreed that we would all flesh him out by committee. But he was straight, to contrast him to Hawkeye. When I say straight, that really brought out some problems. The writers thought straight meant straight—he had no nuttiness to him, he could get boring very quickly. We had a lot of discussions, not battles, to make him less predictable.

"The tendency was to put Alan into a scene and let him clean up. Whenever it got sticky, they wrote to Hawkeye. I said, 'Hey, you've got some other surgeons in there. It's personally insulting for Hawkeye to do the critical work in one area and then leave his patient to do something else. So we slowly worked on it. We were the pros on the basketball court, and I had to stand my ground for B.J. or there just might not have been a B.J.

"There wasn't a watershed year or season when B.J. 'arrived', just certain shows we got to look deeper and deeper into this man.

"There wasn't any other way to go. We'd always find ways to isolate two characters together and try to figure out what would happen so you could see more of them. You either go out or you go in. It's to the show's credit that we chose to go out. You can't keep bringing in new characters or go for the disease of the week."

Mike Farrell

Gene Reynolds rehearses a scene with two of his leads

Year Five (1976-77

GENE REYNOLDS, Creator/Writer

"With Larry Gelbart leaving the show, I hired Don Reo and Alan Katz as co-producers. They were a good writing team that had done a lot of comedy. Like everyone else who joined the show later, they brought a lot of fresh ideas. There is a genuine loss when a fine mind like Larry Gelbart's departs. He's one of the finest comedy writers of our time. When he walked away after being so devoted, it was hard. Losing him was a blow, but I think we did very well. The writers rose to the occasion. I certainly didn't feel panic with Gelbart gone. We had good stories. The shows had always been based on research, and we still had plenty of research. We had gone to Korea, then I had started tracking down veterans and MASH doctors in Los Angeles and then all over the country. We would call them up and record our phone conversations. We talked to nurses, doctors, chopper pilots. Some from Korea; some from Vietnam. We got a lot of good things in talking to people.

"We very much wanted our characters to progress. So this was the year that Margaret got married. It was my expectation that she would stay married, but it didn't turn out that way. The thought was to give more life and something new to the character. Here's a woman who had always wanted to get married. We thought we'd have some fun with it.

"We had no cast problems in Year Five. With M*A*S*H, we never had any serious cast problems. I think Five was the year that Bill Christopher was out with hepatitis. We even did a show about it. When he came back to work, they had painted his chair on the set yellow.

"True, some people left the show, but it was because the show had done them so much good. They all had the Hollywood disease of greener pastures. It was the time to make their moves, so they did. There were certainly no problems with Gary. He held the women and children for us. I've been proved wrong, but I always used to say back then that we couldn't do the show without him. If Larry Linville said he was leaving at the end of the show, I don't think I knew it. Maybe by the last show, or something like that, I heard it around, but I was going on to *Lou Grant* then. In the last days, I guess I remember Larry saying he wanted to go. The character he was playing, Frank Burns, was very far from himself. The others played close, but he was forced to be this shrill, bigoted, hysterical 'nerd,' and it was the toughest part on the show. Linville should have stayed the full eleven years, though. He could have retired by now.

"I think that Years One through Five have a certain similarity to them. They are very much of the character of the early shows. After that, with Gelbart and I gone, there're different hands at work and, as the show progressed for eleven years, it naturally became different. The Vietnam war was over, and the element of peacetime tended to take the edge off the show. The show was rolling along emphasizing its comedic elements, so it was a slightly different orchestration after Year Five."

CHAPTER VI

Above and below: Lt. Radar O'Reilly

BUG-OUT

A bug-out was an order to move camp. On the double. MASH units were accustomed to bugging out. After all, the big "M" stood for Mobile.

B.J. and Hawkeye were supervising the building of a latrine when the rumor of a possible bug-out spread around the 4077, causing a "sit-down" on the job. No one much wanted to build a latrine he would soon have to dismantle or abandon—especially a fine executive latrine such as this one.

The rumor was so convincing that Potter called HQ for the official word and then made his announcement: word of a bug-out was pure rumor. Seconds later, Radar handed him the TWX—the 4077 had orders to bug out.

Bug-outs were organized so that surgery and critical patients were moved last; nurses and mattresses went first. As the shelling began, all but Hawkeye, Hot Lips, and Radar had moved out.

The others went to a location chosen by HQ, but they found themselves, in effect, in occupied territory. A group of local prostitutes were holed up in the schoolhouse that HQ had designated as the new OR. When Potter approached the building to move them out, he was turned away at the door.

"Sorry. No appointment."

"Don't give me that static, lady," he ordered in his heavy-duty voice, the one he reserved for official occasions. "We're here to establish the 4077. Now, get your concubines outta there. We're here by orders of I-Corps, General Irving K. Hamilton, commanding."

"Ohhhhh . . . Binky!" said the madam, evidently recalling the gentleman.

It was Klinger's wardrobe that lured the girls out. Just as the new MASH was set up, word came from I-Corps that the Chinese had been beaten back. The 4077 was ordered to bug out again and return to its previous location. On the way back to camp, they bumped into Margaret, Hawkeye, and Radar, who were finally able to join them.

Some people miss all the fun.

MARGARET'S ENGAGEMENT

Nurses were also included in the medical conferences held in Tokyo, so as chief nurse of the 4077, Margaret frequently went to Tokyo Gen for a back-to-school session. She was the type who took notes assiduously and never took time off to play golf.

She returned from one of those meetings with big news. She was engaged to be married to Lieutenant Colonel Donald Penobscott, a shining brass star in the Army hierarchy who was stationed in Tokyo.

"How'd Burns take it?" Potter asked.

"Hard," reported Hawkeye. "He was clucking like a chicken last night. For nine straight hours."

Then he went a little bit bonkers. He arrested an entire Korean family because he suspected they were spies.

Just a little more paranoid than usual. Radar had to call Frank's mom to calm him down.

"He's heading for a Section Eight," said Potter with concern.

Klinger was green with envy.

OUT OF SIGHT, OUT OF MIND

The Army issued each tent one type G18A76 kerosene stove to take the chill out of winter nights. When a stove broke down, there was only one thing to do at a MASH unit—call a surgeon for an emergency operation. If they could put people back together, surely they could fix *anything*.

Unfortunately, Hawkeye was more gifted with his hands in other areas. While he was bent over a malfunctioning stove in the Nurses' Tent, the gas built up a pocket and then blew—causing flash burns and immediate blindness.

A blind surgeon.

He never panicked.

His eyes swathed in bandages and gauze, Pierce took to a bed in postop hoping that blindness would prove temporary so he could keep his nickname. His good spirits cheered the other patients and rallied the depressed medical staff. He even stood in at surgery to give tips to other surgeons.

"Who was that masked man?" asked B.J., incredulous at Hawkeye's marvelous ability to keep going.

When the bandages were finally removed, Hawkeye was able to see. "It was a lucky thing," he announced. "First I got a chance to see without my eyes, and then I got them back."

Only Hawkeye would see it that way.

LT. RADAR O'REILLY

The regular Swamp Low Life and Aces High Poker Game was held every other Thursday, wounded permitting. Master Sergeant Randy Woodruff from I-Corps was sitting in on one game when Radar absolutely cleaned up. Then Woodruff confessed he couldn't pay. This was his second default in a month, so the Swampmen wanted him to ante up something of value. In exchange for his debt, Woodruff agreed to process paperwork that would promote Radar to second lieutenant.

It proved to be anything but a gift. Radar hated his promotion. Klinger became company clerk and felt betrayed by Radar; the enlisted men who had been his buddies now considered him a fink for becoming an officer; and the officers had trouble accepting Radar as an equal.

"How'd it go, Sherm?" Radar asked the colonel while Klinger stood by, mouth agape.

"You call the Old Man 'Sherm'?"

"Sure," said Radar. "Officers call each other by their first names."

Lt. Radar O'Reilly

Disgusted with his new life, Radar begged the surgeons to get him demoted. "But no lower than corporal," he pleaded. "I need to keep up the payments on Ma's electrolysis."

THE NURSES

Margaret Houlihan represented the best and the worst of the Army. Margaret had taken officer-training school a little too seriously and, as a result, did not play well with others.

When Nurse Baker had a problem with Frank in OR, a problem that was Frank's, not Baker's, Margaret confined the woman to quarters despite the fact that her husband had just arrived on an overnight pass.

Outraged at the injustice, Hawkeye and Hunnicutt sneaked the Bakers into Margaret's tent and told her that a quarantined patient had been put inside so she couldn't enter. She bunked in the VIP tent while Baker spent the night with her husband and even had breakfast in bed, compliments of Radar. Then Hot Lips caught her sneaking back into the Nurses' Tent the morning after.

Baker was in a lot of trouble.

Furious at the escapade, Margaret decided to tell the nurses exactly what she thought of them.

"Did you ever once show me any friendship?" she asked the dumbfounded group. "Ever ask my help in a personal problem? Include me in one of your little bull sessions? Can you imagine how it feels to walk by this tent and hear your laughter and know that I'm not welcome? When did one of you ever even offer me a lousy cup of coffee?"

"We didn't think you'd accept," said one of the braver nurses.

"Well, you were wrong," said Margaret.

HAWK'S NIGHTMARE

It wasn't the first time the strain got to Hawkeye. This time it was so bad that Sidney Freedman had to be called in.

Hawkeye was sleepwalking, calling out for his childhood friends, and jabbering about his past. Then he began to wake from the nightmares screaming his head off. Even *he* thought he was cracking up.

"Not so," Freedman assured. "You're just going back to Crabapple Cove, to a time of no responsibilities, no life and death decisions. You dream to escape, but the war invades the dreams, so you wake up screaming. The dream is peaceful; the reality is the nightmare. Actually, Hawkeye, you're probably the sanest man I've ever known. If you were crazy, you'd sleep like a baby."

Klinger was very impressed by the proceedings.

"It's an act, isn't it?" he asked Hawkeye after Freedman left. "I've been kicking myself for not coming up with it myself!"

THE GENERAL'S PRACTITIONER

Colonel Henry Bidwell came to the 4077 on a recruiting mission. He needed a personal physician for General Theodore A. Korshak, I-Corps commander.

Dr. Benjamin Franklin Pierce was not standing in line for the appointment. He didn't like Korshak's reputation as a tough Army type. Nonetheless, he got the nod. He went to Seoul to examine his new patient.

"I'll sign on as your personal physician," he told the general, "if I can go back to the 4077 after your funeral. The stroke headed your way is a lulu, and you've got six months at the most. There are only two ways to avoid it—check into a hospital in Tokyo and start taking care of yourself or sit on a land mine."

"If you're trying to scare me," the general said, "you're doing a fine job."

Hawkeye grew angry. "You're lucky. You have a choice. Most of the other guys who come my way don't get a choice."

The general went to Tokyo. Hawkeye went back to Ouijongbu.

THE ABDUCTION OF MARGARET HOULIHAN

Klinger was on guard duty when he said good-bye to Margaret, who was leaving the camp to deliver a baby at a nearby village. He warned her about the escaped North Korean prisoners who were thought to be in the area, but Goldilocks was not afraid.

No one else had seen her go; Klinger remained on guard duty. Frank didn't know where Margaret had gone and began to worry. Then he decided she had been abducted, and he got hysterical. Soon everyone was certain she had been abducted by the North Koreans.

"Let's turn this over to Intelligence," Colonel Potter suggested.

"That lets you out, Frank," sighed Hawkeye.

Intelligence sent in Colonel Flagg, who did little except to stir up the hysteria, which, with Frank around, was not hard to do.

The baby safely delivered, Margaret returned to camp. Klinger was still on guard duty.

"Anything happen while I was gone?" she asked.

"Nawww," the unknowing Klinger said. "I just ripped my pink pedal pushers."

DEAR SIGMUND

Dear Sigmund,

I've been feeling somewhat frustrated lately so I came to a kind of a spa. The waters are pretty good; that is, they mix a mean martini and the inmates have an interesting defense against the carnage. Insanity in the service of health.

One of them is particularly good at it—name of Hawkeye. Couple of weeks ago, he made rounds in postop with a personality that had split two for one...wearing a tuxedo with swim flippers and a pair of sunglasses.

I guess what draws me to these people is that faced with aggression in its most brutal form, they've regressed to a state of antic, if not lunatic pleasure. As you pointed out, Sigmund, there's a link between anger and wit. Anger turned inward is depression. Anger turned outward is Hawkeye.

If there's a way to preserve your sanity in wartime, they've found it here. They slide their patched-up patients into the evac ambulance like loaves in a bread truck, and yet they never forget those packages are people.

Your friend,
Sidney Freedman, MD

THE COLONEL'S HORSE

There was some question around the compound as to which female Colonel Potter considered more like a daughter to him—Margaret Houlihan or Sophie, his horse. While the man was in Tokyo for a rest and to see his other favorite—Mrs. Potter—both his girls at the 4077 took sick. No one dared wire him about the problems. The doctors simply worked feverishly to bring the girls back to normal before the Old Man returned.

Frank volunteered to operate on Margaret, whose gastritis looked suspiciously like appendicitis. Margaret, however, announced that if she needed surgery, Hawkeye should do it. Meanwhile, Hawkeye and Hunnicutt were using their skills on Sophie, who had a case of equine colic.

Margaret did, indeed, need to have her appendix removed. She paid a late-night call on Hawkeye that was different from his usual visits from the nursing staff and asked him to do the honors.

Hawk's Nightmare

"Pulse rapid, temperature elevated. I can't stand it any more," she whispered in his ear.

"I should be doing this surgery," shouted Frank. "I know Major Houlihan's appendix better than any of you."

"Listen to these lips, Frank," said the patient before she went under. "Listen to these hot lips. Get out, Frank. Get out."

MULCAHY'S WAR

Hawkeye suggested that the Fitzsimmons boy talk to Father Mulcahy. Private Danny Fitzsimmons had come in with a self-inflicted wound, having shot himself in the foot to avoid combat. Frank wanted to patch him up and have him court-martialed. Hawkeye thought a chat with Father Mulcahy might help.

"I imagine it's very difficult up there," Mulcahy sympathized.

"You *imagine?*" Fitzsimmons asked. Realizing the

priest had never even been to the front, Fitzsimmons refused to discuss it any further.

Father Mulcahy immediately felt guilty. After all, he was a Catholic... guilt was one of his specialties. He asked permission to go to the front.

"But the line officers don't want chaplains up there. You're another unarmed man they have to be responsible for," Potter argued. Father Mulcahy went AWOL to get to the battle. He bumped Igor from Radar's Jeep for a ride to the aid station to help pick up a badly wounded GI.

On the way home, their passenger began to choke on his swollen tongue. Radar radioed back to the 4077. Hawkeye came on the line and clearly and patiently gave Mulcahy instructions for an emergency tracheotomy.

The trio finally returned home, somewhat the worse for wear—but alive.

"Father," Hunnicutt said, "I thought we had a deal. We save the bodies, and you save the souls."

"My," Mulcahy said. "I hope I didn't violate union regulations."

HAWKEYE GET YOUR GUN

North Korean troops outnumbered their southern brethren about three to one, and the ROK (Republic of Korea) forces took many severe beatings. Despite handling a deluge over the previous twenty-four hours, the 4077 was requested to send two surgeons to help a local hospital handle its casualties.

Potter and Hawkeye lost the draw. "Load the Jeep with supplies and don't forget my Geritol," ordered Potter. "Pack your gun, Pierce?"

The road to Kumba and Korean Hospital 426 was not pretty. The men were tense as they drove through the area.

"Don't look now," quipped Hawkeye, "but I think we're being followed by the war. If they keep shooting at you, Colonel, I may have to ask you to leave. They can't be shooting at me. I'm a pacifist."

Once at the K426, the doctors saw how desperately they were needed. Wounded lay on the floor; blood-stained clothes were heaped in a corner; supplies were low. Quickly, they pitched in.

To top it off, on the return to camp, they were ambushed by North Koreans. Hawkeye refused to shoot back. "I'll treat their wounds, but I won't inflict their wounds," he told an incredulous Potter.

"You're a crazier soldier than you are a surgeon," said the older man.

"Thank you."

THE KOREAN SURGEON

Dr. Syn Paik was not the average Commie surgeon. In fact, he had gone to medical school in the States at the University of Chicago. He checked into the 4077 with a group of North Korean wounded who had been given the heave-ho by the Aussies.

"I didn't come to Korea to treat *their* wounded," Frank said when he saw the new patients.

"I'm sure they're glad to hear that," Hawkeye commented.

Paik began to help out in OR. Frank and Hot Lips automatically assumed that Paik was a spy. B.J. and Hawkeye thought he was a fine doctor who should be on their side. Even Potter admitted the man did beautiful work. But HQ would hear none of it. Although ninety percent of the prisoners of war chose not to return to North Korea, HQ considered this a political matter.

"Colonel," asked B.J. "you're not going to throw away a good doctor on a technicality are you?"

"Technicality?" Potter asked. "This man's the enemy."

"Maybe," ventured Hawkeye, "they'd be interested in an exchange. We could keep Paik and give them Frank . . . ."

EXORCISM

Korean locals who lived near the 4077 were, of course, Buddhists, and since they were occasionally treated on the base, they erected a traditional religious object—a spirit post—in the compound to scare away harmful influences.

Colonel Potter ordered its removal and—all of a sudden—the spirits turned bad tempered. First, a Korean bicyclist collided with a hut; then Potter's brand new cigarette lighter stopped flicking; Hawkeye broke a mirror; the PA system conked out; Margaret got her finger stuck in a clamp; and then a gauge broke on an important piece of equipment so that a patient almost lost his life.

"How do you explain this, Father Mulcahy?" asked B.J.

"Bishop O'Hara at the seminary had a brilliant explanation for phenomena such as these. He said, 'That's the way the ball bounces'."

But the coincidences were uncanny. When a Korean grandfather was brought in for surgery, he refused to give his consent for the operation until an exorcism of the evil spirits was performed. By now convinced that something out of the ordinary was going on, Potter gave his permission, and a local priestess appeared.

"That heathen display was ridiculous," Frank sniffed.

Except that afterward, the PA fixed itself, the gauge came unstuck, and Potter's lighter began to flick.

END RUN

The 4077 took great pride in the fact that so many of its patients went home alive. That's not to say that they went home whole. Billy Tyler was not one of the lucky ones. In a battle near the ridge, he ran for a wounded buddy and took a load of shrapnel in his leg. The All-American football player from Iowa would never fulfill his contract with the pros.

"Doc," said the boy, "if you can't save the leg, don't save me."

Hawkeye did not take the patient's advice, though he did take his leg. Tyler didn't take it well. "Why don't you go to hell," he stormed, thunder in his voice, bitterness in his eyes.

It was Radar who got Tyler out of it. "Remember the Iowa-Minnesota game? Iowa couldn't move the ball at all. They had us stomped cold. You went to the short pass and then dove over in the last twenty seconds. What a game!"

"Those short passes did it," Billy remembered. "There's always a way to beat 'em. You just have to keep trying until you find it."

Billy Tyler wrote his own prescription to recuperation.

PING-PONG

Lieutenant Colonel Harold Beckett needed thirty days on the line to get his Combat Infantry Badge. "With that on my record, the boys in Washington can move me up. I'll retire a full colonel."

In his anxiety to secure his own future, Beckett jeopardized the future of his boys.

38 Across

"If it wasn't for that stupid Colonel Beckett" sneered Sergeant Bob Blanchard, "I wouldn't be here and most of these other guys wouldn't, either. The colonel panicked. He didn't react to orders to withdraw. He stood there screaming orders out of an Army manual."

When Potter called him on it, Beckett said, "Army intelligence let us down."

"I hear you screwed up. You blew it!" Potter retorted.

Then Potter reported the man to HQ. End of Combat Infantry Badge. End of promotion. Amen.

THE MOST UNFORGETTABLE
CHARACTERS

Staff Duty Log: 13 June
Corporal Walter O'Reilly, Company Clerk

The friendly old sun showed his friendly hot face over the mountains of purple majesty. As though he was saluting good morning to all. Alas alack, the peaceful quietness of the morn was detonated by a herd of choppers transporting punctured person-

nel. But our gallant doctors, the miracle medical mortals, are ever ready to treat the sick and heal anyone they can lay their hands on. The wounded were aided copiously by super smart surgeons whose knowledge is superseded by nobody I know. Together or apart they worked as a team.

Corporal Klinger was in his last grizzly hour on guard duty little knowing the fate that destiny had planned for him. The Chinese were giving up in hordes. Sgt. Fierman brought in four prisoners he had just captured after they had surrendered voluntarily. The vainglorious Corporal Klinger ran like a bird to the nearest Jeep and sped off in quest of Chinese giver uppers. But destiny determined his luck. The Chinese GI's had not seen women in an overexcited period of time. Corp. Klinger barely escaped with his purity still clean....

* * *

Dear Mom,

I gave up the writing course on account I found out I can write better as myself than as Hemingway, O'Neill, or any of those other bums.

Simplistically yours,
Walter

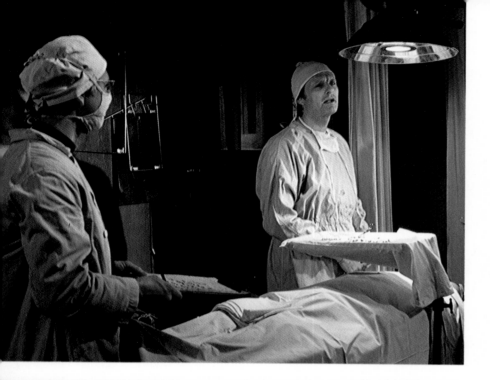

38 ACROSS

Hawkeye could never finish a crossword puzzle. Once, when he got stumped with only one word to go, he was really frustrated. Determined to finish, he began the search for a five-letter word meaning "bedbug" in Yiddish. No one at the 4077 knew the word, so Pierce called his pal, Tippy Brooks, on board the USS Essex to come to help him out. Brooks thought it was a medical emergency, brought his admiral with him, and, together, they risked life and limb to get to Ouijongbu.

When the admiral found out there was no medical emergency, he was not amused. In fact, he ordered an investigation and would have busted not only the Swampmen but Brooks as well. Incoming wounded interrupted his wrath and the admiral joined the others as they scrubbed for surgery.

"You want to sign up for a year, Admiral?" an impressed Hawkeye asked afterward.

"No, thanks. You guys work too hard. But tell me, just why did you get us up here?"

"I'm sorry," confessed Hawk. "It was a misunderstanding. I wanted help with a crossword puzzle. I'm stuck for a five-letter Yiddish work meaning bedbug."

"You mean you dragged us all the way up here to get the word *vontz*?"

HANKY-PANKY

It wasn't just the men who got Dear John letters from their loved ones back home. Nurse Carrie Donovan got a Dear Jane from her hubby. She buried the pain in extra duty and worked well into the night with Hunnicutt and his patients.

"You sure there's nothing going on between you kids?" Hawkeye asked B.J. "No hanky-panky after taps?"

"Scout's honor," a sincere B.J. replied. "I'm happily married."

He spoke too soon. A few days later, while consoling Nurse Donovan, the perfectly married man slipped from his pedestal. Hawkeye was understanding and helpful—and quite amazed that B.J. was about to write Peg all about it.

"Beej, you stumbled last night, but that's all. You were helping somebody, and it got out of hand. You made a mistake. Do not tell Peg. You made one lousy goof, and you want to punish yourself. Okay. Don't make it worse and tell Peg. This will pass. You're human."

HEPATITIS

Father Mulcahy came down with hepatitis and put the whole camp in a frenzy. There are two common types of hepatitis, and one of them is extremely infectious. The

Above left: 38 Across

Below left: Rumor at the Top

last thing the doctors needed was an epidemic. Hawkeye had to examine the rest of the staff and administer gamma globulin shots; Radar had to check out the latrines and the water supply to see if they were contaminated; Potter talked to the cook.

"Isolated for a week?" the quarantined priest asked. "How will I hear confession tomorrow night?"

"Maybe they could write down their sins on a piece of paper and slip them under the door," suggested Hawkeye. "Then we could auction off the paper and make a fortune for the orphanage."

No further cases turned up. Potter was pleased. Nonetheless, he took his gamma globulin in the butt like the best of them and announced: "A patient we had up here three weeks ago showed up in Seoul with a case of infectious hepatitis. Let's hope Father Mulcahy caught it from him, and this will be the end of it."

MOVIE TONIGHT

Movies were considered a necessity for the good of a unit—morale was important. But first-run movies were not on the Army's list. It took Colonel Potter several months to secure *My Darling Clementine*. When it finally arrived, he made an event of it. Everyone was invited to the premiere in the Mess Tent.

Klinger, the projectionist, did not have very good luck with the reel—or the guests. The first kept breaking down and the latter breaking up. During the pauses, Father Mulcahy played the piano; Radar did imitations. The guests even ad-libbed their own dialogue and provided a shoot-out in the best Zane Grey tradition. They had a helluva time.

The party was interrupted by another type of shoot-out—the war. As the staff filed into the OR for the next deluge, at least their spirits had been lifted—they were all singing the movie's theme song.

SOUVENIRS

The souvenirs of war usually have emotional value to those who claim them. Sometimes they also have financial value. Like the ancient vase that Frank Burns bought from a fast-talking street dealer for $27.75. Frank, of course, denied that he had even seen the vase. Meanwhile, Colonel Potter had to give a lecture on the problems of souvenir collecting—especially after the surgeons treated several kids who were injured by enemy booby traps in vases.

Hawkeye and B.J. were forced to ransack Burns' things to get back the vase—a priceless antique that belonged to the national museum—and return it to its rightful owners, the Korean people.

"Why would people want to take home souvenirs of this lousy war?" B.J. asked.

"It helps them remember what they're trying to forget," Hawkeye explained.

POSTOP

It was the Battle of Munsan that did it. The fighting yielded enough wounded to keep the 4077 team on its feet for eighteen hours nonstop. Postop filled while the blood supply emptied.

"Dracula wouldn't find a snack here," Potter announced while trying to rustle up some corpuscles from the 325th Evac.

In postop, those who could talk were anxious to tell their stories.

"It was the weirdest thing. I was sitting in this foxhole. Seemed like nothing was happening, so I was reading one of those Communist leaflets. Suddenly I look and there's this Chinese GI standing over me. We both fired. I got hit in the shoulder, and it knocked me flat. Medics said I got his number."

"I thought I had it made. Stay in the rear and clear out minefields. It's great . . . no one shoots at you. Take your time and snip wires. I just happened to forget that we lay our mines in patterns so we know how to pick 'em up, but we booby-trap a few to fool the bad guys. Next thing I know, I'm lying across the road saying to myself, 'Herb, I think you've got a problem'."

"When I was a kid, I used to fight all the time when people put me down. I believed what they said about me. Not any more. I've been up on the line. I had the guts to go out there and drag 'em back to the aid station. No one's gonna get me again with any verbal abuse because I got something guys like that will never have—self-respect."

MARGARET'S MARRIAGE

Margaret and Donald had been engaged for eight long months without setting the date. Everyone began to wonder—especially Frank.

"No ring. No wedding date. I think it's 'thanks for the buggy ride.' "

That did it! Margaret called Donald in Tokyo, asked him to hop the commuter to Seoul, get a Jeep to the 4077, and take the plunge.

Klinger donated the wedding dress, the very same one he had worn when he married Laverne Esposito. Frank Burns was the best man. Colonel Potter gave the bride away. Father Mulcahy performed the ceremony.

Of course, Hawkeye and B.J. didn't want to be left out—so they gave a bachelor party for Donald the night before the wedding. The groom got a little drunk, as grooms often do, and the doctors decided that a groom who was plastered deserved to be plastered. So they covered his entire body with a body cast. He showed up at the wedding more than a little tight.

"Can she get him out of the cast?" B.J. asked Hawkeye with a touch of concern as the newlyweds took off for their honeymoon.

"Are you kidding?" Hawkeye asked. "She'll tear it apart with her bare hands."

YEAR FIVE (1076–77)

NAME: LINVILLE, LARRY
CHARACTER: BURNS, FRANK, MD
RANK: MAJOR, USAMC
SERIAL NUMBER: ER61109398

"My contract was up at the end of Year Five and I had the option to negotiate or take a walk. I felt I had done everything possible with the character, so I told them I was leaving. I'm not sorry I left. I went on to do television, movies-of-the-week, and theater. I was saturated with playing only Frank.

"The people at Fox thought it was some kind of ploy. They like a successful package to stay the way it is. But I wanted to leave. If I had had a seven-year contract, I would have stayed seven years. I had a five-year contract. I'd done Frank so well no one could see me doing anything else, which is a difficulty for an actor. I was hungry to broaden my experience acting. Frank was not a buffoon or a cartoon character. Frank was a study of subjective and objective reality simultaneously, and a lot of what you saw on the screen was surrealism.

"My life is very peculiar. I end up in trouble while doing the right thing. It's not a contradiction for me. It's part of the growing process. If I wanted to work forty hours and down a can of beer while I watch the Super Bowl, it's easy enough. I either work fourteen hours a day or not at all; I don't drink beer and I didn't watch the Super Bowl. But it's never dull around here.

"Playing Frank Burns was the hardest part in M*A*S*H but I think the most rewarding. It was dangerous. With Frank, you were on thin ice. I could have drowned at any minute, but I got to the other side. Without an element of danger, life gets dull very quickly. Frank Burns could have been a total cartoon—you had to know that he could feel pain like anyone else … maybe more than anyone else. He had his guises to protect himself, that's what made him ridiculous and provided the fun. I could have played him as insensitive, which would have been as easy as throwing myself on the floor and having a tantrum. Any baby can do that. The reverse was much more difficult.

"He was a prototype. If you look carefully at every other sitcom since M*A*S*H, they have all tried to have a Frank Burns and they have all failed miserably. A lot of the credit goes to Larry Gelbart. Burns was a combination of all the things that irritated the hell out of me. He was a walking case history for a shrink. You could see all the elements in him at the same time. There was nothing hidden, and you didn't have to go through years of therapy to get some kind of reaction out of him. It was all simultaneous. It was a bloody dangerous role. Burns was displaying his genuine kind of insanity as if it were conscious and objective behavior, and people reacted to that as if he were a conscious, objective, functioning human being.

"For example, once when he was in the operating room, he got so uptight with Trapper and Hawkeye that he launched into a speech: 'Boy, you guys really think you're something. Well, other people are not necessarily. Someday you'll find that out, and I just hope you're there when you do.' Then Hot Lips says, 'Frank?' and I say, 'Margaret, I've just got to tell them off,' and she says, 'I think you did.' That kind of senseless double-talk, where the man didn't even know he sounded like a complete idiot, is part of what made him such a dangerous person.

"If you look at Burns not as a cartoon, I think you'll find some frightening and dark elements there. There's a mind that stripped its gears, obviously. And yet he is functioning with a knife in his hands on other human beings. You're not playing with cartoons there. Those are nasty and dangerous things. You can't have the reality of M*A*S*H, which is people and bodies and blood and pain and agony, and have a maniac running around the operating room working on them and then come up and say that's a cliché.

"I remember most fondly the excitement of Gelbart trying to push me, saying, 'Let's do something outrageous and insane and see if you can get away with it.' It was like running down a razor blade. You fall down on either side or on it and you're dead. Running with that role down the blade and keeping your balance, that's what it was all about. Seeing if you could get to the other end and not make a fool of yourself … not overdo it or underdo it. I didn't feel anything negative about the show or Frank's part— that's not why I left. I had expanded my abilities enormously, and it seemed all the energy was being expanded on a single point. It's not the ability, it's having the damn material.

"When Frank and Hot Lips were no longer a duet, I think there were structural problems. The writers were writing for her and writing for me, and the Katzenjammer kids were divided. After Gelbart left, it was easier to run Frank into a scene, dump on him, get a laugh, and run him out the door. I think Hot Lips and Frank's relationship was pivotal to the show. Once it dissolved, there were a goodly number of problems. Loretta wanted her own identity separate from Frank Burns. I'm not sure, but I think that's what was involved and why changes had to be invoked.

"I think the finest example of what we all did was *Sometimes You Hear the Bullet*, a first-year show. It was the most beautiful balance we ever hit—the best, by far. There were some stunt shows, some gag shows, some shows that displayed our expertise by being different—and they were wonderful in their way. But for teamwork, for being what the show was always meant to be, it was *Sometimes You Hear* *the Bullet.* People may disagree with me, and I couldn't care less. This show contained the comedy, which is obviously the staple of the show, but it also contained an element of horror. And that, to me, is the finest thing we could do, because the show was very definitely an antiwar, antimilitaristic theme. People that you know really do die in wars. If there were any faults in M*A*S*H at all, I think it would be the parade of wounded that go through it without us getting to know them genuinely.

"I think part of what made the show work so well was that many of us were actor-writers. I counted up one day and we had nine writers on the set, many of them the show's actors. We were also theater people and knew what we were doing. Comedy is not just acting silly. That's why I keep doing plays. You have to be in front of an audience to see what people laugh at.

"What I remember most about M*A*S*H was the dark. We worked twelve-hour days. We went to work in the dark, we left in the dark. In the studio next door to us, they were shooting something or another and were happy to get two pages a day. We shot fourteen pages a day. When we were on location, the weather was actually hostile. We had one day out there that I believe started with below freezing and, at the end of the day, the temperature had risen over seventy-five degrees.

"The third year was probably the best; by Year Five, it was very different. I kind of divide the years that I was on the show into two beats—at the end of the first three and then, of course, the end of Five was the totality. For me, the end of Year Three was a distinct point, and then it's what happened later. Three was the high point of the show. I didn't much want to come back for a good-bye show at the beginning of Year Six, so it was never seriously discussed. The period had been put on a run-on sentence, and that was it."

Larry Linville

Potter's Retirement

Year Six (1977–78)

BURT METCALFE, Executive Producer

"I remember Year Six vividly because it was the first year I produced M*A*S*H alone, and I was scared stiff. Gene and Larry were both gone and only one person on the writing staff, Jay Folb, had been there. I added Isaacs and Levine [David Isaacs and Ken Levine] to the staff; we had used them freelance.

"I guess the major element of the year was the arrival of David Ogden Stiers. Larry Linville had made it clear he wasn't returning after Year Five. We started off the season with an hour show devised to account for Frank's demise and Winchester's arrival. I had been thinking about the new character during the hiatus. I didn't want a straw man or a cartoon figure. Frank Burns's character was too easy a joke, he was such a fool. I wanted to bring in a very good doctor, a formidable man with dimension and complexity. Actually, I kept thinking of William F. Buckley. I had known a guy in the Navy who was something like the character I wanted—that's where it really started.

"One Saturday night, I was home with the flu watching TV, and I saw *The Mary Tyler Moore Show* with Stiers playing the station manager. He had an upper-middle-class Midwestern temperament with a way of saying, 'I'll see you in the gutter,' and just chopping Lou and Mary to pieces, and I said, 'Oh, my God. That's perfect.' He could offer the conflict we needed without us being repelled by him. I never saw or considered another actor.

"The shake-up of David arriving and Gene leaving gave us new blood and new stories and new enthusiasm for the new season. It was a very exciting time. We didn't feel stale at all. We didn't think it was time to go off the air. We were nervous but excited, ready to go get 'em.

"Alan got more involved starting in Year Six and wrote some memorable shows. The episodes are definitely different in Year Six. We didn't want to try to imitate what had gone before. We couldn't be the comic genius that Gelbart was. We had to find our own ground. I think the stories became more poignant, more Frank Capra-ish—he's symbolic for what I try to say. Some people will say we got into sentimentality, but we had used many of our best guns comically. We went for more depth and for stressing personal relationships."

CHAPTER VII

FADE OUT—FADE IN

Hot Lips was on her honeymoon in Tokyo; Frank was on much needed R&R in Tokyo. Never the twain did meet—except in Frank's demented mind. He went AWOL stalking Tokyo, certain that every blonde woman he saw was Margaret.

"I've gotta get on the horn to I-Corps," swore Potter. "Let's see if they can trace Burns. He should have been here yesterday. We've gotta have another surgeon."

At the very moment, Dr. Charles Emerson Winchester III, a Boston Brahmin who had the misfortune to be human enough to be drafted, had beaten Colonel William McDermott Baldwin in cribbage. Winchester was anxious to collect $672.17. Just as the colonel was to pay up, Potter's request for a new surgeon came through. Baldwin didn't have a lot of surgeons himself at Tokyo General, but one look at Winchester's smug expression and he decided to help out his old buddy, Potter. Winchester was sent packing.

Back at the 4077, there was general concern—and some mirth—over Frank's disappearance. Word from Tokyo began to filter through that Burns had, indeed, cracked up. He assaulted a blonde on a bus, called her Margaret, tried to lick the buttons on her uniform, and then escaped the MPs. He was finally caught after he followed Brigadier General and Mrs. Horton P. Kester into a public bath and got into the tub with them—all the while certain that he was trailing Margaret and Donald.

Hawkeye and Hunnicutt packed their bunkmate's things. They knew he would never return. Gleeful as they were, their merriment faded when they met the new man, who arrived wearing his Class A uniform, a double-breasted camel hair topcoat, leather gloves, and a cashmere neck scarf. He even managed to maintain his dignity while being towed into camp in an ox cart. (His Jeep and driver were long gone.)

Winchester made it clear from the beginning that he was not one of the boys, but he pitched in immediately and did a great embroidery job on Dr. Leon Berman. Berman suffered from a ventricular aneurysm that was producing blood clots and would have died without immediate open-heart surgery. None of the Swampmen knew the technique, but Winchester took the tricky task in stride.

"The whole family has gifted hands. Mother's a concert pianist," he sniffed. His true arrogance hadn't begun to show because he still thought he was going back to Tokyo Gen. Then Potter gave him the news.

"And if I refuse to stay in this hellhole?" Winchester questioned grandly, one eyebrow raised.

"You'll be making gravel at Leavenworth," Potter explained.

FALLEN IDOL

Hawkeye blamed himself. After all, he was the one who suggested that Radar go to Seoul for some recreation. When Radar came back as a casualty, the stunned doctor insisted on performing O'Reilly's emergency sur-

Fade Out—Fade In

gery. Then he went to Rosie's Bar to drown his sorrows in sake and Coca-Cola.

He was so hung over the next day that he had to leave surgery in the middle of a bowel resection. Charles closed for him.

Pierce's bedside manner was no better. He soon stormed out on Radar as well.

"You walked out on a patient," Radar reminded Hawkeye from his sickbed. "A lot of people look up to you here. They admire you and they want to be like you, and when you walk out, they feel like you let them down. If they can't depend on you, then maybe there's no point in depending on anything."

"Don't lay all that on my shoulders," snapped Hawkeye as he stalked out of postop. Later, when Hawkeye tried to apologize, Radar would have none of it. The boy was suffering his own hurt at the realization that Hawkeye, too, had human failings.

It took a man-to-man chat with Colonel Potter to make the company clerk realize that he had grown up a lot when he discovered that even doctors can't be idolized.

LAST LAUGH

"Provost Marshal's office is sending a colonel up to investigate B.J.," announced Potter, his face as white as a clean surgical gown. "They claim he's an impostor. Not even an MD."

"I could have told you that," Hawkeye volunteered. "He's a piano player in a bawdy house."

"Aw, c'mon," said Dr. Hunnicutt. "The Army has all my credentials. The Acme School of Medicine; residency at Joe's Hospital and Auto Supply; and my private practice at Schultz's Mortuary."

When B.J. found out that his investigating officer was to be Leo Bardonaro, everything snapped into place. Bardonaro was a pal from undergraduate days at Stanford and an infamous practical joker. He arrived at the 4077 complete with palm buzzers, exploding cigars, and whoopee cushions. But the humor turned nasty when Beej was actually arrested for a crime that Bardonaro trumped up. Hunnicutt was sent to Seoul for an inquiry.

Hawkeye cornered Bardonaro, got Hunnicutt cleared, and managed to secure the last laugh. He sent the man off without his traveling papers in a Jeep with too little gas.

IMAGES

Eddie Hendrix was a walking tattoo museum. He bore eagles, anchors, women, ships, and more women all over his hefty body. One look was all Radar needed to convince him that he, too, needed a tattoo or two.

Klinger tried to dissuade him. "A blue dagger would clash with a pink organdy or a basic black sheath! Tattoos are feh!"

Then Potter tried. "They're dumb. Back in World War I, I had a friend got himself tattooed. Put his girlfriend's face smack dab in the middle of his chest. Couple of years later, he sprouted hair on his chest and turned her into a bearded lady."

Radar remained adamant. So Hawkeye and B.J. went with the boy to make sure the conditions would be sterile. To buoy their courage, they stopped at Rosie's, where they met Sergeant Artie Rimmerman, a teetotaler who explained that he was off the booze due to hepatitis B caused by a dirty needle at a tattoo parlor. Even that didn't change Radar's mind!

"It's a teddy bear," shouted Hawkeye after a forced inspection of Radar's bare bottom.

"But I was afraid of the dirty needle, so I had him draw it in. It'll come off when I take a bath," Radar sighed.

"My God!" Hawkeye hooted. "It's permanent; you never bathe!"

WAR OF NERVES

Sidney Freedman usually came to play poker or to poke around among the psyches of the staff. This time he came as a casualty. He had made a house call to a foxhole when the Chinese decided to overrun the field. Freedman and his patient both landed at the 4077. Freedman had a minor head wound; his patient was in more serious shape.

"First time I saw this boy," Freedman explained to Hawkeye, "he had to be carried to my office. Wasn't wounded. Hysterical paralysis. Had seen three of his buddies killed in twenty-four hours. We used to send these cases home. We found the problem stuck with them for the rest of their lives. Now if the trauma has been recent enough and their defenses haven't built up to a point where they'll resist treatment, it yields to talking. But you've got to get them right back to their unit. That's how I got there. I was doing a follow-up. You can't send them out and forget them."

The patient was not appreciative. "I'll never forget what it felt like being put back in that foxhole when you knew what I'd been through. I'll never forget having my legs all shot up, and I'll never forget how much I hate you."

THE WINCHESTER TAPES

Dear Mother and Dad,

I've only been here a short while, but it seems forever. MASH 4077 is truly a nightmare. I won't be happy until I am out of here. I've even contemplated shooting myself in the foot. But you know how much I enjoy the annual Deb's Cotillion.

I live with two heathens named Pierce and Hunnicutt. Their version of wit is dirty laundry and nose hair. Constant exposure to these cretins only aggravates my misery. I am endearing myself to the CO— the man responsible for my presence in this cesspool. He's a tough, bandy-legged little mustang, but he paints. He's somewhat of a primitive, no Churchill, but I've agreed to pose for him if it will help my case.

Above and below: Images

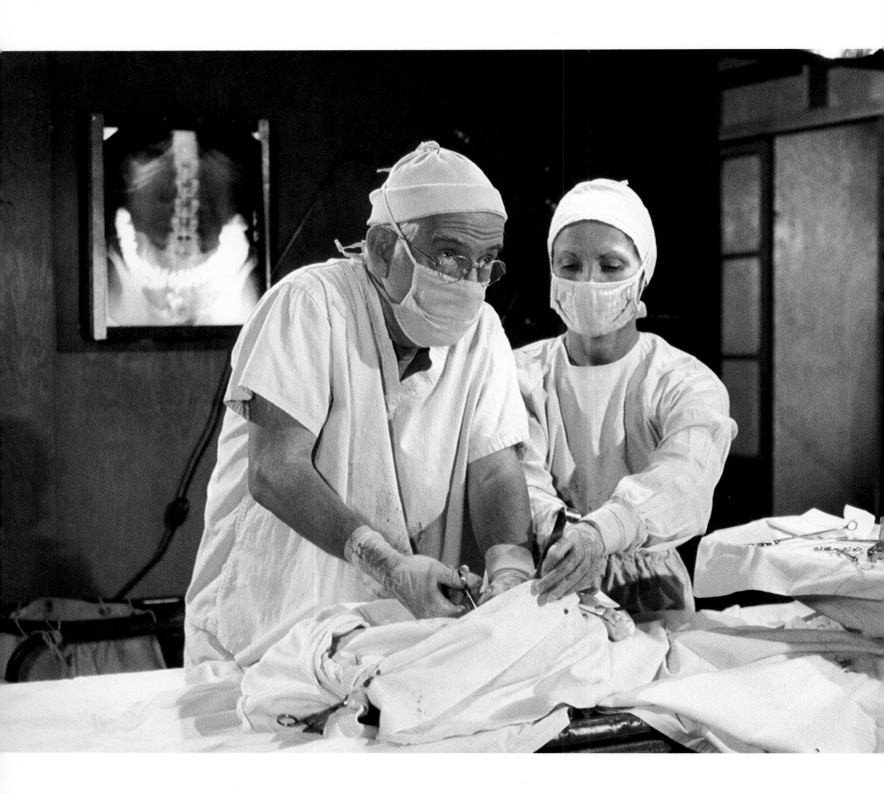

Father, you must know someone influential who can get me out of this rattrap. Talk to Senator Griswold. After all, you paid good money for him.

I must conclude this now to catch some sleep. Another thirty-eight-hour day is done. Now Mother and Dad, I'll put this as succinctly and eloquently as possible—get me the hell out of here.

Your loving son,
Charles

THE LIGHT THAT FAILED

There was a backup generator at the 4077 to provide light in the OR when shelling shut down the power. But when you were out of light bulbs, there wasn't much a generator could do. There didn't seem to be much the Army could do, either. They sent a truckload of mosquito netting instead.

In the darkness, it was easy to make a mistake, and Charles accidentally injected his patient with curare instead of morphine. Curare is a poison that causes temporary paralysis of all muscles in the body, including the diaphragm, so Hawkeye and B.J. had to quickly resuscitate the man to save his life. Charles was almost in shock himself.

"Dammit," Hawkeye said. "Will you stop worrying about yourself, Charles, and think about your patient."

"I'll admit that what I did was inexcusable. Maybe not totally. I've gone fourteen hours straight in the OR. And it was dark. But is that any excuse for misreading a label? Not really. If that man had died, his blood would have been on these hands. You could at least acknowledge, Pierce and Hunnicutt, that it takes a courageous man to admit when he's wrong."

TEA AND EMPATHY

Black marketeers had broken into the supply room again and looted all the penicillin. That left the 4077 in sorry shape.

When Corporal Benny Bryant confessed to Father Mulcahy that, among other things, he trafficked in stolen medical supplies, Father Mulcahy was in a religious jam. He, of course, was not allowed to reveal anything spoken to him in confession, but he knew how badly the penicillin was needed. Wounded would succumb to secondary infections and death in a matter of hours without the medication. And the British had just sent in several men who were developing peritonitis—infection of the abdominal lining—because they had been served tea after they were wounded, ostensibly to calm their nerves.

Mulcahy's lips were sealed. But not his feet.

The padre grabbed Klinger and they went after the drug. Bryant had revealed his hiding place in the confes-

sional, so the dutiful duo drove directly to the schoolhouse, dug up the old temple bell in the yard, and retrieved the penicillin. They were shot at by North Koreans as they scrambled back to the Jeep. They escaped with their lives, but Klinger suffered a casualty—his dress.

They returned to the 4077 and saved the day.

THE GRIM REAPER

Colonel Victor Bloodworth had the Battle of Hill 403 down to a matter of numbers. A hardened battle commander, he measured the risks of any attack in terms of gains and losses, not real people's lives. His strategy reduced a battle plan to a matter of numbers, and he briefed Potter and the medical staff accordingly.

"All right, gentlemen. Let me tell you what to expect in casualties for the next twenty-four hours. We come up with an anticipated 280 to 290 men passing through your unit. Do you think you can handle that?"

"Why don't you try for Hill 404 instead?" asked Hawkeye, incredulous that men were being reduced to statistics.

"Yeah," Hunnicutt chorused. "It has a lovely view of Hill 405."

Sure enough, as the battle ensued, the wounded began to arrive. When Bloodworth came down to check on his men, an outraged Hawkeye threw the colonel up against a wall and angrily called him "The Grim Reaper." Bloodworth filed charges before he returned to the front.

A North Korean bullet forestalled further proceedings. Bloodworth was sent back to the 4077 with a belly wound and had to rely on Hawkeye to save his life. The "Reaper" came to appreciate the healer, if not vice versa.

THE MASH OLYMPICS

With the 1952 Olympic Games underway in Helsinki, Colonel Potter decided to shape up the whole team by holding the MASH Olympics. The camp divided into two teams: one headed by Hawkeye and one by B.J. The winning team was promised three days leave; the losing captain would have to push the winner around the compound in a wheelchair for a week.

Competition was stiff. Margaret wanted to win so she could go to Manila with her husband, Donald. Although not a member of the unit, Donald was allowed to sub for Klinger in the Nurse Carry race. When the score tied at 5-5, Potter had to draw one name from each team to run an obstacle course. Donald went up against Sergeant Ames—an out-of-shape Army regular. Donald had it made but turned to look over his shoulder and bumped into a tree branch. Ames won and brought home the passes for Hawkeye's team. Jesse Owens couldn't have done better.

IN LOVE AND WAR

A shiny 1948 Chevrolet pulled into the camp. Out of it emerged Kyung Soon, a gorgeous Korean dish wearing an expensive Western-style dress. She certainly didn't look like she came from a country whose per capita income was under $25.

Her pretensions alienated everyone, especially Hawkeye, who resented it when Potter sent him to her home for a house call.

"I know it's very lower class of me to be upset, but when the local countess butts in line ahead of sick people, I get a fast case of rising gorge," he said in his most sarcastic manner.

But at her bombed-out home, Hawkeye discovered that his "countess" was using all her ways and means to care for the homeless. Pierce changed his mind as his animosity turned to admiration. In fact, he soon found himself falling in love with the woman. They spoke French together; they pretended the war had gone away together; they danced to records on her old Victrola in the remnants of what had been a grand old house.

"War and love don't mix," Potter philosophized.

"Let her go," B.J. warned.

"I can't let her go," Hawkeye lamented. But he could not keep her. She thought it her duty to take the people she cared for to a safer place, south of Ouijongbu, where there was no fighting. Nothing Hawkeye could say would get her to stay.

"I'll never see you again," he said as tears filled his eyes. "We'll write a few notes as a graceful gesture of futility and then I'll never see you again."

CHANGE DAY

To pay the troops, the Army sometimes coined its own money, called scrip. Scrip had to be changed frequently to foil counterfeiters and black marketeers. Color codes were used and then rotated at an appointed moment chosen by HQ and appropriately called "Change Day."

To make "Change Day" really pay off, Charles made a deal with his Korean tailor to buy up old scrip at ten cents per dollar. Charles promised a cut of two percent to the tailor if the man helped him rook the locals. Then he would take the old scrip and change it for new, making a tidy profit.

While exchanges took place, no one was allowed off or on the 4077 grounds, so Charles was stopped by MPs and routed back. As he ran to the barricade, he was stopped again.

"Permission to come aboard denied, sir," said Klinger, on guard duty in a sailor suit.

"I've got to exchange all this money!" Winchester shouted.

"Deep-six it, sir. I have to keep out the riffraff and the profiteers."

Every now and then, the rich don't get richer.

PATENT 4077

Hawkeye was forced to use a hemostat on an artery when what he really needed was a vascular clamp small enough to control an artery without crushing it. Such a clamp did not exist in 1952.

"Chalk it up to the insanity of war," B.J. said. "The Army can make a gun that will level a village thirty miles away but they can't come up with a tiny surgical tool that'll help save a man's leg."

Sergeant Zale designed what the doctors were looking for but Engineering said it would take ninety days for delivery. In ninety days, a hundred men could become amputees. Then Hawkeye and B.J. found Mr. Shin, a local peddler who made all his own trinkets. He made the new clamp in three days, and it proved so successful that Mr. Shin decided to go into the surgical supply business.

There's no business like war business.

THE SMELL OF MUSIC

Hawkeye and B.J. just didn't like Charles very much, that's all there was to it. And they liked his French horn playing even less.

"Make a deal with you, Winchester," B.J. suggested. "You knock off the horn, and we'll shower."

"Reek away, gentlemen. I shall continue to play as long as there is breath in my body and music in my soul."

Reek they did. A separate table was set up for them outside the Mess Tent. They would have been kicked out of OR if possible. Their body odor was so bad that the rest of the staff took after the trio with a water hose—to clean up Hawkeye and Hunnicutt and to rust up Winchester.

"I love it," shouted Charles, "Drown the cretins."

"I don't care what you guys did to me," said Hawkeye, "but those lice you just drowned were women and children."

Then Margaret grabbed Charles' precious French horn and placed it under the wheels of an oncoming Jeep.

"You barbarians!" Charles screamed, as he began to whimper.

COMRADES IN ARMS

Hawkeye and Margaret were sent to the 8063 MASH to demonstrate one of Hawkeye's procedures. When they arrived where 8063 was supposed to be, they discovered just how mobile a MASH could become. The unit had bugged out, leaving the two visitors stranded in enemy territory.

Hawkeye was turning the Jeep in the opposite direction when it conked out. Margaret was not amused. Neither of them could fix it. When some North Koreans came toward them, the two abandoned the Jeep and took to the woods. The North Koreans started the engine right up and drove off, leaving Pierce and Houlihan stranded in not-so-friendly territory.

The Merchant of Korea

Above right: The Grim Reaper
Below right: Comrades in Arms

They took cover in an abandoned hut. Then Pierce decided to make a house call in the middle of the road, where he spotted a wounded man. The man was dead. Returning to the retreat, Hawkeye attracted a burst of enemy fire. In the shelling, timbers of the hut began flying, and Hawkeye took a splinter in the thigh. Margaret was able to remove it, but the minor surgery left the patient unable to walk any distance. They were stranded.

Resigned to huddle there for the night, Hawkeye and Margaret drank some Japanese Scotch they had and talked heart-to-heart about Margaret's problems with her husband.

"I'm nothing to him. If I were a half-ton truck, he'd be more lyrical about me. Do you know how it hurts to give your heart to somebody and then find out he's got a little darling named Darlene?"

They drifted to sleep, but shelling woke them and drove them into each other's arms.

The morning after, she made him breakfast from K rations while he made small talk.

"Well, here we are, two sleepy people at dawn's early light hoping they don't get shot before lunch."

"I love how brave you are," sighed Margaret. "It's thrilling, really. I love a strong man who takes charge. Now walk out that door, and let's get out of here. Do what I tell you."

They walked toward Ouijongbu and spent the next night under a palm tree in a rainstorm. Margaret adjusted Hawkeye's collar as she snuggled next to him.

"You know, all the time when we were insulting each other, every once in awhile I'd wonder what it would be like to be, you know, close to you. And there you were wasting time with other women."

"Waste not, want not."

They were finally rescued. "Margaret," Hawkeye laughed with tears in his eyes, "we're safe. It's all over."

"Oh, no, it isn't!" she swore. "Not by a long shot!"

THE MERCHANT OF KOREA

Peg wired B.J. to send $200 so she could buy some land they had had their eyes on. But Hunnicutt didn't have the money. So he borrowed it from The Swamp's wealthiest tenant, Winchester, and promised to pay up in twenty-four hours—payday.

Charles soon began to treat B.J. as his servant.

"Close this patient for me, will you? I'm due in postop in an hour, and I'd really like to get a bite."

"I think I should have stolen the money," B.J. said under his breath. "I think I've become a $200 houseboy."

The next day, Radar announced the HQ had sent the company pay to Guam by mistake—there was only enough scrip for the enlisted men. Hunnicutt had to get a second mortgage from Charles, the "Merchant of Korea."

To earn back some money before the pay arrived so that Charles would leave him alone, B.J. decided to take

him on in a not-so-friendly little game of poker. But Charles—who whistled grand opera while he played—had beginner's luck and was winning, until B.J. discovered that Charles whistled his arias a little louder when he was bluffing.

"Think of all those years I hated music," Hawkeye gloated, as they cleaned out the unsuspecting Charles.

WHAT'S UP, DOC

Margaret suspected that she was pregnant but refused to fly to Tokyo for a test. The only rabbit at the 4077 belonged to Radar. But a pregnancy test usually involved killing the rabbit, which was not acceptable to Radar. So "Fluffy" underwent the knife. Hawkeye removed her ovaries for the test.

Meanwhile, Charles was held hostage by a slightly deranged patient who demanded a chopper, civilian clothes, and transportation to Ohio. When he heard that someone wanted to go to Ohio, Klinger volunteered to be the hostage. He barged in and exchanged himself for Charles.

"Okay, okay," the patient said. "Anything's better than this whiner."

Charles breathed a sigh of relief.

"I don't mind being brave," Klinger insisted. "I'll go all the way to Ohio if I have to. It's in the line of duty."

Klinger was ready and willing to leave, but, alas, the patient was not. He had lost so much blood during the standoff that he passed out and had to be rushed into surgery.

"Come on, kid," wailed Klinger. "You can't do this to me."

Twenty-four hours later, both patients were greatly improved. Fluffy healed nicely and proved that Margaret was not pregnant; the patient was mending while waiting for a visit from Sidney Freedman.

POTTER'S RETIREMENT

General Waldo Kent called Colonel Potter to Seoul for what was expected to be a routine visit. Once there, however, Potter got a big surprise. Kent threw the book at him, then sent him back to the 4077 with his butt in a sling.

Potter returned as "El Groucho," but took several days before confessing his troubles to Hawkeye and B.J. The surgeons insisted that there must be a company spy who was sending bad weather reports to Seoul. It had to be Charles!

Charles only denied the charge and suggested that they look through the mail pouch to discover the traitor. Sure enough, they found a letter from a spy in camp.

Potter was still hurt.

"Sherm," said Hawkeye, "you can give me a hundred good reasons to leave, and I can't give you one good reason to stay. Stay anyway. Think about it for a while."

Your Hit Parade

Potter looked at his watch for a second or two. "What the hell. I'll stay."

MAIL CALL THREE

No mail for three whole weeks! But when it came, there was plenty for everyone. Hawkeye received a huge stack of love letters addressed to Benjamin Pierce but erroneously delivered to him. He read them anyway and couldn't wait to meet the other Benjamin Pierce.

Charles got a lot of mail from home, including one piece addressed to Master Charles. Radar's mail included a letter from his Mom that mentioned she had a boyfriend. Father Mulcahy got a postcard from his sister "the sister" that B.J. classified as a nunogram.

But Klinger was the most hurt when he opened a Dear John letter from his wife, Laverne. "She took my allotment checks, built up a nice bank account, and now she's found another guy. She had no right."

He decided to go AWOL to straighten it out. Radar found him at Kimpo airport and brought him back to camp. "I was this close," Klinger told Potter. "I had deluxe class in the baggage department of a C-47. I bumped a general's poodle to get on."

The two men talked. And Klinger decided to stay at the 4077 and let Laverne go her own way.

"I may not have a family in Toledo," he said, "but I got one here."

YOUR HIT PARADE

The pressure was on. Chinese troops were close by. The 8055 had already bugged out; the 8063 was overrun with wounded, so they put up a "For Sale" sign and sent their patients to the 4077. To keep up spirits during the deluge, Radar went on the PA as a disc jockey.

The Officers Club, the Mess Tent, and The Swamp were turned into operating rooms as more and more wounded poured in. Then a real crisis hit—no more AB negative blood. The only donor in the neighborhood was a bomb disposer on R&R, who was eventually tracked to Rosie's Bar and brought to the 4077 in a semiconscious state.

"This guy's a bomb disposer? He's bombed, all right!" said B.J. But his blood was as good as gold—gold with a high alcohol content.

The surgeons worked through two days and nights before the deluge was over.

'This is Radar mike-side signing off with the twenty-third playing of *Sentimental Journey*. How about that, you hot potatoes in MASH land?"

TEMPORARY DUTY

It was regular procedure for MASH units to exchange cutters for temporary duty. Hawkeye and Nurse Bigelow went to the 8063; Captain Roy Dupree and his nurse, Lorraine Anderson, came to the 4077. Dupree was a top-notch surgeon but boisterous and obnoxious; Anderson was a school chum of Margaret's who made eyes at Winchester while they operated across a crowded room.

Offended, Margaret reminded Lorraine that surgery was not "a sexual sandbox" and kicked her friend out of her tent. Potter, on the other hand, was so impressed with Dupree that he arranged for the man to be permanently attached to the 4077.

Charles and B.J. needed a scheme to get rid of their unwanted new roommate. They encouraged Dupree to take the prized Sophie—Potter's horse—for a morning gallop through the camp. Potter kicked him out, and Charles welcomed Hawkeye back with a giant hug.

"God, I'm so glad you're back," Charles told the astonished Pierce.

DR. WINCHESTER AND MR. HYDE

To better deal with the incredibly long operating shifts, Charles turned to amphetamines. The side effects made him work faster, eat less, and sleep little. He became a zombie. He even doped up Radar's pet mouse, "Daisy," for the big race against the Marines' mouse, "Sluggo."

Upset by the sudden change in Charles's personality, B.J. and Hawkeye went through their roommate's footlocker and found the pills. They faced him.

"Admit you're not Superman, Dr. Pasteur, and Al Jolson all rolled into one," Hawkeye suggested.

"It's hard to take, Charles," said B.J., "but you're just like the rest of us . . . human."

Finally, they had to toss out the drugs to bring Winchester back to normal. Of course, normal he was no bargain, either.

MAJOR TOPPER

Klinger hated the new man almost immediately. His name was "Boots" Miller, and he was a clear Section Eight if there ever was one.

He played the soup ladle like it was a trombone; he talked to his shoes; he shot real bullets at make-believe planes and then went after pretend pilots. Potter shipped him home as fast as he could.

Later, Potter got a package from a man at the Novelite Toy Company. Boots had become a rich man with a sock puppet that he had invented while talking to his shoes at the 4077. Now, he wanted to make toy planes, like the ones he "shot down" at MASH.

"I'm now vice president in charge of development of this company," he wrote. "I want to make a new toy called Enemy Glider. Did you happen to photograph the one I shot down there? Please send me one of your pictures by registered mail since this company is filled with spies who are out to get me."

Major Topper

YEAR SIX (1977–78)

NAME: CHRISTOPHER, WILLIAM
CHARACTER: MULCAHY, FATHER JOHN FRANCIS PATRICK
RANK: CAPTAIN
SERIAL NUMBER: RA11295403

"I always thought that M*A*S*H was about a chaplain in the Korean War, and Burt had to keep reminding me that it wasn't, so you'll have to excuse my perspective. Year Six was my first year back after being out much of Year Five with hepatitis. It was fortunate how it worked out or I might have been taken out of the show. But it was the year that Fox had a new deal out at the Ranch. The expectation was that we wouldn't have the Ranch, so we had done all the exteriors at one time, early on. I was doing interiors, back at Stage 9, when I got sick. They had to rewrite me, but I was established enough so that I got paid and didn't get written out of the show totally. I was in bed for eight weeks, and I could have never missed that amount of work if we shot in the normal way, so I guess 'Someone' was watching over me.

"By the sixth year, I was in every show. You know, I was not a regular like everyone thought. I was a day player, like Jamie. We both started out in a few episodes and worked our way up to full contracts. I got my contract the year after he got his, that must have been Year Four, and then I think it took them a year to correct the billing. It wasn't much of a transition, but it was nice to get 'up-front' billing. And there were certain other things—a parking space, a dressing room. I'd been doing about twelve shows a season, then in Year Five, I was ill, but I know I was in all of them in Year Six, which was very gratifying because they didn't *have* to put me in. There would be scenes where I was doing very little, but I was in them. That was nice. It showed I was considered a part of the whole picture, even if it was just standing around OR or having only one line. As an actor, you have to have faith; as a priest, you have to have faith. I'm always impressed when I see an actor come in and do a couple of lines and do them well, and I think, 'Boy, that's zingo! That's great!' You can have a very small bit to contribute and then you're not small anymore. It's kind of hackneyed to say there are no small parts. I hope that Mulcahy does get some focus in the small parts. I like the big parts better. But if you can crystallize the small parts, that's great.

"I never thought of Father Mulcahy as the Angel of Death in the operating room. The opposite, I'd say. He was standing by to bring comfort. I wore that purple sash or stole in the OR to make it clear which figure was Mulcahy and what he was doing there. He also wore one in the movie, if you'll recall. That projection is a conscious effort on my part. I liked the color purple, and I wanted to introduce a different color into the darkness; I wanted to stand away from the doctors but in the right way. Some doctors were uncomfortable about my being in the OR. I was a very strong image.

"I mumbled around with the part in the first years. I went to see a number of priests, particularly the Irish priests at St. Timothy's down the road from Fox. I wanted to feel comfortable playing a priest. The show had a medical adviser but not a religious one. I learned how to cross myself, give a benediction, learned Latin prayers, and how to give last rites. I went to the library to read government records on the chaplain corps. I found that priests are very human and that I should avoid doing any stereotyping of a saintly nature. I wanted to play away from making Father Mulcahy too innocent. He acted as kind of a balance, a sane balance, to the wackiness of the doctors. Not that there was any antagonism there. He could look the other way. He represented the point of view of the audience, I think. The audience may very often have felt as he did, and it was nice to see someone on the spot feeling that way. He began and ended a dedicated priest. I played the character against the cross. He is a simple man, well meaning but intuitive. I let anybody else feel however they want. I personally wanted to get away from religious jokes. I thought he could be amusing without having to turn on a religious joke. Every once in a while, you can make allusions to the Bible, but if every time Mulcahy came into the room and made a remark that turned on his being a priest, that gives a terrible burden to the character, and the writer, and probably the viewer. I wanted him to be more human.

"The part did get meatier over the years, starting in Year Six. It was inconsistent, though. Some shows I had a small part, other times a large one. During hiatus, I used to take story ideas to the writers who were still working. None of them ever came to fruition, but it insured that they were thinking of me.

"Sometimes I was frustrated by seeing things I thought Father Mulcahy could do very well being done by other people, but M*A*S*H was so good that no matter how small a part was, it was wonderful to be there at all. But there were times I had a problem with what was going on. In the first show of the sixth year, I had to make some reference to Major Burns and Hot Lips and was supposed to act as if I had never known that they were having an affair, and I had a problem. I thought, 'How naive can I play that?' I decided to go for the thin line as if it were a joke because people assume priests don't think about sex, but it was silly to me that Mulcahy be that naive.

"Otherwise the sixth year went very smoothly. I thought there was some intention that the Winchester character come in and be a romantic interest for Hot Lips. I thought it would be the reverse of Hot Lips and Frank now that she was married, and then she would take up with the new doctor. But that was either my imagining or my projecting. Maybe I invented it. I thought it was a great way to go.

Loretta didn't want too much to be married. I think Father Mulcahy should have been more involved in the disintegration of her marriage. He married her. I thought there was a great scene there for him to ask if there was something he could do to save her marriage. I think she uses Colonel Potter as the father rather than Mulcahy.

"They tended to keep Father Mulcahy around but didn't allow him to grow as much as he could. The last couple of years, things worked out better. He became a more complete character. He's probably the longest running religious character in prime time. It's hard to find what people are comfortable with when it comes to religious characters. Also, among writers and actors, you don't find as many religious people as you do in the country as a whole, and that makes the writers unsure of how to write for a religious person. Even his activities were kept to what writers thought the public would accept—the orphanage, for example. There were a good number of foxhole conversions in the war, but we never dealt with that. Chaplains spent a lot of time in postop, but Mulcahy rarely went. A lot of the time, he drinks coffee in the Mess Tent as if there were nothing else to do. Sidney Freedman would come in and do a lot of talking to patients that I think Father Mulcahy could have done. I never really knew why that character was invented. Mulcahy could have expanded to handle all that.

"But M*A*S*H had a wonderful ensemble, and everyone was always treated as part of the ensemble. There was never the feeling that M*A*S*H was the setting for just one person's talent, and the show was never written that way. I think all the characters added a different color, a different kind of humor. Father Mulcahy's humor was occasionally whimsical, which is my kind of humor. We all brought our own color to the lines. Alan had his own way of working that makes Hawkeye's lines, which are sometimes thin on paper, work wonderfully. I wouldn't be able to do his lines. I wouldn't be able to do Jamie's lines, nor could they do mine.

"M*A*S*H had a lot of serious things under its belt. We did a lot of serious shows and broke some new ground. That's what makes it a classic."

William Christopher

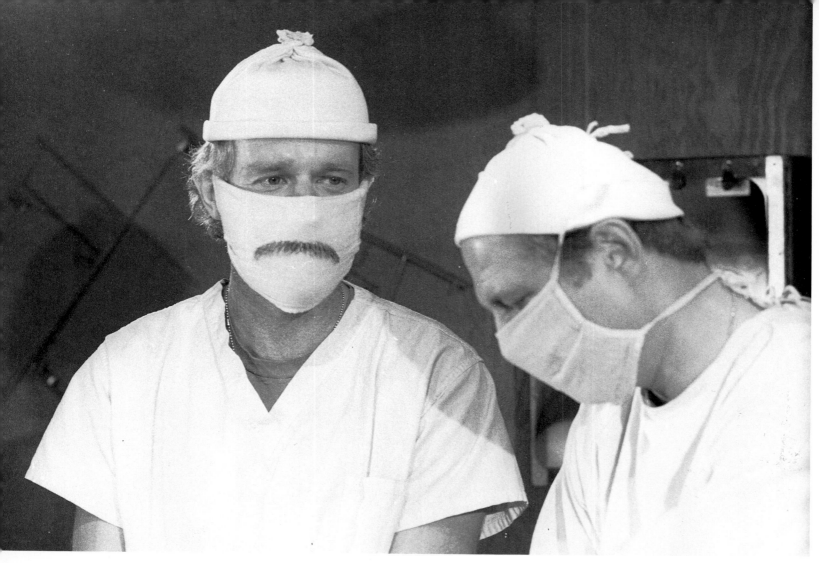

Mike Farrell tries out his moustache on a surgical mask.

The Swamp, with its roof exposed, on Stage 9 at Fox during the filming of *April Fools*

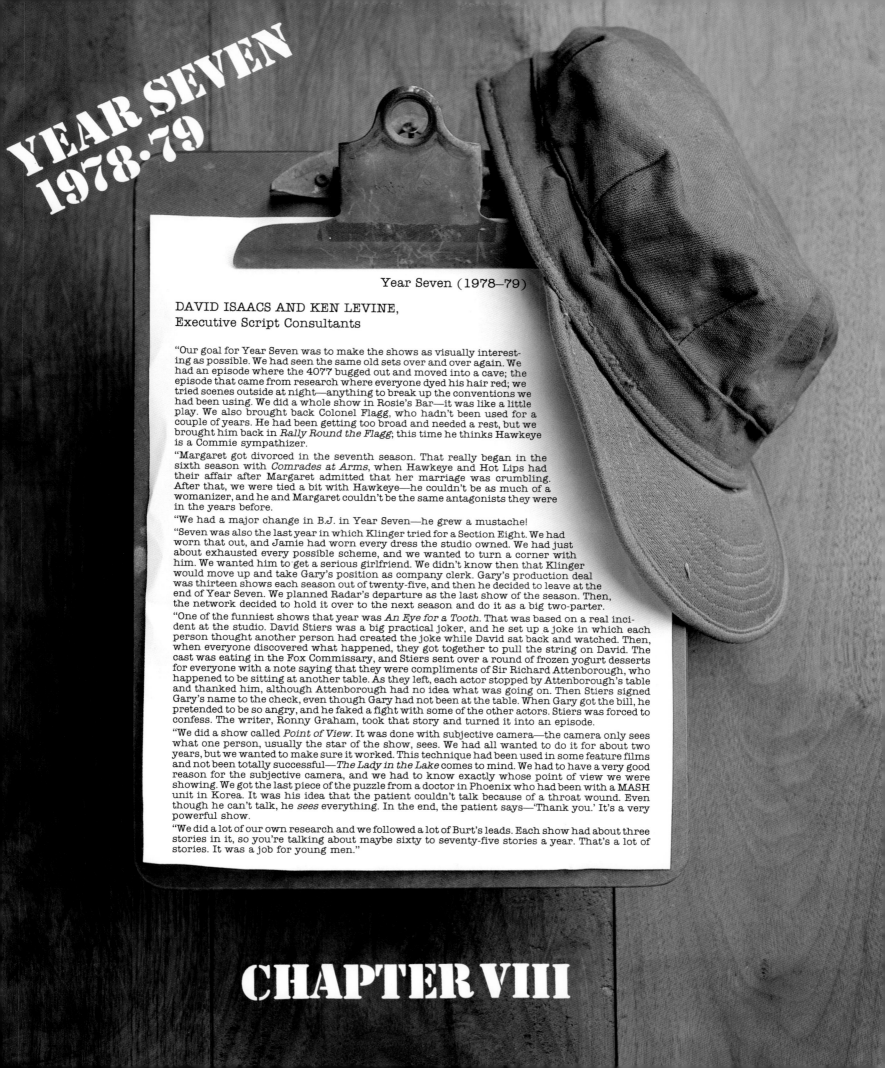

Year Seven (1978—79)

DAVID ISAACS AND KEN LEVINE,
Executive Script Consultants

"Our goal for Year Seven was to make the shows as visually interesting as possible. We had seen the same old sets over and over again. We had an episode where the 4077 bugged out and moved into a cave; the episode that came from research where everyone dyed his hair red; we tried scenes outside at night—anything to break up the conventions we had been using. We did a whole show in Rosie's Bar—it was like a little play. We also brought back Colonel Flagg, who hadn't been used for a couple of years. He had been getting too broad and needed a rest, but we brought him back in *Rally Round the Flagg*; this time he thinks Hawkeye is a Commie sympathizer.

"Margaret got divorced in the seventh season. That really began in the sixth season with *Comrades at Arms*, when Hawkeye and Hot Lips had their affair after Margaret admitted that her marriage was crumbling. After that, we were tied a bit with Hawkeye—he couldn't be as much of a womanizer, and he and Margaret couldn't be the same antagonists they were in the years before.

"We had a major change in B.J. in Year Seven—he grew a mustache!

"Seven was also the last year in which Klinger tried for a Section Eight. We had worn that out, and Jamie had worn every dress the studio owned. We had just about exhausted every possible scheme, and we wanted to turn a corner with him. We wanted him to get a serious girlfriend. We didn't know then that Klinger would move up and take Gary's position as company clerk. Gary's production deal was thirteen shows each season out of twenty-five, and then he decided to leave at the end of Year Seven. We planned Radar's departure as the last show of the season. Then, the network decided to hold it over to the next season and do it as a big two-parter.

"One of the funniest shows that year was *An Eye for a Tooth*. That was based on a real incident at the studio. David Stiers was a big practical joker, and he set up a joke in which each person thought another person had created the joke while David sat back and watched. Then, when everyone discovered what happened, they got together to pull the string on David. The cast was eating in the Fox Commissary, and Stiers sent over a round of frozen yogurt desserts for everyone with a note saying that they were compliments of Sir Richard Attenborough, who happened to be sitting at another table. As they left, each actor stopped by Attenborough's table and thanked him, although Attenborough had no idea what was going on. Then Stiers signed Gary's name to the check, even though Gary had not been at the table. When Gary got the bill, he pretended to be so angry, and he faked a fight with some of the other actors. Stiers was forced to confess. The writer, Ronny Graham, took that story and turned it into an episode.

"We did a show called *Point of View*. It was done with subjective camera—the camera only sees what one person, usually the star of the show, sees. We had all wanted to do it for about two years, but we wanted to make sure it worked. This technique had been used in some feature films and not been totally successful—*The Lady in the Lake* comes to mind. We had to have a very good reason for the subjective camera, and we had to know exactly whose point of view we were showing. We got the last piece of the puzzle from a doctor in Phoenix who had been with a MASH unit in Korea. It was his idea that the patient couldn't talk because of a throat wound. Even though he can't talk, he *sees* everything. In the end, the patient says—'Thank you.' It's a very powerful show.

"We did a lot of our own research and we followed a lot of Burt's leads. Each show had about three stories in it, so you're talking about maybe sixty to seventy-five stories a year. That's a lot of stories. It was a job for young men."

CHAPTER VIII

Above and below: Peace On Us

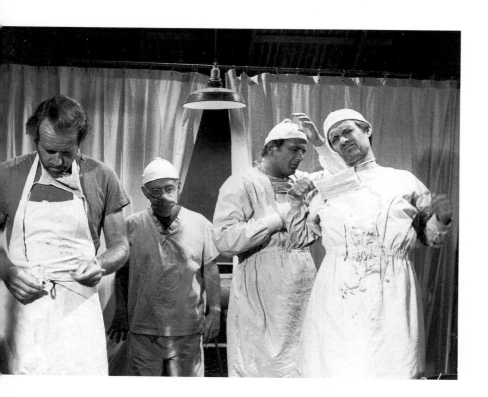

COMMANDER PIERCE

Colonel Potter went to Seoul and left Hawkeye in charge. "There goes the war!" B.J. laughed.

He was wrong.

Hawkeye took the responsibilities to heart and turned "all Army." He was disgusting. In fact, it got so bad that after Hunnicutt made a trip to an aid station without permission, Hawkeye fumed that his heretofore best friend had gone AWOL.

"I don't believe what I'm hearing," sighed Margaret. "Since when did you join the Army? If only Frank Burns could see you now. It's not so easy to play the clown when you have to run the circus, is it?"

When Potter called from Seoul to check in, he realized that he had to return to the 4077 on the double. He found Hawkeye at his desk, two days behind on the paperwork and feeling belligerent and mean. Potter undertook to get his replacement drunk just to calm him down. Then he patched up the rift in The Swamp with a few more drinks.

A CO's work is never done.

PEACE ON US

Peace talks to settle the Korean conflict dragged on for more than a year. It was frustrating for the negotiators, the soldiers, their families, and the 4077.

"Peace talks!" spouted an angry Hawkeye, "I love it! They talk, and we get blown to pieces. The four or five eternities I've spent putting kids back together gives me the right to complain about this lousy, crummy, stinking war."

He got even more upset when Colonel Potter announced that due to a lack of surgeons, the Army had raised the number of points needed to go home from thirty-six to forty-five. That put Crabapple Cove just a little further away. If that weren't bad enough, Margaret tearfully confessed to Hawkeye that her marriage was officially over.

"It's all my fault," she sobbed. "Look at the place I picked to have a marriage . . . the middle of a war!"

That was the last straw. Hawkeye jumped into a Jeep and drove to Panmunjom to the peace talks.

"Thirty-five years in the Army," said Potter shaking his head. "I thought I'd seen it all."

He tried to have Hawkeye stopped enroute but had no success. Pierce made it into the conference room and onto the speaker's floor. It was not one of his more eloquent get-'em-in-the-guts speeches but rather a lunatic plea. The guards dragged him away. "People are dying out there," he shouted. "You've got to stop this war!"

B.J. PAPA SAN

MASH doctors all over Korea spent their spare time giving free medical service to the locals. B.J.'s moonlighting brought him to a family that touched him more deeply than his usual cases. The entire family lived in a tiny hut in squalor unknown by most Americans. The father lay dying of pneumonia and was infecting everyone else.

B.J. treated them all, then tried to make their lives a little bit better. He brought them food, medical supplies, and all but moved in with them. He got them mattresses; he fixed the hole in the roof. He worked long shifts in OR then rushed to his Korean family to work harder still. Hawkeye was concerned.

"Beej, these people have a lot of sadness in their lives. It comes with the territory. No matter what you do, you can't really change that all by yourself."

But B.J. had to try. He thought of them constantly. After a siege of heavy shelling, he rushed to the hut. They had gone.

He was heartsick. "First they take me from my wife and kid, and just when I find something to help fill the gap, they take that away, too."

His voice broke with sadness; tears brimmed in his eyes.

BABY, IT'S COLD OUTSIDE

The high temperature at Ouijongbu that winter was thirteen degrees Fahrenheit. Everyone at the 4077 was miserable, except for Charles, who got a special delivery package from Mummy—a fully winterized polar suit. It was bad enough to lord the suit over the staff, but when he showed up for triage to treat frostbite cases while he was snug as a bug, tension increased.

It was so cold that all the stoves had to be moved into postop to keep the patients from freezing to death. Staff had to huddle together in the Mess Tent around one measly heater. Only Klinger was outside—on guard duty. Then a shell burst, wracking the camp and rendering Klinger deaf.

"Deafness will get you out of the Army," Potter told the man, "but if this is a scam, I'll nail your sorry hide."

It was no scam. Klinger really was deaf. But there was another crisis in the camp, and Hawkeye and Potter had to save the life of a patient. They emerged victorious just as Klinger's hearing miraculously came back.

THE BILLFOLD SYNDROME

Billfold Syndrome is a type of amnesia in which the victim keeps looking at the ID in his wallet to try to remember something about himself or his past in hopes of regaining his memory.

It happened to Sergeant Jerry Wilson, a young medic from the 5th Regimental Combat Team. He used to haul wounded into the 4077 on a regular basis and knew the gang well. Then he arrived one day, looking at his name tags and unable to identify himself.

Potter called in Sidney Freedman, who decided to hypnotize the boy to get to the root of the trauma that had induced the memory loss.

"All right, Jerry. We're at Hill 403. The Chinese just threw a battalion at us. Confusion. Shells all around. Your buddies are falling."

"Thompson!" called Jerry in his trance. "Thompson! Where's Stevie, my kid brother? He's in your platoon. Have you seen him? Oh, God . . . Stevie . . . I've got to find Stevie . . . Where is he? I promised Mom I'd look out for him. I'm the oldest. It'll kill her."

"What happened to Stevie?" asked Dr. Freedman.

"Oh, Stevie! Stevie, no! Please, no! He never got out of the bunker. He never made it. I'm sorry, Mom. I'm so sorry."

LIL

Colonel Lillian Rayburn was yet another visiting dignitary making a tour of the beauty spots of Korea. She came to inspect the nurses at the 4077. Rather than a routine visit, the inspection turned out to be a special moment for both Lil and Colonel Potter. Radar thought it was a bit too special, but the two colonels did hit it off.

"I don't think it looks right," said Radar.

Hawkeye tried to calm him down. "The colonel's just looking for a little companionship, someone closer to his age and hair color than us."

"Those two are becoming an item," Klinger announced after the colonels picnicked together near the minefields. They returned to Lil's tent for a nightcap.

"Is what's happening what I think is happening?" Potter asked Lillian as the evening warmed up.

"Did I get my signals crossed?" Lil asked, a little surprised.

"You didn't," Potter responded. "I just gave you the wrong signals. There's a girl at home with my picture on her piano, and I guess I can never forget that."

THEY CALL THE WIND KOREA

"Heavy winds with temperatures below freezing," said the weather report from I-Corps.

The bad weather meant no choppers would be incoming, so Charles decided to drive to Seoul in an attempt to catch the last commuter to Tokyo for his R&R. Klinger volunteered to drive him and checked out a Jeep. On the road, a convoy slowed their progress almost to a stop. An MP advised an alternate route—which Klinger never wrote down and Charles promptly forgot.

Lost in the middle of nowhere, Klinger and Winchester came upon an overturned truck carrying four wounded Greeks, all of whom required immediate medical attention. With only his doctor bag, Charles performed emergency surgery on one man while Klinger made bandages out of the Bostonian's custom-made silk shirts. They spent the night sheltered from the windstorm in the back of the truck and tended the sick. The next morning, Klinger went to look for help. That's when he discovered that they were only two hundred yards from the 4077.

"Klinger made a wrong turn and got us hopelessly lost. I was obliged to save these poor sons of Greece," Charles

*Clockwise, from above: Baby, It's Cold Outside;
None Like It Hot; Baby It's Cold Outside; None
Like It Hot; Peace On Us; Baby, It's Cold Outside*

said as they got back to camp. "Be it ever so crumbling, there's no place like home." He headed off to The Swamp for the remainder of his R&R.

OUR FINEST HOUR

War correspondent Clete Roberts came back to reevaluate the conditions at the 4077 for another of his famous television talks.

"It's been two years since I was here and, in spite of the ongoing peace talks, an end seems nowhere in sight. How do you deal with it, Dr. Pierce?"

"I usually close my eyes and hope it'll all go away. It doesn't seem to work. Most times you just do your job and try to ignore the fact that the war is going on right outside your window."

"Captain Pierce, when you leave here, what memories will you take with you?"

"That's easy. The face of every kid who comes through here."

NONE LIKE IT HOT

The 38th Parallel was one of the hot spots of the world. Temperatures consistently rose above one hundred degrees Fahrenheit in the summer. But relief for the 4077 was just a package away. Hawkeye and B.J. ordered a rubber bathtub from Abercrombie & Fitch. When it arrived, the whole camp went into a state of hydromania.

Officers and noncoms were soon lined up for ten-minute dunks. But those standing in line started to get rowdy, even nasty. Potter finally suggested that the tub leave town. A certain Sergeant Clifford "Scrounger" Rhoden had already expressed keen interest in the tub and was drooling for a trade.

"Oh, yes, Sergeant Rhoden of Sears and Rhoden," Hawkeye said. "Supplies a large variety of contraband even if he has to rob his mother to get it."

"So you read my brochure," Rhoden grinned.

The Swampmen drove a hard bargain. They swapped the tub for a case of Scotch and ten gallons of strawberry ice cream. They had just removed Radar's tonsils, and ice cream was exactly what the doctors prescribed.

OUT OF GAS

A gas crisis at the 4077 meant that precious supplies of sodium pentothal—which was used as an anesthetic—were low. Sergeant Zale, the supply officer, had made what he considered one of his best deals. He had traded the pentothal for plasma. But a deluge was expected, and it was feared that there wouldn't be enough gas.

Father Mulcahy decided to put in the fix himself. "I could make, uh, a drop with the black market. I have connections. I've dealt with them to obtain supplies for the orphans. You can get practically anything. You'd be surprised what a priest can get away with."

Winchester volunteered to see just how much that was, and the two arranged a rendezvous to exchange a case of Chateauneuf du Pape—Charles's tent wine—for the much needed pentothal. But Charles blew the swap with his haggling. The racketeers stripped the two men to their underwear then drove off with the wine. No pentothal!

In their skivvies, the priest and the surgeon were about to hike back to camp. Then they realized that the thieves would probably stop and drink the wine, which would make them susceptible to a sneak attack. Charles and the priest waited for the men to pass out. "Have you ever seen such boors?" sniffed Charles while watching from the bushes. "Drinking red wine with poultry!"

At the appropriate moment, they stole the Koreans' truck with its seven cases of pentothal—and returned to the 4077 triumphant. "Remember the Boston Tea Party!" shouted a jubilant Charles.

MAJOR EGO

It wasn't unusual to lose a patient on the table and be able to bring him back to life with heart massage. If less than three minutes passed, it was unlikely that the man would suffer any brain damage. It didn't happen often, but it was a last-ditch method to try to save a life. All the doctors used the technique when needed. But when Charles used it one time, he decided to call *Stars & Stripes*.

A reporter came to the 4077 to get the scoop.

"This is my first interview since I graduated summa cum laude from Harvard with one of the highest grade point averages ever seen at that institution," Charles told the reporter in his inimitable way.

The reporter stayed through an operating shift to observe Charles in another difficult procedure. This time, Charles was so busy showing off that he almost bungled the job. When the patient began draining blood, Hawkeye suggested that Charles reopen and check for hemorrhage. Charles hotly said that Hawkeye was merely trying to make him look bad in front of the reporter.

"The only thing that's keeping me from knocking your block off for that little remark is the thought that I'd have to treat you afterwards," a furious Hawkeye shouted.

As the patient's condition worsened, Hawkeye was forced to go in and save the man's life.

Charles admitted his error. When the reporter showed the laudatory story to him, he tore it up.

"Charles," announced Hawkeye, "you're pompous, arrogant, conceited, and a total bore, but you're all right."

DEAR COMRADE

Dear Comrade,

As instructed by the Intelligence Section of the People's Army, I have begun surveillance of the 4077 MASH. I have taken a job as a houseboy for a doctor

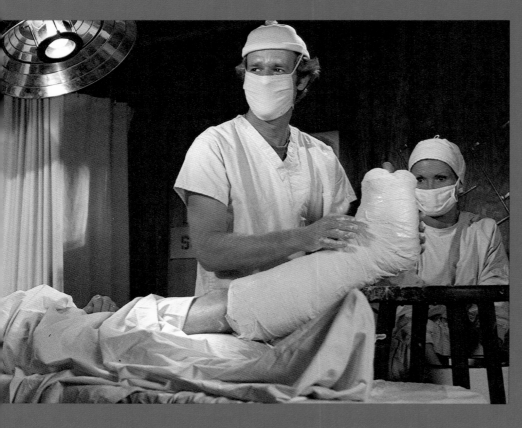

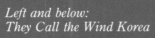

Left and below:
They Call the Wind Korea

Above: Our Finest Hour
Left and below: Major Ego

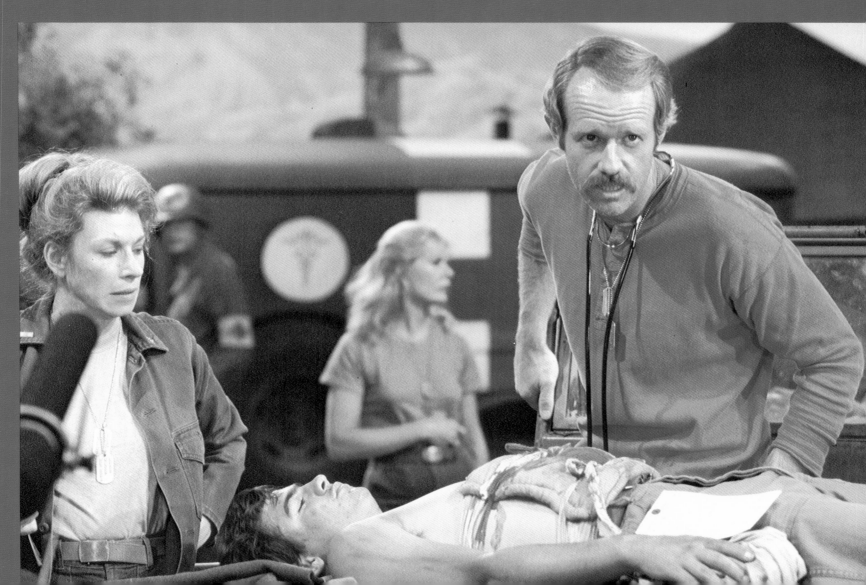

None Like It Hot

from Boston at some place called The Swamp, and I will remain here until I learn the methods they use to achieve their remarkable record of success.

For such an efficient unit, their behavior in surgery is extremely haphazard and undisciplined. As for their off-duty behavior—decadent is the only word. I find no evidence of leadership here, although they do have a commander. He has the roar of a tiger but the bite of a kitten.

The Americans are as soft and weak-willed as we have been led to believe, comrade. They're supplied with an abundance of rations and yet they whine and complain about its quality.

My conclusions are as follows: their success record is, indeed, valid, but their methods are so unorthodox that duplication on our part would be difficult— if not impossible.

Yours truly,
Comrade Park

AN EYE FOR A TOOTH

Passed over once again for promotion, Father Mulcahy was uncharacteristically angry. When he met a chopper pilot who had been promoted twice in six months, he saw purple.

This pilot flew with a man-sized, 150-pound dummy named Little Mac that served to counterbalance the empty pod when there was only one patient on board. But when Little Mac was destroyed, the pilot, Toby Hill, was left without a partner. So, always anxious to help and wanting to attract some attention so that he'd be promoted, Father Mulcahy sneaked off with Hill on an emergency flight. When he returned—in a pod—he was badly shaken but alive.

"Padre," said Potter when they returned, "as soon as you've got your stomach back, I'm going to give you the chewing out you deserve. In the meantime, I'm putting you in for a commendation. Next time promotions come up, your name better be on the top of the list."

POINT OF VIEW

He was another one of the wounded: Private Hank Rich from San Antonio, Texas—went to Alamo Heights High School, then he got drafted. He was on patrol with his platoon, over near Hill 447, when the Chinese hit. Rich was one of the first down. A medic picked him up, tagged him, and got him into a chopper. The boy had a throat wound, so he couldn't talk, but he saw and heard everything that was happening.

"Hi. I'm Corporal O'Reilly, the company clerk. They call me Radar. If it's okay with you, I'm gonna take your valuables for protection."

* * * *

"Hello, Private Rich, I'm Father Mulcahy. I'll be your spiritual leader for the next few days. I see you're Protestant—well, no problem. Just close your eyes now and rest easy. Remember, He's watching over you."

* * * *

"Okay, fella. I'm Klinger. Don't mind the outfit. We're gonna take a quick X–ray now. What's your good side? Makes no difference. This camera sees right through you."

* * * *

"Hi, there. I'm Captain Pierce. I want to peek under your bandage. Army regulations. Okay. What I'm going to do is take that shrapnel out of your neck and put a tube in so you can breathe easier. When the swelling goes down, your voice should come back. I know you're thinking, 'This guy looks as if he couldn't fix a bicycle tire.' Well, I can't, but I'm gonna get you through this."

It took two operations, but they patched the kid up and put him on the wagon for that glorious trip to Evac, Tokyo, and then home. Rich spoke his first words as he was leaving: "Thank you, doctors."

Dear Sis

PREVENTATIVE MEDICINE

It was another deluge, only this time neither the Chinese nor the North Koreans were totally responsible. Colonel Binghamton Lacy was a careless son of a bitch who knowingly sent his men into battle even when he expected a higher than usual casualty count.

When he came by the 4077 to visit his men and hand out Purple Hearts to those who were still alive, he bragged to the doctors about the next mission he had volunteered his boys for.

To protect the innocent, Hawkeye decided to give Lacy a little emergency surgery—just to keep him away from the front as long as possible. He spiked the man's drink, diagnosed the ensuing cramps as an attack of appendicitis, and asked B.J. to assist.

B.J. refused to do unnecessary surgery. "We're doctors. We're supposed to put bodies together, not take them apart. Some things are wrong. You're going to hate yourself tomorrow and for the rest of your life if you do this."

"I hate myself right now," countered Hawkeye. "I hate me. I hate you. I hate my whole life here. If I can get this maniac off the line by some simple surgery then I can hate myself with a clear conscience."

DEAR SIS

Dear Sis,

Received your letter. It's a shame Sister Lombardi was transferred to St. Cecilia. I know the basketball team will miss her hook shot. As I write this, no one has shown up for my 10 A.M. ecumenical service, but I'm not disappointed yet. It's only 11:30. I guess my sermon is not exactly what you'd call a hot ticket.

I realize you'll get this letter around Ash Wednesday, but here in Korea, it's right before Christmas. It's a time for anticipation and hope. Unfortunately, it's also the time when both sides get in as much destruction as they can before the traditional truce.

When you're faced with such overwhelming physical misery, it just doesn't seem enough to offer spiritual comfort. I keep wanting to do more, but more is never enough. I'm almost desperate to be useful, Sis. No one comes for confessional. I have no one to grant absolution to, no one to comfort, no one who wants to bend my ear. At times like this, I head for the bar at the Officers Club...I tend, you see. You hear a lot of confession that way.

Yours in Christ,
Francis

Above: An Eye for a Tooth

Right: Dear Sis

Below: The Price

THE PRICE

Cho Pak was one of those ancient Koreans whose age was impossible to determine. He could have been seventy or seven hundred. He and his daughter, Sun, did laundry for the 4077. Unfortunately, they were treated with the disdain one comes to use with servants who do not speak your language. Cho Pak had been a great warrior and a national hero. He did not wear the title of laundryman easily. He felt he had lost face with the world, and the embarrassment had a crippling effect on him.

When Sophie—the colonel's mare—disappeared, no one thought to make the connection to Cho Pak. Instead, Potter called I-Corps, got out a helicopter search, and made rounds of the neighborhood. The horse could not be found.

The next day, Pak rode Sophie into camp. He was dressed in his old military uniform, his back was straight as he rode proud in the saddle—a man transformed. When he dismounted, he became a little old man again.

"This horse means as much to me as any animal I ever owned, but I give her to you," Potter said to Cho Pak. It was the gesture of one cavalryman to another.

Three days later, Cho Pak's daughter, Sun, returned the horse to Colonel Potter.

"My father died during the night. His last hours were his happiest because of you. He left this world with dignity and with honor and pride. He left with the memory of what he did for his people. In his mind, he was no longer a laundryman. He died remembering he was a hero."

HOT LIPS IS BACK IN TOWN

After Margaret's divorce came through to chase away the blues she set to work devising a new system for triage. The nurses would take over for the doctors, freeing them for more time in OR. To show off her new plan, she invited an old acquaintance, General Lyle Weiskopf, to the 4077. She drilled the nurses; he arrived for the inspection; everything went perfectly.

Wieskopf was very impressed.

"There's an opening on my nursing staff for a lieutenant colonel. We could do some wonderful things together. It'll be like the old days—romantic suppers in the Officers Club, late night strolls through the cherry blossoms, then my billet for a nightcap and a game of escaped convict and the warden's wife."

"I'll be colonel in charge of what?" countered Margaret, her consciousness and her voice raised. "I'm a head nurse and a damn good one. I'm not going the pushover route any more. Find yourself another clay pigeon. And get the hell out of my tent."

Then she poured herself a drink. "Here's to me," Margaret said with pride.

INGA

Inga Halvorsen was a lady doctor for the Swedish Red Cross Hospital. Sent to the 4077 for a short tour of ob-

servation, she ended up doing more demonstrating.

First she criticized Hawkeye's handling of a patient. Then she showed everyone a brand-new technique that would improve the man's mobility after recovery. Then she made advances to Hawkeye even though she had rebuffed *his* advances the night before. On top of all that, she took over on one of Charles's patients.

Before you could say "Swedish-meatball surgery," the 4077 was filled with wounded men—not wounded bodies but wounded dignity. When Charles launched into a tirade about Inga, Hawkeye suddenly realized how awful she made all the men look and was determined that he would not remain a fool.

"Listening to you, Charles, I get a clear and sharp picture of the world's most perfect ass—me."

He and Inga then sat down and discussed why men have problems learning from women and letting women make the first move. They discovered that they had a lot to give each other. But it was time for Inga to ship out.

THE YOUNG AND THE RESTLESS

Medical techniques advanced rapidly after World War II and the Army made every effort to train doctors in the latest methods. During the Korean War, field units were often visited by demonstrators.

Captain Ralph Simmons was a hotshot medical demonstrator stationed at Tokyo Gen who came to the 4077 to present new methods for treating penetrating wounds of the heart. His speech was interrupted by incoming wounded, so he scrubbed up. It took him a while to get the hang of the pace, but he adjusted and fit in quite well.

Too well, Colonel Potter thought. Potter had been enduring an attack of phlebitis, but when Simmons arrived and took over in OR, the colonel gave in to the pains in his leg and took to bed. The better Simmons did, the worse Potter got. Then Charles began drinking heavily after Simmons showed *him* up.

"This Simmonsitis is some disease," Hawkeye quipped.

RALLY ROUND THE FLAGG, BOYS

That crazy Colonel Flagg came back to the 4077. This time, one of the patients called him in, claiming that Hawkeye was a Commie sympathizer because he had taken a seriously wounded North Korean patient ahead of him. The North Korean was a Number One in triage and the American a Number Two, but the American still thought he should have been treated first. So Flagg came to investigate. He loved the whole brouhaha, but Charles had the most fun.

Flagg asked Charles to help spy on Pierce, never suspecting that the Bostonian would dare to set him up. Charles planted a map under the North Korean patient's pillow—a map that seemed to designate a secret meeting. Flagg was certain that he was about to bust a spy ring. Instead, he merely broke up a weekly bridge game among Hawkeye, Potter, and two locals who happened to be the chief of police and the mayor of Ouijongbu.

AIN'T LOVE GRAND

It had to happen sooner or later. Charles fell in love—with a working girl at Rosie's Bar. He serenaded her with Tchaikovsky; bought her a dress from Klinger's closet; took her to the Mess Tent for fine dining. At least she thought it was fine.

Her name was Sooni. Charles called her his "lotus blossom." He tried to teach her how to hold a fork properly while he convinced himself that she was from one of Korea's old aristocratic families. It was no use.

"Why do you have to make me into some kind of high-class broad?" Sooni asked. "Your music and poetry are lousy. I'm just a working girl. I pull that stuff on some GI, and I'm out on my butt. Go rhyme yourself, Charlie." And she was gone.

Charles confessed it all to the Swampmen. "How could I have been so blind and stupid?"

"Charles," the ever-patient B.J. said, "you needed someone. It wasn't such a big mistake. We all need someone. It's only human."

C*A*V*E

Caught in cross fire, the 4077 was forced to bug out. And the location chosen was a nearby cave. Once there, Hawkeye confessed he suffered from claustrophobia.

"Ever since I was a little kid. People thought I was sloppy. I just couldn't step into a closet to hang up my clothes."

He hovered near the mouth of the cave until one of his patients turned for the worse. The boy was a bleeder who needed further surgery to survive. The surgery had to be done back at camp.

Margaret and Hawkeye packed up their fears, and their patient, and returned to the abandoned camp. "I'm head nurse," Margaret said. "I'll be damned if I'm going to send someone else out to face what terrifies me."

The operation was a success; the shelling stopped; and the gang returned. They found Houlihan, Pierce, and patient sound asleep in postop.

A NIGHT AT ROSIE'S

Hawkeye was on another of his hate-the-Army crusades. This time, he took up the cause with an AWOL sergeant at Rosie's Bar. Every time someone came to get Hawkeye back to the 4077, Pierce convinced that person to stay at Rosie's. The bar was filling up fast.

They had a wild night. They danced, drank, shot craps, and let off steam. When the MPs came for the AWOL man, Margaret helped him escape back to his unit.

The next morning, the bar was in a shambles. B.J. and Hawkeye slumped over the only upright table.

"We better get back and get some rest," said B.J. "I've got duty in postop this afternoon."

"Yeah," Hawkeye agreed. "We'll probably be getting casualties later. It's been too quiet around here."

THE PARTY

Darling,

It's four in the morning. The party just broke up a few minutes ago. No one wanted it to end. What a beautiful idea you had for us to all get together here in New York. We hugged and hung onto each other for an hour before we said goodnight. We love you and miss you so much that each of the families here felt related through all of you over there.

Mr. and Mrs. Winchester were the hit of the party. I don't know why you thought they wouldn't even come. We cleared the dance floor when they did the Charleston with Radar's mother and Uncle Ed.

Father Mulcahy's sister, Sister Angelica, had the joint jumping with her saxophone. Margaret Houlihan's mother and father danced the whole evening together. Are you sure they're thinking about a divorce? Hawkeye's father took a real shine to Mrs. Potter.

I guess the most touching moment was when Mrs. Klinger saw the group picture under the phony Fort Dix sign. There were tears in her eyes when she said you didn't have to go to all that trouble to make the sign. She's known all along that Max left Fort Dix for Korea, she just didn't let on to his game because she didn't want him to worry about her worrying about him.

Getting all of us together like this was an unbelievable treat that we will remember and cherish all our lives, even when you are all safely back home.

Your loving wife,
Peg

C*A*V*E

Above and below (left and right): A Night at Rosie's

Ain't Love Grand

Dear Comrade

Above, left and right:
Ain't Love Grand

Below and right: Major Ego

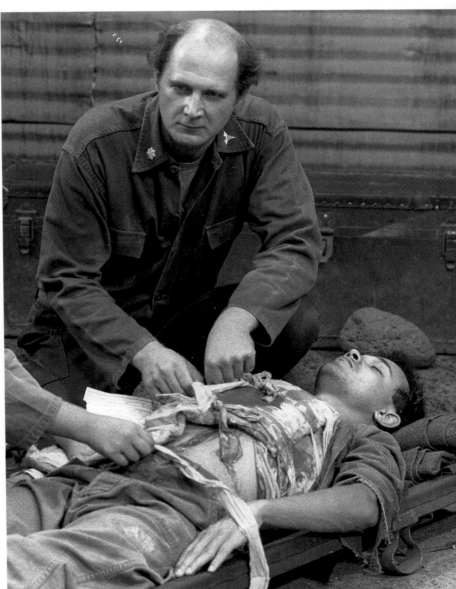

Year Seven (1978–79)

NAME: BURGHOFF, GARY
CHARACTER: O'REILLY, WALTER ("RADAR")
RANK: CORPORAL, USA
SERIAL NUMBER: US56349216

"When God gave the commandments to the Israelites, He just didn't give ten, but He gave a whole system for living. He said if you have a maid or male servant in your service for six years, on the seventh year, that person shall go free. That was over 2,000 years ago, and God knew that after five years, a person has pretty much outgrown an agreement he made. It's a normal biological need for growth, that's what the seven-year-itch is all about. There needs to be a reevaluation of the original contract within the context of change that has taken place in and around a person. So in the seventh year, I notified the producers that I would not be coming back. I felt the public deserved and would enjoy a conclusion to Radar's involvement with the 4077, and I wanted to come back for a final show.

"The network disagreed at first. McLean Stevenson's leaving had caused a big stir, so they didn't want to make an issue of it. There was some mention that when Rob Reiner and Sally Struthers left *All in the Family*, the ratings had dropped. So I concluded the seventh year without a good-bye show. During hiatus, the network changed its mind and we negotiated for the two parter that aired in Year Eight, *Good-bye Radar*. They didn't want to do anything that screwed up the ratings.

"After the first three years, I was in fewer shows because of the strain on my family life. I usually did about thirteen a season. I didn't know it then, but I was beginning to suffer from what's called burnout. My worst year was in the fifth year, and most documented cases of burnout also happen in the fifth year. Year Five was my capacity for doing that character. I had reached my artistic and creative and physical capacity. If people really want to know what happened to me, or may be happening to themselves, no one can explain it better than Dr. Herbert Freedenberger in his book, *Burn-Out*."

"Burnout is a social disorder that has just been identified in the last ten years. It's a work-oriented disorder that derives from the world changing so fast that a person's ethical standards from childhood are no longer standards when he reaches adulthood. I believe in right and wrong and the support system I grew up with, yet I went to work in the industrial world with values from the 1950s. The disillusionment is so great that you work harder to achieve the things you think you are lacking. The harder you work, the less you accomplish, so more panic sets in and you spiral downward to burnout, a nearly total depletion of your vital energies. It is *temporary*. The symptoms are physical and psychological—lower back ache, heartburn, diarrhea, irritability, denial that you have the condition, and a tremendous fear that something is wrong, but you can't identify what.

"People who have burnout need to know it is a temporary situation. They can cure it by either alleviating the problem, like me—I took a sabbatical; or by readjusting their attitude to be better in balance with the realities of modern life. As a Christian, I chose to do the first.

"For seven years, no new person in my life called me Gary. Only Radar. A name is a very important thing. It's one of the first elements of identity. It's primary, and if you're missing your name, you're in trouble. People don't have to call me Mr. Burghoff—a simple Gary would do it. I don't even own the name Radar. It belongs to Fox; they can do anything they want with it, too.

"Radar's growth was very much inhibited by the confines of television. If a character changes too much, the studio gets nervous. In syndication, the shows are run out of order. It's confusing to see a character one way one day and another way the next day. We all fought for growth, but what really happened was that the characters changed within an episode then went back—except in the final show, which was about graduating and then going on.

"Stories have been written about my irritability on the set, which I think were unfair. They never focused on the others' irritability. We all cared a great deal about M*A*S*H and each other. Small disappointments became big disappointments, that's all. The last two years of the show, I'd say I reacted animatedly—not viciously, not without love and respect. People who have burnout are irritable because they are trying as hard as they can to do something that is beyond them. They are trying to do better than they can do. The pressure they put on themselves is unbearable.

"It took me a long time to figure out what was going on those last years. I thought it was only me, but I know now that's not true. I had to leave. I told them that I would not renegotiate my contract, that money was not the issue, that I did not want another show. That really scares the hell out of them. In Year Seven, all I could really think about was being able to take a year off to be with my daughter. That's what I did. I recovered. I began to study the Bible. I work in the theater, and I have new priorities for myself: my family, my friends, contact with nature, and my profession. I am now trying to glorify my concept of God in everything I do. I'm not very adept at it, but I'm working on it."

Gary Burghoff

Filming *Are You Now, Margaret* in the OR on Stage 9

Year Eight (1979—80)

DENNIS KOENIG, Story Editor

"Year Eight will mostly be remembered as the year Radar left and Klinger assumed his job. We did some isolated shots with Gary so we could weave him into a number of shows at the beginning of the season. Then we did the big two-parter when Radar went home because his Uncle Ed died and his Mom needed him to run the farm.

"There were a couple of interesting shows that season that were a bit unusual. *The Yalu Brick Road* took place mostly off the compound; *Dreams* was Alan's baby. He had talked about it for years, but it had never come up. Finally, he just did it. It really got the most letters and positive reaction.

There was a show that didn't turn out great but dealt with a very important story, *That's My Baby,* about Amerasian babies. It was a tough story to do because it dealt with an issue we had a tendency to overlook—what we did to the Korean people by being there. These kids were never accepted in Korean culture; they were shunned by society and had no future.

"*Old Soldiers* is the show about the tontine, where people pledge to meet again. I had read about one in the paper, and I knew it was appropriate for a guy about Potter's age. It got really mushy on the set filming that one.

"By Year Eight, the old Hot Lips as we knew her from the beginning of the show was virtually gone. She was a new character. *Nurse Doctor* made a statement about Hot Lips that was to lay the ground for the new character from then on in. Hawkeye continued in the process of becoming less raunchy. We did *Bottle Fatigue* about his drinking too much. He was more actively compassionate and less selfish; he began to think more about other people.

"One of the big unseen problems in Year Eight was whether or not the actors would go on strike and when. They did strike, but after we had filmed all of Year Eight. Then the air dates for Year Nine were pushed back, so at the end of Year Nine, we had several shows that hadn't been aired. We saved them for Year Ten, but we shot a full season again in Year Ten. We hoped to use the six leftover scripts from Year Ten with the two-hour movie as our half season for the final year. When the network said they wanted nine more scripts, they could just as well have ordered nine hundred. I couldn't believe it."

CHAPTER IX

Right and opposite:
Good-bye Radar

YEAR EIGHT—BATTLE NOTES

TOO MANY COOKS

Dear Sherman,

I am writing you from Pensacola. As you know, I always go to see my cousin Portia when I need cheering up. Yesterday, I met a wonderful young man. Lyle and Mavis Wilson's boy. They're Portia's neighbors. He's back from Korea, where he was wounded, and he told me a MASH unit saved his life. As I listened to him, I could just imagine you as his doctor. The miles between us seemed to disappear and, for a few minutes, it was as if you and I were together. It made me realize how unfair my last letter was. It's just that sometimes I get tired of being alone, and I get angry and I blame you. And when you're not here to yell at, I get even angrier. I hope you can somehow understand what I'm saying. I might let off steam once in a while, but I adore you. I'm very proud of you and I wouldn't trade my life for anyone's.

Love,
Mildred

ARE YOU NOW, MARGARET

R. Theodore Williamson was another one of those snazzy congressional aides who were always popping up taking tours of the various MASH units and making reports. They wore brand-new, spanking-clean fatigues that still had fresh creases and their boots sparkled because they were brand-new. Most of them were creeps. Williamson was no different. He was at the 4077 on behalf of Congressman Daniel Lurie, who just happened to be up for reelection.

Staff, nonetheless, wanted to make a good impression. Klinger kept working on his Section Eight—congressional influence was something he lacked—while he snapped photos of the visit for *Stars & Stripes* with his Brownie. Margaret also wanted to impress the aide; she was always trying to win friends and influence people in high places.

"Don't mind Pierce and Hunnicutt," she said. "They're both first-rate surgeons. Sure, they'll show up for roll call in their bathrobes. They keep a still in their tent. Once they ran my underwear up the flagpole. But I want you to understand, it's an honor to serve with these men."

Williamson knew little of honor, especially Margaret's. He was actually at the 4077 specifically to grill her about an old boyfriend, whom the maniac anti-Communist Congressman Joseph McCarthy now considered un-American. Williamson wanted Margaret to testify against the man, although she had not seen him since school days.

Margaret refused. Williamson paid a late-night call to her tent to convince her to cooperate or to "work these things out"—his way.

"You lecherous hypocrite!" Margaret shouted. "You're sure I'm a Communist, but for a little tumble, you'd let me off the hook!"

As the man pressed himself on Margaret, Klinger popped out of the closet he was hiding in to record the moment for posterity with his Brownie.

A little blackmail went a long way in fighting Communism.

GUERRILLA MY DREAMS

"I am Lieutenant Kung Jae Park and this woman is my prisoner," the ROK officer reported to Hawkeye. The woman was a civilian, wounded with shell fragments. "She is an enemy guerrilla."

"Good," said Hawkeye, "We'll frisk her for bananas."

She seemed harmless enough to Hawkeye and B.J. Even Margaret, the original gung-ho kid, thought there had been a mistake. So they all worked together to postpone the woman's release from the hospital. Lieutenant Park's reputation didn't do much good, either. He was known to be the kind of man who tortured prisoners first and asked questions later.

Park was astounded at the conspiracy. "Your concern for an individual life is admirable, doctors, but impractical. War is like chess. Loss of a single pawn is insignificant. All that matters is winning the game."

Are You Now, Margaret

None of the staff was around when the female pawn quietly arose from her bed, pulled her IV tubes from her arms and hobbled to another patient's bed, where she tried to kill him. But she was too weak to fulfill her mission and fell to the floor. Hot Lips rushed to the scene when she heard a bottle crash.

"She was probably trying to escape before she had to talk to Lieutenant Truth or Consequences," Hawkeye guessed. He wanted so much to be right.

When HQ nixed the idea of sending the woman to another hospital for safekeeping, Hawkeye and Hunnicutt decided to smuggle the woman to freedom. The scheme just about worked when Lieutenant Park caught them.

He reported to Potter, who could do nothing to stop him. In civilian matters, the Republic of Korea took jurisdiction over the US Army.

The woman turned angrily to Hawkeye and cursed him in Korean. "She says she will kill you," Park translated, "as she tried to kill the enemy in the hospital, and she would gladly die for this murder if she could kill but one of you. Can you not see that this woman's life is more important to you than it is to her?"

Hawkeye was stunned. "Why, you son of a bitch," he muttered as Park drove off with the woman.

PRIVATE FINANCE

Just before Eddie Hastings died, he made Hawkeye promise that the money secured in his money belt would be forwarded to his needy parents. It turned out to be a lot of money. The staff immediately guessed that it came from the black market or some other illegal activity. But CID (Criminal Investigations Division) had no criminal record for the boy. Before writing his parents and sending the money, Hawkeye wanted to make sure it was the right thing to do, so he questioned some of Hastings's buddies. That's how he found out that Hastings had no buddies, just men who had known him and had seen him change from a nice All-American type in boot camp to a profiteer and gambler who made Shylock look like a prince. Reluctantly, Hawkeye wrote the boy's parents and forwarded the funds.

A money order came back a few weeks later.

Dear Dr. Pierce:

We don't know what happened to change Eddie during the war, but something did. From his letters, we could tell that he was not the boy we sent off to a place we never heard of until Eddie went there to fight. All he wrote to us was about deal-making and profits. We are a simple Christian family. The money you sent came from an Eddie we never knew. We are returning it to you with the hope you can find someone there who needs help more than we.

Bless you,
Matthew and Betty Hastings

MR. & MRS. WHO

Hemorrhagic Fever ran through the Orient in epidemic proportions. It was a viral infection that caused renal failure. It could kill. There was little to do for the victims. Oral intake of liquids had to be restricted so patients didn't drown in their own fluids. After that, each patient was on his own.

There were several Hemorrhagic Fever epidemics among American troops during the Korean War. In fact, that strain of the disease became known as Korean Hemorrhagic Fever. In the beginning, doctors lost more than fifty percent of their patients. By the third epidemic, they were losing only twenty percent.

Three new cases plagued the 4077. "These kids' blood vessels are so weak the trip to a hospital in Seoul would probably kill them," B.J. said.

"They've sent us a change in treatment for Phase Three of the disease," Colonel Potter announced at a specially convened staff meeting. "Failure to follow this procedure is a court-martial offense."

Shortly after that announcement, one of the patients moved into the last phase of the disease and hovered close to death. B.J. remembered a medical paper he'd read that suggested the use of a low sodium concentration run intravenously. He wanted to try it as a last-ditch maneuver, but the HQ directive opposed it.

"I say we have no choice," Potter said.

Twenty-four hours later, Corporal Shaw awoke in postop. "Hey, doc," he said in a normal voice.

"Who do you have to know to get something to eat here?"

GOOD-BYE RADAR

Radar returned from R&R in Tokyo just in the nick of time. Both generators had gone AWOL—"absent without 'lectricity," as Klinger put it. Klinger just didn't have the know-how, or the connections, to get a replacement, and wounded were expected.

"Welcome, kid," Klinger said. "It's not often we get a savior in the place."

It wasn't as easy as he thought to save the day. Radar, too, had trouble, and it depressed him. He drowned his sorrows in a grape Nehi. "First I have a cruddy time in Tokyo. I meet a girl for the first time, and I get dragged away from her. I nearly die on the trip back here. Now I let everyone down. And my grape Nehi is warm."

The worst was yet to come. Potter got a wire from Ottumwa, Iowa—Radar's Uncle Ed had died.

"Lord knows your mother is strong," Potter said after he broke the news to Radar, "but she won't make it alone. Go get yourself a DA7 hardship discharge and type your name on it. You should be home for Sunday night supper."

Radar was ambivalent. First he thought he should stay because Klinger would never get the hang of being clerk. Then Klinger found another generator, so Radar felt less needed. He decided to leave.

They had planned a big good-bye party in the Mess Tent, but incoming wounded canceled all previous dates.

Corporal Walter Eugene O'Reilly was left standing in his dress uniform with no place to go—but home.

"We got work to do, Radar," shouted Hawkeye as he rushed off to triage.

"It's not exactly the way I wanted to say good-bye," Potter said, "but I've got to get into OR pronto. God speed, son."

Radar said good-bye to his animals, tasted the frosting on his uneaten good-bye cake, and raised his hand in a good-bye salute to Hawkeye as the surgeon looked out the OR window and raised his bloodied glove to the departing young man.

Ten hours later, the doctors emerged from surgery and went to The Swamp for a drink. Potter looked down at Hawkeye's bunk. "Hey, boys, look at this. Radar's teddy. He left it here."

PERIOD OF ADJUSTMENT

Radar went home through San Francisco. Peg and Erin Hunnicutt met him at the airport. Peg wrote B.J. all about it: "He sure is a cute little guy, so nice. It was really funny, when Erin first saw Radar in his uniform, she ran up to him and said, 'Hi, Daddy.'"

B.J. didn't find it amusing at all. It hurt like hell. He tossed, turned, fumed, and finally took to throwing darts at a picture of Radar's face.

He wasn't the only one who had problems when Radar left. Klinger was up to his Mudhens shirt in hot water. He just couldn't do anything right. Margaret didn't get the extra nurses she requested because Klinger never processed the forms; Potter was on his case because all the paperwork was piled up; Charles was mad because nothing worked properly.

"He's done only one thing remarkably well," said Charles. "He's made me realize what a gem Radar was."

Only Father Mulcahy realized that Klinger needed a little on-the-job training. He had a heart-to-heart over a teacup with Colonel Potter and told him about Radar's first days at the 4077. "It was so bad," he concluded, "that folks here were convinced the enemy had sent him to sabotage the unit."

Potter got the point.

"You know," he told Klinger, "I don't mind telling you my first days in Henry Blake's shadow were a mite uneasy. Nobody was jumping for joy over me. Thing is, people gave me a chance to take the job and make it Sherman Potter's. I guess maybe I forgot that when you took over for Radar. What you need to do is make the job Max Klinger's. And if you need some help, just knock on my door. Is that clear, Max?"

Klinger saluted with appreciation.

THE YALU BRICK ROAD

B.J. was actually a motorcycle enthusiast, but he didn't mind a fast spin behind the wheel of an Army Jeep. Hawkeye minded, especially when B.J. turned the thing over

and left them stranded on a country road with a carton of antibiotics that had to get back to the 4077.

They were soon spotted by a North Korean soldier, who surrendered to them just as they surrendered to him. They took turns surrendering to each other until the trio met up with a group of North Koreans who wanted to kill the doctors. Their "prisoner" saved their lives when he talked the NKPA patrol into releasing them to his custody.

"As soon as I put down my arms, I'm going to hug you," B.J. promised to the man, who spoke no English.

Once away from the patrol, "Ralph"—the name Hawkeye gave their savior because he reminded him of a buddy's younger brother, Ralphie, who always tagged along behind—again surrendered to the Swampmen. They continued down the road, surrendering to each other in comic fashion until they found a wounded civilian. They took the man to a farmhouse, where they were given a motorbike with a sidecar and sent on their way back. "Ralph" came with them, surrendering all the way.

"I must come with you," "Ralph" explained. "I am your prisoner."

"Ralph's" insistence on becoming a POW was typical of what would happen later as the war drew to a close. Few Koreans wanted to go north to Communist rule. "Ralph" was one of the lucky ones, and he knew it.

NURSE DOCTOR

Lieutenant Gail Harris didn't fit in with the other nurses because she wanted to be a doctor. She had resigned from the Army, was finishing her tour of duty, and would be returning stateside to attend medical school. Father Mulcahy helped her study for her entrance exams. When Nurse Harris became a little too friendly for it to be fatherly, Mulcahy turned to Hawkeye.

"As soon as I realized what was going on, I put a stop to our lessons," he explained, "but I'm afraid I hurt her rather badly."

"Father, you've got two commandments on the critical list," Hawkeye warned. "I never thought of you as a love 'em and leave 'em kind of guy."

The padre convinced Hawkeye to take up the job as the girl's medical consultant, but Gail was offended that Father Mulcahy had betrayed her and decided to quit the whole thing and get a transfer. Margaret had to step in and settle things.

"The duration of your military service will be spent right here," she told Harris plainly. "Your nursing duties will only be part of it. The rest of the time will be spent under the supervision of Captain Pierce and myself in intensive study for your Medical Aptitude Test. I know it's tough for a woman to become a doctor. But with your background and talent, you've got a real chance. As long as I'm your superior officer, I'm not letting you back out. Understand, Harris?"

"Yes, ma'am."

LIFE TIME

At 2:32 P.M. Corporal George Hudson was flown in to the 4077 with a bad chest wound. As he was lifted from the pod, Hawkeye diagnosed a lacerated aorta and put his hand into the man's chest to compress the aorta against the spinal cord and stop the bleeding.

"If we cut off the blood to the spinal cord for more than twenty minutes, there's a good chance he'll be paralyzed. Hit it, fellas. Let's get this guy out of here," he shouted as the race against the clock began.

They sped to OR in a Jeep, Hawkeye's arm buried in Hudson's chest as the precious minutes ticked away.

At 2:38 P.M., Margaret found the necessary vascular clamps to hold down the bleeding so Hawkeye could remove his numbing fingers.

At 2:43 P.M., blood was typed and matched, and Charles Winchester began donating his own blood to keep the man alive.

At 2:49 P.M., a donor for an aortorial graft was found.

At 2:52 P.M., Charles began the delicate operation that he had only observed once but that no one else at the 4077 had ever even seen.

At 2:56 P.M., the graft was in place and was holding.

They were four minutes over. Only time would tell if George Hudson would ever walk again.

When he came to, the doctors crowded around his bed.

"Wiggle your toes," commanded Hawkeye anxiously.

George groggily wiggled his toes. The medical team whooped with joy.

DREAMS

There was another deluge. The wounded just kept coming...and coming...and coming. The wounded got to sleep. The doctors and nurses did not. It got so bad that Hawkeye allowed naps on a rotation basis only.

Margaret fell into her cot and was asleep immediately.

She dreamed she was in a big open field, dressed in her wedding gown. She met her bridegroom. They embraced and stepped toward her big brass bed. As the groom began to kiss her, wounded soldiers began marching by them like robots. A hand touched her shoulder, and she turned to see another wounded man. More and more wounded were brought in, heaped on the nuptial bed. Hawkeye stepped to the bed and began to operate. She was assisting. He called for an instrument, but when she looked down at her instrument tray to comply—it was empty.

When Margaret returned to OR, it was Charles's turn for some rest. He hit the sack in The Swamp and was dreaming almost immediately. In his dream, he wore a black cape and top hat and stood before his MASH comrades to perform magic tricks. They loved him; everyone clapped and threw money. Then Potter pulled back the drape and revealed a gurney with a wounded soldier on it. The gurney moved by itself toward Charles and then paused in front of him. The man was badly wounded; his

eyes begged Charles to help him. Charles leaned down and deftly pulled a flag out of his own ear; then he began to juggle; finally he started to dance while waving sparklers in the air. The patient grew stiff and rolled away on his gurney.

* * * *

B.J. dreamed of Peg. He was in a fancy club of some kind, dressed in a white dinner jacket. Four couples danced around him. A butler opened glass doors, a mirrored staircase moved forward. Atop the staircase, a woman in silver shoes began to dance toward him—Peg. They twirled around and around until suddenly they were in OR. Potter cut in. B.J. began to operate as the dancing woman moved away, lost to him.

* * * *

While Father Mulcahy was hearing confession, he nodded off to sleep. He dreamed that he was carried on a sedan chair into the Mess Tent by six men in black cassocks. The Mozart Mass in A Minor was playing in the background as all the members of the MASH outfit looked on in awe. They knelt and Father Mulcahy blessed them. He opened his Bible to read from it, but blood dripped onto it from the crucifix above him; he turned back to the congregation in horror, but they were no longer kneeling. Instead, they were performing surgery in OR.

* * * *

Klinger grabbed his nap in the supply room, where he curled up in front of the stove. He dreamed he was on a train and the conductor called out, "Toledo! Next stop, Toledo!" Klinger got off the train and found himself in a deserted street in front of Paco's, his favorite hot dog joint. It was also deserted. He peered through the windows but saw the OR. Potter was operating on a patient. The patient turned his face, and Klinger saw that he was the patient. He awoke drenched in sweat.

* * * *

Hawkeye dreamed of his college professor. The man asked him how to replace an arm, but Hawkeye had

These pages: Scenes from *Dreams*

been asleep and missed the lesson. So the professor took one of Hawkeye's arms. Then he asked Charles to remove Hawkeye's other arm. The arms were thrown into a lake that was filled with mannequin arms and legs. On the other side of the water, a small Korean child called to Hawkeye, beckoning him to heal her wounded belly. Hawkeye bent over her to operate. As the nurse handed him the scalpel, he realized he had no arms with which to do the surgery. His empty sleeves blew like ghosts in the breeze. His lips formed a silent, anguished scream as he howled, "Noooooooooo."

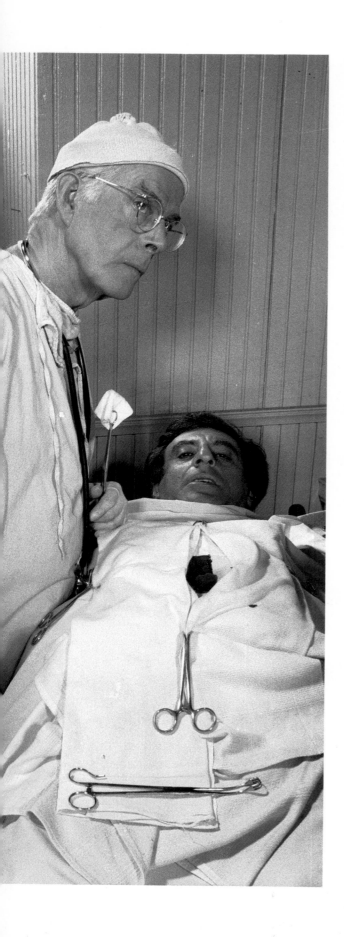

Above, left and right: Dreams

Captains Outrageous

DEAR UNCLE ABDUL

Dear Uncle Abdul,

Boy, am I glad Ma named me after Uncle Max. Please thank Aunt Fatima for the olive marmalade. It was the talk of the whole camp. Mostly sick call. Sorry it's been so long since I have written you, but I have a new job here. I've been busier than a one-armed paperhanger. Right now, there's a cease-fire, so I can write.

I'll never understand the Army. I've done everything I can to get out of this place. Now they've made me company clerk, and I'm responsible for the whole kit and kaboodle.

Good luck on the opening of Abdul's Oasis Drive-In. I bet you won't find a better shishka-burger this side of Beirut.

I have my very own office now, so please tell Ma to send me my lamp with the revolving waterfall in it. Thanks.

Love to all.

Your nephew,
Maxwell Q. Klinger
(the other Max)

CAPTAINS OUTRAGEOUS

A brawl at Rosie's Bar turned the tables on everyone. While trying to stop the fight, Rosie sustained several broken ribs. She soon became a patron of the 4077. While in the hospital recuperating, she was unable to run her business and fretted that she would go broke. Big-hearted Margaret volunteered everyone's overtime to help tend bar at Rosie's while Rosie mended.

Father Mulcahy was the only one who didn't do unto others. He was busy serving another kind of punch—his own right hook—as he tried to take out his frustrations at once again being passed over for promotion.

Potter was almost as upset as Mulcahy. He even called the Pentagon. He was astounded when Klinger put him through. "Klinger, you old camel trader! How the devil did you actually get through?" the colonel asked.

"Proverbial piece of baklava, sir."

By the time Rosie was back at her bar, there were two toasts to be made: to her continued good health and to Father Mulcahy. Hawkeye pinned his own bars on the new captain.

"They have very low mileage, Father. I hardly ever captain in them."

"Well," said Mulcahy, pleased with the whole operation, "this has taught me that the meek may inherit the Earth, but it's the grumpy who get promoted."

STARS & STRIPE

The American College of Surgeons, as prestigious a bunch as there ever was, were so impressed with the work a certain Dr. Hunnicutt and Dr. Winchester performed on a patient with an "air-conditioned" colon that they requested an official paper for their medical journal.

"Some college," a jealous Hawkeye scoffed. "They don't even have a football team."

When the doctors sat down to collaborate on the paper, they squabbled more than the negotiators in Panmunjom. Charles didn't like B.J.'s writing style; B.J. didn't want Charles's name listed first, especially since Winchester begins with a "W". Then they got into even more serious fighting because B.J. couldn't remember the patient very well, and Winchester kept insisting he did more work than B.J., anyway.

"I'm not going to let Dr. Didlittle rob me of the credit I deserve," harrumphed Hunnicutt.

"I've about had it with your snide effrontery, Dr. Hunny-twit," Charles countered.

Potter couldn't take it. "I've been thinking about all the people who had a hand in your little stitch and sew contest, boys. There's a lot of them. So why don't we submit this paper from the entire MASH 4077?"

He should have been named Solomon.

HEAL THYSELF

Colonel Potter was quarantined in his tent with a case of mumps that he probably caught when Meg Cratty stopped by with a bunch of her orphans. Mumps are contagious, but most adults have antibodies to the disease from having had it as children. Somehow, that perennial child, Charles, had missed the mumps.

"I have nothing to fear. The superiority of the Winchester genes has rendered me immune. I've been exposed countless occasions and always emerged unswelled."

Except for his head.

The next day, he moved into Potter's tent—another victim of Meg Cratty's kids' generosity.

"He was caught with his genes down," Hawkeye smirked.

With two docs in bed, the 4077 was short of surgeons and put in for a replacement. Steve Newsome arrived the next day. He seemed like a great guy—good sense of humor, good hands, good heart. He fit in perfectly.

But a few days later, he cracked. He just kept staring at his hands in horror. "The blood won't come off. No matter what I do, it just stays there. No matter how much I wash. No matter how much I scrub. It's always going to be there."

"I thought he was as strong as any one of us," B.J. mused.

"He was," Hawkeye agreed. "That's what scares me."

YESSIR, THAT'S OUR BABY

The baby was left on the doorstep of The Swamp. "This is my baby," the note said. "She is good baby. Strong. Beautiful. Father American GI. Gone now. Baby American, too. Please care for her. I cannot, but I love her."

Top and above: Heal Thyself

Everyone but Father Mulcahy fell in love with the child. He was too concerned with the realities of her future to be taken in by the romance of having a tiny bit of life in the camp.

"Children of American soldiers and Korean women are not treated well here," he said sadly. "When people in the villages find out, their lives become a horror. They are outcasts of society. Little boys have been emasculated. Girls are killed outright. Korean babies with blue eyes are shot on sight. Even at the orphanage, she will be ostracized. The child has no future here."

So Hawkeye took her to the Red Cross, but they were no help. Then he went to the Army, and they were no help. The Republic of Korea offered no help, either. Charles and Hawkeye even flew to Tokyo, to the American Consul. No luck—the child could not be admitted to the United States without a relative there.

Father Mulcahy suggested sanctuary in an old Catholic mission where the girl would be sheltered and educated until she was fifteen or twenty. Everyone agreed it was the only chance. She had to be anonymously left on the doorstep of the mission, as was the custom.

"In nomini patri et fili et spiritu sanctu. Go in peace, child."

BOTTLE FATIGUE

Drinks were not very expensive at the Officers Club, so when Hawkeye got his monthly tab he was shocked. After all, he was also drinking at Rosie's and at home sweet home—Tent #6, The Swamp.

"We're talking serious boozing," he said. "My bill is twice what B.J.'s is. I could have bought a used Studebaker for this."

"Relax," admonished Charles. "When we go back to civilization we will return to normal."

But Hawkeye decided to stop drinking immediately. The first day wasn't hard. He woke up singing "Oh What a Beautiful Morning," but got progressively worse as time went by.

"Four more days of his sobriety will drive me to drink," swore B.J.

The war was sobering enough.

A Chinese patient was brought in in such serious shape that he was rushed to surgery before his clothes were removed. From his pocket, he pulled a live grenade.

"I'll take you with me, Imperialist Yankee dog!" he shouted to Hawkeye as he pulled the pin.

Hawkeye was an awfully quick-witted Imperialist Yankee dog. He clamped his hand over that of the Chinese soldier, preventing him from releasing the trip lever.

"How long can you hold on, Hawk?"

"For the rest of my life."

While Father Mulcahy and Margaret searched the floor for the grenade's pin, the rest of the staff sang chorus after chorus of "Hush Little Baby" as surgery continued in the tense atmosphere. Mulcahy found the pin, Hawkeye got it back in the grenade.

Old Soldiers

Hawkeye then operated on the man successfully. When he was finished, he walked right into the Officers Club and ordered a drink.

Some things aren't worth being too sober for.

MORALE VICTORY

Even Charles was pleased with his work on Private David Sheridan, and no one expected more of himself than Charles. "Thanks to my incomparable display of surgical prestidigitation this lad will still have two legs to stand on when he gives me the ovation I so richly deserve."

When Sheridan came to, Winchester was at his bedside and told him of his good fortune—only slight damage to his hands; perfectly restored legs.

"I don't care about my legs, dammit," said the patient in agony. "My legs are nothing. My hands are my life. I am a concert pianist!"

Charles went limp with anguish. But he didn't give up on the patient, or himself. He sent Klinger to Seoul to get some sheet music.

"Your right hand may be stilled," Charles told the boy when he gave him the music, "but your gift cannot be quenched. Ravel took the challenge to write music for an Austrian concert pianist who lost an arm in World War I. This is Ravel, for you. I cannot perform music, though I have hands. You can shut your gift off forever or can find new ways to use it—through baton, the classroom or the pen. There is a true gift in your head, your heart, and your soul. These pieces are for you when you are ready to be as one."

Above: Lend a Hand
Left: Morale Victory

172

OLD SOLDIERS

Potter took the call at 3:00 A.M. then left immediately for Tokyo, saying something about a sick friend. When he returned he was melancholy, listened to old French records, and stayed away from everyone except the kids who had come around for some vaccinations. The staff was concerned.

Then he wrote notes to the staff. "You are invited to my tent tomorrow night at 1900 hours. Cordially, Sherman Potter. P.S. That's an order."

"He's been antsy ever since he got this package in the mail from some lawyers," reported Klinger.

Hawkeye thought that meant a divorce—or a lawsuit. Charles guessed that the sick friend was just a ruse, perhaps Potter had had some tests and was sick himself. "This waiting around is killing *me*," moaned Margaret.

When they finally met at Potter's tent, their CO was wearing his World War I uniform.

"I guess you're all wondering why the getup. Well, it was a long time ago, 1917 to be exact. We were in France under a heavy artillery barrage. Me and my buddies laid low in an old French château. We were quite a group, the five of us. Went through hell together and lived to get drunk about it. Anyway, there we were in this château. So Stein finds a cache of this fine brandy and we sat up the whole night. Shells were screaming and we were singing and toasting our friendship. Then we got down to the last bottle. This bottle here. Do any of you know what a tontine is? It's a pledge. The five of us made a pledge. We'd save the last bottle, let some legal eagle store it for us. Whoever turned out to be the last survivor would get the bottle and drink a toast to his old buddies.

"For good or bad you're looking at the last survivor. I got the job when Grusky passed on in Tokyo. He had the bottle sent here, God rest his soul. I was feeling real sorry for myself, getting along in years and all. But I'm looking at it differently now. As much as my old friends mean to me, I think you new friends mean even more. So I'd like you to share this bottle with me."

LEND A HAND

Dr. Anthony Borelli returned to the 4077 early in 1953 to demonstrate a new graft technique.

"Nerve grafts sound damned ambitious for a bunch of meatball surgeons," said Potter, not convinced that his men would have time to use the technique.

Borelli began the lecture in Potter's office but was soon interrupted by an emergency phone call from Battalion Aid. One of their surgeons had been injured. They needed another doctor—to save their man and to handle the wounded. Borelli volunteered to go with Hawkeye.

Although Borelli and Pierce began work on a cooperative basis, the two men were soon bickering as they labored to save their patient.

"What the hell kind of doctors are you?" asked an incredulous medic who had to stand by while they argued. "Save the patient's life and then you can kill each other."

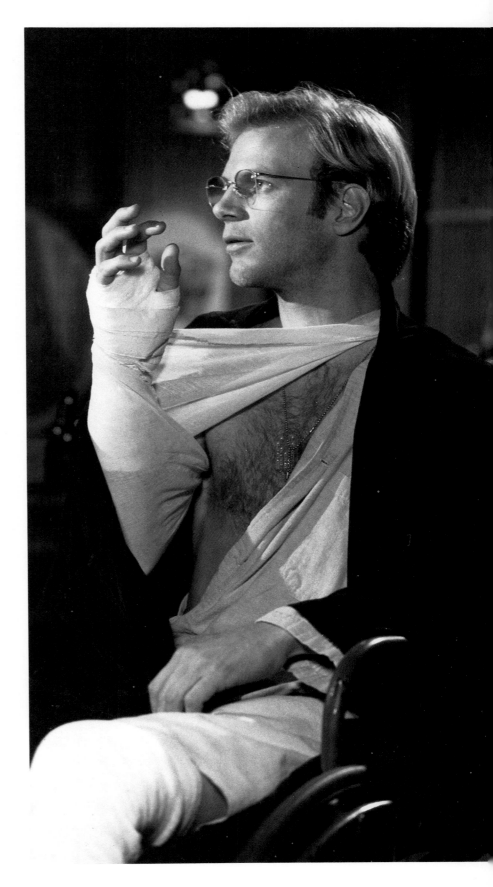

Morale Victory

173

Old Soldiers

Back Pay

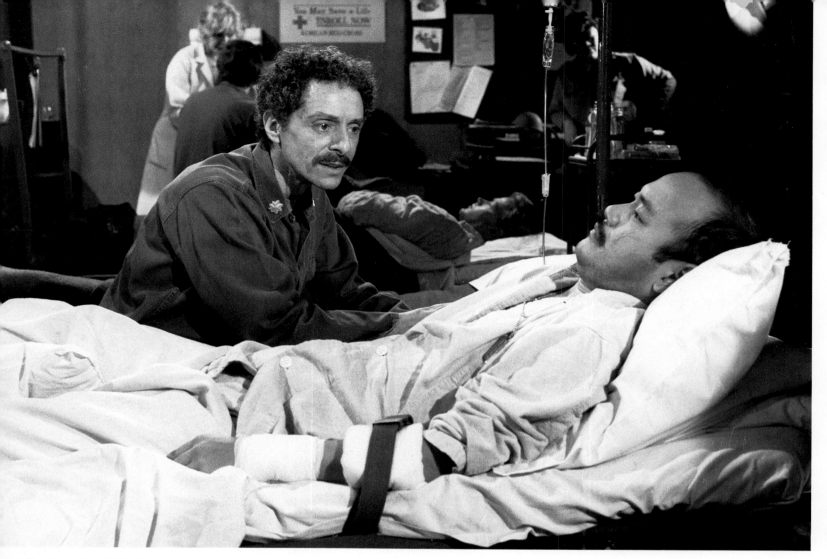

Goodbye, Cruel World

They heard shelling nearby and worked faster. Then an explosion rocked the hut. Hawkeye covered the patient with his own body, Borelli was thrown to the floor. When the dust settled, Borelli had a broken arm and Hawkeye a sprained wrist. Together they had only one working pair of hands. But they finished the surgery.

"We're a team," said Borelli with admiration for their work. "I should have broken my arm an hour ago."

"An hour ago," admitted Hawkeye, "I would have gladly broken it for you."

GOODBYE CRUEL WORLD

Sgt. Michael Yee was a bonafide, decorated war hero who had even been written up in *Stars & Stripes* as one of America's leading soldiers. When he arrived at the 4077 he was a VIP.

"A Very Injured Person," said Hawkeye.

Yee was anxious to get back to his unit, but Hawkeye decided to send him home. "Back to San Francisco, where the only taps you have to worry about are the things Shirley Temple wears on her shoes."

Pierce thought the man was happy about it. When Yee attempted suicide, the doctors realized there was something very serious going on beneath his patriotic surface. They called in Sidney Freedman.

"Most attempted suicides over here are young kids going to war for the first time. But Yee fought in Europe in World War II. I think he's got a guilt problem. In his ten years in the service, this is the first time he's fought an Asian enemy. He's been looking through a gunsight at people who could be members of his own family. He's got to kill Chinese to be a good American. To be a good Chinese he's got to kill himself."

"Will he try a second time?"

"Second time? He's been trying since the outbreak of the war. That's why he volunteered for all those dangerous missions."

APRIL FOOLS

Potter was far from pleased when he got the wire that announced Colonel Daniel Webster Tucker was on his way to the 4077 for an official observation.

"This fella can observe you to smithereens. He's a stickler's stickler, they say. He quotes Army Medical regs by memory, especially the part on court-martial. For the sake of these hard-earned eagles, boys and girl, there will be no larks, antics or shenanigans while Tucker is here. Got it?"

Their mouths said yes, but their hearts said no. When Tucker arrived, Margaret had just taken on the Swampmen in a pillow fight. Feathers were everywhere. Things were no more impressive in OR.

"They've all been to medical school. Do they expect a round of applause for doing their jobs?" griped Tucker.

The only man who impressed him was Maxwell Q. Klinger, who had never done so much saluting in his whole life. Everyone else was disgusting. "As of right now," he told them all, "you're on report. I'm going to make life miserable for you clowns. If I have my way, you'll all be court-martialed."

In his rage he turned to Klinger for support. Only Klinger was dressed as Cleopatra. Tucker was stunned.

"The only decent soldier here and they've broken you. You're ill, son, lay down. You'll be stateside in seventy-two hours."

Then he grabbed his chest and fell to the floor. The doctors ran for their cardiac kits. Potter opened Tucker's shirt and began a chest massage. Tucker hoarsely whispered a message, as if it were the last thing he would ever say: "April fools!"

Then he sat up, shook hands with Potter, and congratulated all of them on being taken. Colonel Potter danced a delighted jig.

WAR CO-RESPONDENT

Aggie O'Shea was a war correspondent. She arrived at the 4077 when some of the men in the unit she was covering were wounded.

Noticing her, B.J. remarked "When did this line start using stewardesses?"

Everyone in the camp was impressed with the reporter, but B.J. became the willing object of her attention and affection.

"You haven't said or done anything that could even remotely be considered a pass in spite of all the openings I've given you," she reminded him when they talked over their predicament.

He talked it over with Hawkeye.

"C'mon, Beej. We're big boys. You went down this road once before."

"No Hawk, you don't understand. That was just a matter of cheating on my wife, which isn't happening now.

It's worse than that now. It's that Aggie's all I can think about. And not just being in bed with her. I'm thinking about being with her."

"Funny thing about war," Hawkeye reminded him, "two people with absolutely nothing in common get thrown together and really start caring about one another."

"Yeah," said B.J. "I'm a prisoner of war. Every day is what it is because of this war. I met my friends because of this war. I found Aggie because of this war. I guess you can't go from 'how do you do' to 'I love you' because of the damn war."

Aggie left the next day.

BACK PAY

Hawkeye's Dad sent him a clipping from *Newsweek* about a doctor who was "making a killing" stateside doing X-rays for Selective Service. Sort of a killing before the killing. Hawkeye was furious. He dove into Klinger's files and did a little arithmetic of his own.

"Okay, I average seven tracheotomies a week so that comes to 546 tracheotomies. Type that in, Klinger. I'm sending my bill to the Surgeon General's office. Let's see, tracheotomies at $7 per, that's $3,872."

By the time he went through all the records, his final bill was $38,215.11. CID sent in a man to investigate.

"Captain Pierce, this is Korea. We're at war. This bill could be construed as an attempt to defraud the US government. This is hot-headed, self-righteous nonsense." Then he left the 4077.

But Hawkeye *was* still hot-headed and self-righteous. He kidnapped a Jeep as partial payment of his "bill." The investigator returned.

"I didn't steal it," said Pierce, "one man's theft is another man's justice."

Finally he lowered his stakes. When the investigator injured his foot and needed X-rays, Hawkeye agreed to do the work if the man paid $4 cash. Money in hand, Hawkeye treated the foot and then took the man to Rosie's to buy him a drink. He left the rest of the $4 as a tip.

Some things are purely a matter of honor.

YEAR EIGHT (1979–80)

NAME: MORGAN, HARRY
CHARACTER: POTTER, SHERMAN T., MD
RANK: COLONEL, USAMC
SERIAL NUMBER: RA41021629

"M*A*S*H has been the highlight of my career and my life, too, I think. This was the eighth series I've done. At the end, I felt I'd invested a part of my life in this show. I don't know any other show I can say that about. There was a nobility about M*A*S*H and what those people were trying to do. The characters, for the most part, had a code of honor to them. Potter was a once-in-a-career role; he was such a warm, basically sympathetic character. I even love his name. I loved it when Jamie, you know, as Klinger, would sign his name with a flourish and announce, 'Sherman T. Potter.' I wondered what the 'T' is for. Tecumseh, I would guess, as in General Sherman. Larry Gelbart actually named me for his family doctor, I hear.

"Potter really went from A to Z. He got involved in the worst shenanigans. When I came in, I had to remember that I'm not playing McLean Stevenson or any character he was playing, and they had to either accept me or not. I really didn't have too many fears in that regard. I mean, if they do or they don't, it doesn't matter because if they don't, the whole thing is down the drain anyway. If the feeling off camera is just as strong as it is on camera, then you can't beat it.

"Strangely enough, Potter developed almost a father-daughter relationship with Hot Lips, which I don't think would have occurred to anybody when the show was being contemplated. It kind of developed out of what happened off camera. Loretta and I became so close. I think eventually Potter had a kind of father-son relationship with everybody else in the camp.

"It was the greatest set to work on. We had a day of rehearsal and then shot for four days, which is quite rare. The studio left us alone. It was almost an asylum being run by the inmates. Almost all of us directed. I used to direct a couple of shows a year. I don't like it that much. It's very draining to act and direct at the same time. Exhausting.

"There will never be a more relaxed set than M*A*S*H — or a more intense one. We were always horsing around, throwing sponges at each other, throwing food in the dining room. One of the things we used to do when we were waiting around in the operating room was take the clamps from the instrument trays and try to see how many we could hang on somebody's surgical gown before he noticed. Mike Farrell held the record with twenty-three hung on David Stiers's gown before Stiers noticed.

"My favorite episode of all was in Year Eight, where I drank the bottle of brandy from my old World War I buddies and cried. *Old Soldiers.* We had made a pledge, a tontine, that the last one of us alive would drink the bottle of brandy and toast his old comrades, and it was easy to take that and apply it to my new comrades.

"The eighth year was my fifth year on the show. It was a bit different from the others because we lost Radar and, essentially, we lost Klinger, too. I don't know if the audience noticed. Klinger as clerk no longer did his thing. Klinger was no Radar, and it was a compromise that had to be made, but Radar's presence was missed.

"Colonel Potter is very close to me. Before I got the part, I played in an episode called *The General Flipped at Dawn.* Not that many people know I was a general before I was demoted to colonel. Anyway, that part was one of the most fun in my life. Really silly stuff. Very different from Potter, but I think related to a part of me also. In every case, whatever part the actor is playing comes from something within him, but most of us on M*A*S*H played pretty close to the heart. In my case, to a great extent, there wasn't much difference between me off camera and me in front of the camera, particularly with the relationships. Gary had been like a son to me; Loretta like my daughter. She and my wife and I used to spend Saturday afternoons together; Loretta brought the champagne. It was a very tender relationship. The only case that was different was Larry Linville, whom we were fond of. But once we moved onto the set, no one was fond of Frank Burns; he was nothing like Larry Linville in the flesh. He was brilliant in that part.

"I think Year Eight was the last honeymoon year for everyone. M*A*S*H would still be going on today if Alan and Mike and Loretta and David hadn't said they'd had enough. By Year Nine, the cracks were beginning to show; Year Ten was going to be the last year and then we decided to go for one more. The decision to end was really based on Alan. I guess I could have kept on forever. It was just that kind of role, that kind of show."

Harry Morgan

Year Nine (1980—81)

JOHN RAPPAPORT, Supervising Producer

"In the early years, there were a whole lot of ideas from the research to draw upon. A lot of stories came to us almost full-blown. Later on, as our story sources started to dry up, as the doctors we talked to repeated stories we had already heard or used, we would get a germ of an idea as a starting point and then work to develop it into an actual flowing story line. In the last four years, because a lot of initial story ideas had been pretty well mined out, we would try to deal with the personalities of the characters, dream up things that would happen to them. Sometimes we would start a story conference with, 'What would be an interesting way for Charles and Hot Lips to get together?'

"The changes in the characters come from this sense of evolution—where the stories go and what the actors felt about what might happen to their real characters. But it really became organic. 'How might we further plumb Charles's behavior? How would he react to a specific circumstance and how and why would Charles react differently to this than B.J. or Hawkeye?'

"If a story was being written by us rather than a freelance contributor, we used a very detailed twelve-to-fourteen page outline of the story, and then a first draft would be written. Thad Mumford and Dan Wilcox, for example, would sit in an office and kick it around, writing it line by line, talking back and forth. After a draft was done on the story, the entire writing staff, including Burt Metcalfe, would gather in a conference room across from my office. There was a long couch in there, two easy chairs, a large brown table with five or six chairs grouped around it. We polished each script in there two or three times.

"I was on call twenty-four hours a day practically. We would sometimes sit in that room for eight hours. It was somewhat of a miracle that we were able to survive and emerge from there pretty good friends."

CHAPTER X

Left: Your Retention, Please
Below: The Red/White Blues

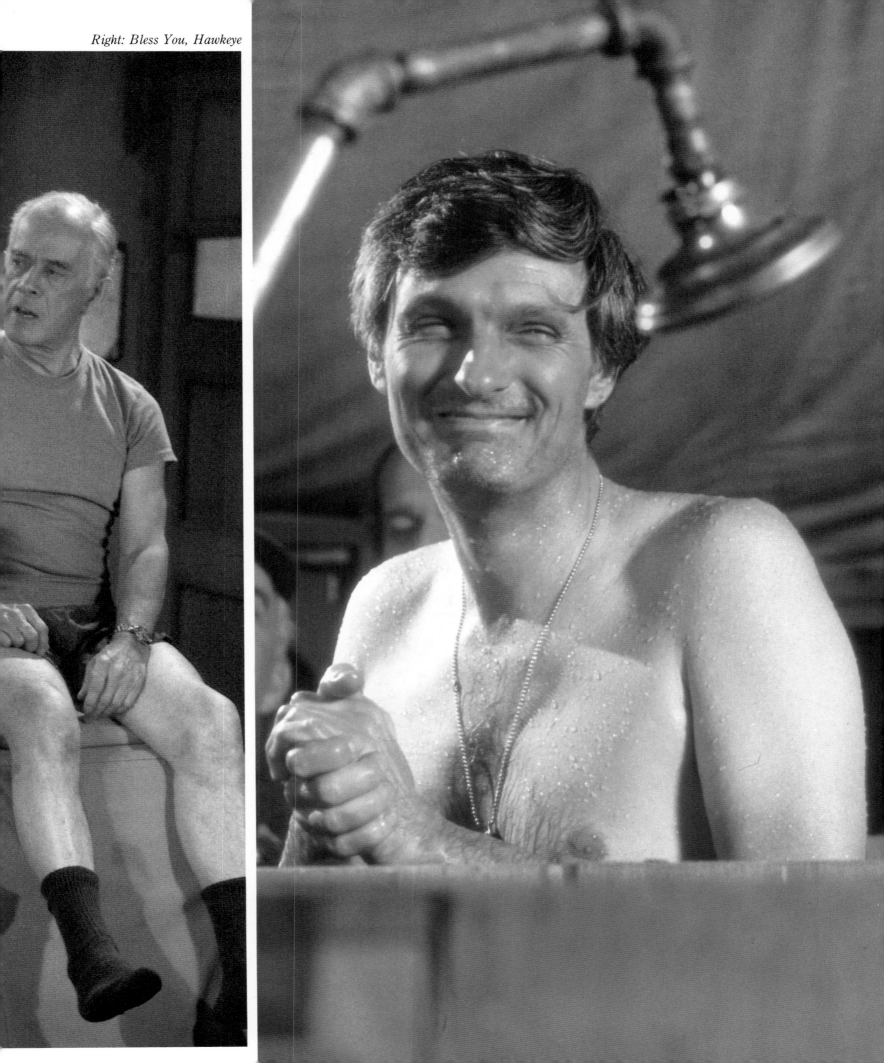

THE BEST OF ENEMIES

Hawkeye got a twenty-four-hour pass out of hell and into purgatory—destination Seoul. Dressed in clean fatigues, shaved, and cologned, he was singing a song while driving along a deserted road when a bullet ricocheted off his Jeep. Frightened, he lost control of the wheel and swerved into a tree. The sniper came down the hill to claim him.

"Look," the panicked doctor said. "I'm sorry I took your parking space. I'll be out of here in a jiffy as soon as I can get my motor started."

Li Han, Hawkeye's captor, would not allow retreat. Pointing to Hawkeye's Red Cross doctor bag with his gun, he gestured Pierce into the woods at gunpoint. "Well, I think I should warn you," Hawkeye shouted. "I am not a tree surgeon."

Li Han took his captive to an unconscious buddy propped up next to a tree hidden in a dense forest. The man was wounded badly and needed treatment.

"Ah, ha! I get the picture—even with subtitles. As long as he stays alive, I stay alive. Then we have to get him to a hospital. He's bleeding into his brain. He'll die if we don't move him."

Han did not understand what Pierce said, but his gun made it clear that he would not allow the patient to be taken to the 4077. Time was running out. A frantic Hawkeye performed an emergency tracheotomy. It failed. The man died.

"I'm sorry," said Hawkeye, close to tears. "I just didn't have the equipment to save him."

Li Han angrily motioned his prisoner to leave. Hawkeye gathered his things, grateful not to be shot, and started away. He looked back over his shoulder and saw the forlorn Li Han digging a grave with his bayonet. Hawkeye returned, knelt alongside the North Korean and, with his hands, began to dig the grave with him.

CEMENTING RELATIONSHIPS

Just as many a soldier met God in a foxhole, many a wounded man saw Venus in a nurse's uniform. Corpsman Ignazio De Simone was with an Italian battalion from the UN Special Forces. He was wounded in the leg and shipped to the 4077. Once there, his pride was more hurt than his body when he received a Dear Giovanni letter from his girl back at home.

"You've got to forget about her," Margaret innocently counseled. "Any woman would be thrilled to have you."

De Simone took her to heart. He serenaded her outside her tent. He tried a little more inside her tent.

"I am an officer in the United States Army, and I order you out of my tent," Margaret shrieked.

A few days later, and with great relief, Margaret said good-bye to De Simone as he shipped back to his unit. He returned the next day.

"Your lips said go away," he explained, "but your eyes said go AWOL."

"Look," said an angry Margaret, "I fixed your leg. Now walk back to your company on it."

"Then there must be another man."

"It's Dr. Winchester," lied Margaret, naming the first doctor who walked past her. Ignazio assaulted him with a stream of half Italian–half English, begging him to claim Margaret or leave her.

Charles had no idea what was going on. "My good man, I have better things to do than listen to someone make no sense in two languages."

"Watch your mouth," Margaret said, "or I'll get lover boy to say *arrivederci* to all your teeth."

NO SWEAT

Potter took a sleeping pill in order to get a good night's sleep. He should have handed them out at the staff meeting—no one else could sleep, either. The night was filled with mini-crises.

Hawkeye unloaded a patient in such critical condition that he needed to be stabilized and flown to Evac first thing in the morning. Only the sleeping Potter could call I-Corps to order a chopper. Potter was awakened and pointed toward the phone.

Then Charles needed some carbon paper. But carbon paper was much more dear than penicillin, so it was kept in the safe. Only Potter knew the combination. He had to be awakened one more time.

When Margaret discovered that a chopper was coming in the morning, she had to awaken Potter to request that the pilot bring her some lotion for her prickly heat. As she and Potter were discussing it, Klinger accidentally switched on the PA system. The entire camp heard the conversation.

"You don't understand, sir. This is Margaret. Wake up. Please wake up, sir. I have prickly heat. A severe irritation on my gluteus maximus.

"Oh, I get it. A bad case of keester itch. Ain't nothin' more bothersome than a case of the old fanny fungus. With all this heat, that cute little caboose of yours must be red as a beet. I don't know how bad off your whazoo is, but I bet it don't come close to the rump rots I had in the Big War....

"Sir...sir...uh..."

LETTERS

Hawkeye got a big manila envelope filled with letters from the fourth graders taught by an old friend of his back in Crabapple Cove. She had the class write their questions about the war directly to the doctors.

"Oh, this is cute," Margaret said. "Here's a boy who thinks MASH people sit around all day making potatoes."

"Oh, dear," said Father Mulcahy, "I got one from a girl who wants to know how many lives I've saved this year. I specialize in souls—not lives."

Cementing Relationships

"That's nothing," Hawkeye said. "My kid has the makings of a US senator. He goes on for five pages and says nothing. Here's one. Uh-oh. 'Doctor, my brother was a soldier in Korea. He got hurt but some doctors fixed him up so he could go back and fight some more. Then he got killed. Now I'll never see Keith again. You doctors just make people better so they can end up dead. I hate you all. Signed, Ronnie Hawkins.' "

"Dear Ronnie," Hawkeye wrote, after much consideration and pain. "It is a shame you let the love you had for your brother turn to hate for others. Hate makes war, and war is what killed him. I understand your feelings. I often hate myself for what I'm doing here. It fills me with anger and a sense of futility. But sometimes in the midst of all this insanity, the smallest help can make my being here seem worthwhile. I'm sorry, Ronnie, but maybe that's the best answer I have to offer you, that you look for good wherever you can find it."

FATHER'S DAY

"Howitzer Al" Houlihan, otherwise known as Colonel Alvin Houlihan, was also otherwise known as Margaret's dad. He came to visit her at the 4077 after wangling a business trip to the Orient. After retiring, he had become a civilian consultant to the Army. Margaret was thrilled. She ran out to hug him when he arrived.

"Please, Margaret," he said as he pulled away. "Not in front of the troops."

Colonel Houlihan settled into the VIP tent, then went into OR to observe. Margaret was tense. "Just once," she begged the Swampmen, "could you conduct yourselves with the tiniest trace of professionalism?"

During the surgery, she knocked over an IV stand. Her father walked out, a look of disgust on his face.

The next day, he announced he was leaving early. Margaret thought it was all her fault. She was hurt and angry, but mostly blamed herself for once again not living up to what her father wanted.

Potter talked it over with Colonel Houlihan. "Margaret's busted her britches trying to please you, but you don't seem to give a tinker's damn."

"My daughter knows perfectly well that I love her. I flew halfway around the world to see her. That should say it all."

"You're so busy being 'Howitzer Al' you can't even let your daughter know you love her. She thinks you're leaving because of her. She doesn't know you had to walk out of OR because you had to toss your cookies. If you ask me, which you didn't, I'd say you're running away from the person who you should be gettin' close to."

Father and daughter said a tense good-bye. Colonel Houlihan signaled his driver to pull away, but after a few feet, he stopped and walked back to his daughter.

Above: Father's Day   *Below: Your Retention, Please*

Your Retention, Please

"Margaret, I'm very proud of you and your work here. I can arrange to be in Tokyo next month. I'd love it if you'd come up there and see me."

YOUR RETENTION, PLEASE

Max Klinger got a letter from his ex-wife, Laverne, announcing that she was about to marry yet another of their mutual friends. Max's heart was broken—again. Unable to hide his chagrin, he went to the Officers Club to tie one on. That's where he ran into Vickers, the Area Retention Officer, whose job was to reenlist men. He signed Klinger up for six more years, effective as soon as Klinger took the proper oath.

Hawkeye couldn't believe it. "Give me some credit, Captain," said Klinger to Hawkeye. "I may be a rummy but I'm no dummy. The Army provides a home and a career. The Army's my best friend. It won't stab me in the back like that ex-wife-stealer, Gus Nagy." Then he trotted off to take his oath from Colonel Potter.

Potter decided to bamboozle Klinger. He knew that the man did not want to spend another six years in the Army. He just needed time to come to his senses. But Klinger was so insistent that he be given an oath, Potter thought the best way to shut him up was to give him one. He just didn't give him the *proper* oath. Instead, he administered the oath of office of President of the United States.

When he snapped back to reality, Klinger could not believe what had happened. He had no way of knowing that Potter had protected him with the wrong oath, so he decided to take matters into his own hands. It was time to pull some of his old tricks.

He swiped Sophie from her corral, dolled himself up in a cotton-ball wig, took off all his clothes, and rode bareback through camp in his best imitation of Lady Godiva.

"This is a protest. I was drafted behind my back."

"I'd say your back is pretty drafty, too," Hawkeye laughed.

TAKING THE FIFTH

"If we get out of here before we lose our looks, we could meet in the storage room and take inventory of each other. Wear your rubber gloves. I love watching you take them off," lover boy Hawkeye Pierce whispered to Nurse Able, one of the objects of his affections.

"No gloves, no store room, no date," she replied tersely. The mighty Hawkeye hath struck out.

In fact, he struck out with every nurse he went to bat with. Then Klinger gave him a bottle of 1947 Château Margaux that an English supply officer had given him as a gift. The Limeys got it cheap, but to the Americans, it was an incredible luxury. Hawkeye decided to let the wine sing his love songs for him.

"Savor a vintage evening with Hawkeye Pierce," read his announcement on the bulletin board. "Trade your boredom for some Bordeaux. In one hundred words or less, tell why you should be in a glass by yourself."

"No self-respecting nurse will have anything to do with this," B.J. cautioned.

"That's exactly what I'm counting on."

The winning wine entry was as smooth as the grape: "I find you an incredibly exciting, vibrant man. I must admit wine makes me a little crazy, but I'm sure it's nothing you can't handle."

They met for their date. Lieutenant Palmer whispered urgently, "Hawkeye, I just don't know if I'm woman enough for you." Then she whistled through her teeth. Margaret and all the nurses barged in, each with a wine glass in her hand.

"It's such a wonderful moment," Palmer said smugly. "I wanted to share it with all my friends."

DEATH TAKES A HOLIDAY

Potter was on as Santa Claus; Hawkeye and B.J. were on as doctors that Christmas Day. Despite the cease-fire, one customer did appear at the 4077, a man who had been found at roadside—mortally wounded.

Margaret found a photograph in his pocket of his wife and children. The snapshot jolted all of B.J.'s emotions into a very unmerry Christmas. "If we can keep this guy alive until midnight then his kids won't have to remember Christmas as the day their daddy died."

The three of them worked feverishly all night, using every procedure they knew to keep the man alive. At 11:25 P.M., they ran out of tricks. Father Mulcahy administered the last rites.

"Give me ten ccs of Adrenalin," B.J. ordered. "C'mon, kid. Let's give it one more shot."

"No," Hawkeye said gently. "It's over. Let him rest."

Margaret reached for the death certificate. Hawkeye stared at the clock powerlessly, then slowly got up, walked over to it and moved its hands.

"Look, he made it. Time of death, 12:05, December 26."

"Christmas should be thought of as a time of birth," Father Mulcahy said as he gave his final blessing.

A WAR FOR ALL SEASONS

The 4077 did not have an artificial kidney machine. In fact, there was only one in the entire Far East. But B.J. and Hawkeye had a patient whose kidneys were not doing a very good job of keeping him alive.

They consulted with doctors at the 8228 MASH, they talked to locals, they read medical papers. Finally they decided to build their own kidney machine.

Margaret got them some parts while in Tokyo for R&R; Sears & Roebuck delivered some parts from their catalogue; and Paco's of Toledo, home of the most heavenly hot dogs in Ohio, sent the most important item—sausage casing for tubing.

"Thanks to the brilliance of your doctor, who shall remain me," Hawkeye reported to his patient, "your kidneys are beginning to work like kidneys. You're well enough for us to ship you to Oinju, where they have one of these machines that doesn't look like it was built by Mr. Wizard. Then you're going home."

TELL IT TO THE MARINES

Private Jost Van Liter was a naturalized American citizen who joined the Marines to show his appreciation to his new country. He won two Purple Hearts and two Bronze Stars before he ended up wounded in the 4077. He told Margaret his story—how he had only three weeks left to serve in his tour of duty but that his mother was being deported because she divorced her American husband. By the time he got home, she would be back in Holland. Margaret went to Hawkeye with the story. Hawkeye called the boy's CO to arrange an early release. No deal. Marines don't go in for motherhood and tulip stories. So Hawkeye wrote an angry article for *Stars & Stripes*. The Marines killed the story.

"Be a Jost writer," B.J. suggested. He and Hawkeye went to the press train at Moonsan and told the boy's story to the war correspondents gathered there. Murray Thompson put the piece on the wire service for newspapers all over the United States.

"How will that help my problem?" Jost asked.

Death Takes a Holiday

Tell It to the Marines

Depressing News

DEPRESSING NEWS

The Army likes things in triplicate, so it should not have surprised Hawkeye so much when his order for tongue depressors came back with some extra zeroes at the end. He asked for five thousand but he got five hundred thousand—a small Army snafu.

He decided to use the extra four hundred and ninety-five thousand to build a monument to the Army's inefficiency by putting the names of all the soldiers who had passed through the 4077 on tongue depressors and then building them into a tower. Klinger alerted *Stars & Stripes* because he thought it was such a hot story. An Army information officer named Maury Allen came along with a photographer.

Allen was impressed. He liked it so much he suggested a national promotional tour. "We'll ship your hoozie-whats to the States, put it in parades, lots of brass bands, display it everywhere. Be great for enlistment. 'Doc Gives Recruiting Drive Shot in the Arm,' I can see the headlines now."

Hawkeye was appalled. He was the last person in the world who would help the Army with a recruiting drive. He stalled for time to get ready for his picture, then rigged some dynamite to his tower. As the photographer snapped, the entire tower blew to smithereens.

Allen was stunned. "You spent two days and nights building this and now you've blown it to kingdom come? What the devil for?"

"Senseless destruction is what war is all about," sighed Hawkeye as he walked away.

OPERATION FRIENDSHIP

When a mortar shell cut the power to the generator, the autoclave—a clever little machine that sterilized instruments—built up so much pressure that it exploded. Klinger saw it coming and threw himself on top of Charles to save his life. B.J. was thrown across the room—and landed with his arm wedged between a table and the wall.

"Charles is fine," announced Hawkeye, "but Klinger has damage to over fifty percent of his body. His nose is broken."

Although B.J. said he was fine, Potter sent for a replacement surgeon who happened to be a specialist. Dr. Norman Traeger arrived from Tokyo the next day. Hawkeye was insulted.

"I'm B.J.'s doctor, and I don't like you to go behind my back," he fumed.

"I am also a doctor," B.J. said, "and I don't need me or him or even him." He pointed a finger at the other men.

But he was wrong. Suddenly his hand went white and grew numb.

"If that hand's not operated on immediately," Traeger said, "he could lose the use of it."

Just the words a surgeon loves to hear. B.J. was pre-medicated, rushed to surgery, and restored to good health.

"It's called public opinion," Hawkeye explained. "People read about an injustice, and they rally around to change it. That's the American way."

Sure enough, the Dutch Consul General in San Francisco read the story. He hired Van Liter's mother as a secretary, thus providing diplomatic immunity. She would no longer be deported.

"Just consider it my Dutch treat," Hawkeye beamed.

NO LAUGHING MATTER

Colonel Horace Baldwin had a cushy job in Tokyo. He was the sore sport who had exiled Charles to Ouijongbu because he owed Winchester over $600 in a cribbage game. Potter was not certain how Charles would react when he discovered the man would be visiting the 4077.

"I shall personally perform elective surgery on the first organ of his that presents itself," Charles swore when Potter told him about the guest.

Charles did get a bit agitated. Both Potter and Klinger tried to calm him down. Klinger coyly reminded the major that he would catch more flies with honey than vinegar. By the time Baldwin arrived, Winchester was as sticky nice as maple syrup. He was determined to charm his way back to Tokyo. He played cribbage and lost gracefully—intentionally. He flattered; he cajoled; he even tossed in a bottle of his finest cognac. Baldwin got to feel so chummy with the major that he asked him to get some feminine companionship. When Charles trotted off to Rosie's Bar with a $10 bill in his hand, Margaret entered the colonel's tent with some papers she wanted to show him. But Baldwin assumed that she was the evening's main dish and pounced on her—black mask, whip, chains, and all.

Margaret was aghast. She reported him to Potter. Baldwin countered by accusing her of improper behavior. To corroborate his story, he put the pressure on Charles.

Charles came through like a gentleman. "As painful as this is," he announced, "I must tell you that Colonel Baldwin is lying through his teeth. He offered to have me reassigned to Tokyo if I would bear false witness against Major Houlihan. I will not, even for a return to that pearl of the Orient, lie to protect a person while destroying another's career."

OH, HOW WE DANCED

May 23 was B.J. and Peg's wedding anniversary, only B.J. had to spend it with Hawkeye instead of his wife.

"Hey," Hawkeye said. "I've never had an anniversary. Tell me about it."

B.J. waxed eloquent on the details of what the day would be like if he were home. Hawkeye surreptitiously taped it all. He sent the recording to Peg, who sent him a small package in return.

On the night of the 23rd, B.J. walked into Potter's office for the surprise party he was expecting. Then he got the surprise of his life. Hawkeye flicked on Charles's tape recorder and played the recording of B.J. talking about the perfect anniversary day. On the movie screen flashed the home movie Peg and her dad made to accompany the tape—each scene depicting the events B.J. talked about so longingly.

"Hi, darling," Peg said. "More than anything, I wish we could be together today. I know you feel the same way. Your wonderful friends know that, too. So we put together this little movie. It's not anything Hollywood

would care about, but we care about you and hope you'll like it."

As the movie ended and B.J. wiped away a tear, Peg's voice came back on. "At the end of the day, we'd dance and talk and hold each other. B.J., I know that film and tape can't replace the real thing, but this particular anniversary will always be special to me. I love you, my darling."

BOTTOMS UP

Captain Helen Whitfield was an old friend of Margaret's who was tranferred to the 4077 near the end of 1952. Margaret was delighted to have a friend she could talk to finally. The women were close friends, but Margaret did not know that Helen had become an alcoholic.

Then Klinger found the woman locked up in the supply room hunched in the corner, hugging a bottle of booze. In a panic, he went to Colonel Potter.

"I have a friend in a MASH unit who has a problem—back in Toledo, not here. My friend knows something bad about somebody but he doesn't want to be a dirty, low-down, squealing stool pigeon but he thinks it's important and . . ."

"Klinger, you're the unknown soldier. Now tell me already."

Potter had a talk with Margaret. Margaret covered perfectly for her friend. Then she went to Helen.

"Helen, you've been drinking for years. Things were different in the old days. In this unit, you can't be the party girl you used to be. You almost gave a patient the wrong type of blood last week. I can't let you in OR. Your career and mine are at stake here. I went out on a limb for you with Potter. I gave him my word on you. The only way I can help you is if you level with me."

Helen turned in her last bottle of booze and swore she had no problem. Margaret believed her. The captain was cool as a cuke for two days. Then she broke into the DTs in the Mess Tent and went wild, knocking over trays and scratching invisible bugs off her arms.

"She fooled a lot of people," Potter said, "but worst of all, she fooled herself. Let's get her some good help."

THE RED/WHITE BLUES

Two weeks before his annual physical was due to be sent to Washington, Potter asked Hawkeye to do the honors. Potter was as shocked as his doctor when his blood pressure read 165/93—too high to stay in a combat zone. He had to get the second figure to 90 or below. Potter saw himself being assigned to a "weenie job" at a desk for the rest of his Army career. He only had a few months left in the service and, while the 4077 wasn't paradise, he was in no hurry to swap it for a desk job.

Hawkeye agreed to hang on to the test for the two weeks until it was due so Potter could improve his blood pressure. He tried to eliminate stress for his regular

Bless You, Hawkeye

routine. Margaret took away salt shakers from the mess tables; Father Mulcahy nixed coffee. B.J. brought him breakfast in bed. Cigars, liquor, even salted pretzels were denied.

Finally Potter exploded. "The next person who is nice to me is going to die with boots on. Mine. I'll have no more of this mollycoddling from any of you. Understood?"

Two weeks later, Potter went for his visit to Dr. Pierce. His blood pressure was 137/88. Home free.

He celebrated with a shot of whiskey and a good cigar.

BLESS YOU, HAWKEYE

It started with an attack of sneezing. Then Hawkeye's hands swelled, his eyes began to run, and his skin blotched over with hives. He tested negative to all known allergens. But his condition deteriorated so much that he had to be put on an IV and isolated in the VIP tent. He was convinced he was going to die.

"We've gone as far as we can with his body," Colonel Potter reported. "It's time we found out what's going on in his mind."

Sidney Freedman came the next day. "Think of the problem as a land mine that's been inside your head for a long time. Something happened the other night to trip it."

Freedman reviewed all the patients Hawkeye had admitted and came up dry. Then he got Pierce to talk about his childhood. As Hawkeye clenched and unclenched a fist, Freedman knew he was on the right track. Hawkeye told of a traumatic incident with his cousin, Billy, at the fishing pond. The teenaged Billy had thrown seven-year-old Hawkeye overboard and then saved the boy from drowning.

"Private Caputo came in here drenched wet and that's what did it," explained Freedman, the master sleuth. "The odor triggered the sneezing. Your sense of smell is the strongest link back to a memory. Your life and death incident with your cousin when you were seven came to the fore. The battlegrounds of childhood sometimes leave the worst scars."

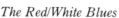

The Red/White Blues

THE LIFE YOU SAVE

A sniper bullet grazed Charles's head and left him obsessed with death. He sat up all night with an unconscious patient whose life he had saved. When the patient came to, Charles was loaded with questions.

"Do you recall what you felt? Did you see anything? Was it like dreaming? Did you hear voices?"

B.J. admonished Charles for his "graveside manner," but Margaret thought perhaps he was troubled. No one understood his burden, so Charles took off for the front, where he teamed up with the surgeon at Battalion Aid.

"I still don't understand why you're here," the surgeon said, "but I'm glad for the extra hands."

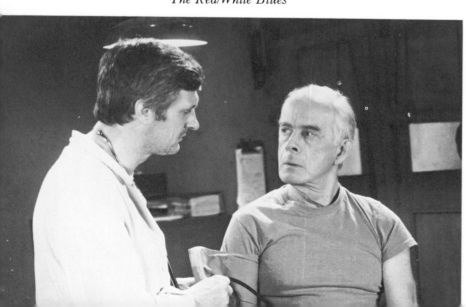

A mortally wounded patient was brought in. "What's happening to you? Do you feel anything? Do you see anything?" Winchester asked him urgently.

"I . . . I smell bread," the soldier said. Then he died.

Charles realized there were no answers, tossed his bullet-creased hat away, and went back to the 4077.

BLOOD BROTHERS

Privates Gary Sturgis and Dan Lowry came into the 4077 by way of Hill 1223. Lowry was in bad shape, touch and go all the way. Sturgis volunteered to give blood. "We're both the same type, A-positive. That sort of makes us blood brothers," Sturgis said.

When the lab ran a blood count, they discovered that Sturgis couldn't possibly donate blood—he was in the early stages of leukemia.

"At the outside, he could have three years," Charles predicted.

"And his buddy who got blown over three parallels is going to be okay," said Hawkeye. "You get used to kids coming in here in pieces, and you do your best to put them back together again. But dammit, there's hardly a mark on that kid, and he's still going to die."

Hawkeye broke the news to the patient, then went to Father Mulcahy, who talked the case over first with Pierce, then Sturgis. They recommended that Sturgis go immediately to Tokyo General for another lab test, chemotherapy, and a trip home. But Sturgis wanted to stay with Lowry at the 4077.

"Dr. Hunnicutt told me my being here was helping Dan. What do a few more days for me matter anyway? It seems I've got a right to do what I want with the time I've got left. I'll go, but I want to nurse Dan back to health first."

THE FORESIGHT SAGA

Radar wrote to the gang at the 4077 and boasted of his success as a "gentleman farmer." Seems that his fiction was better in letter writing than it had ever been in his correspondence writing course. When Klinger patched through a call to Ottumwa, he reached Radar's mom.

Radar wasn't home, it turned out, because he had to work at a night job just to keep up the mortgage payments on the failing farm.

"Seems Radar exaggerated a mite in his letter," Potter told the disappointed crowd. "He was embarrassed to say how tough things are."

"Gee," B.J. said. "Radar needs help on the farm and we have that Korean patient here who's a farming whiz but doesn't have any place to live. Let's get Radar to sponsor him, and they'll both be happy."

It was a match made in heaven.

Blood Brothers

YEAR NINE (1980–81)

NAME: STIERS, DAVID OGDEN
CHARACTER: WINCHESTER, CHARLES EMERSON III
RANK: MAJOR, USAMC
SERIAL NUMBER: US21020980

"All along, in my entire life, I've had a sense of a hand guiding me along. M*A*S*H fitted into my life really honorably. Every time I've turned around, someone has offered me a job, a plum role, or something really good. Of the twenty years I've been an actor, I've only been out of work unwillingly for a total of six months, and then only for brief stretches. I'm not being an egoist, but I was good enough not to dishonor any project I worked on. I earned it through good work.

"When I first came to Los Angeles and televisionland, I despised it. For a young actor not conversant with videotape, it was very shocking to walk into a factory atmosphere like that. You're being paid an inordinate amount of money to exercise a minimum of your abilities in material that will not touch, instruct, illuminate, uplift, or last. I wasn't prepared for the speed at which they shouted, 'Print.' Things improved when I did a guest spot on *Rhoda*—it was as warm as any theater company I'd ever known. Before M*A*S*H, David Doyle and I were the original two male members of *Charlie's Angels*. I did the pilot. I remember distinctly Mr. Spelling [Aaron Spelling, *Charlie's Angels'* executive producer] neither liking nor trusting me, and I gather he was as happy to have me leave as I was to leave.

"I did three *Mary Tyler Moore Shows* in the last year of the show, and the fellow who was executive producer of M*A*S*H [Burt Metcalfe] saw the three episodes that I shot as the stuttering station manager—a barracuda of a man with a perfectly wonderful smile and a gutter attitude toward people. Burt's point of view was that that sort of behavior on *Mary* was 'lovably unlovable.' He thought that I could really be a despicable person and a bastard to people who were loved and manage not to be so hate-able myself. You didn't want not to see the character again.

"I started in Year Six. They were really good to me for like the first three weeks or so, then one day I was standing in the operating room. I'd just finished something in a close-up and a piece of surgical gauze whizzed across my face and I, Jesus, I thought, I'm so bad they're throwing things at me. I didn't realize that's the way they joked.

"Obviously, I had worried that they were going to be so tight that there wouldn't be room for me. I had been very concerned about them absorbing me into their unit, the ensemble, so their reinforcing the friendship with jokes was very nice. You worry that a show that's been very popular and very strong is going to take a dive suddenly because you've joined it. Farrell went through that period when he came in after Wayne left. The same thing happened to me when I joined. It's a regular phenomenon. At the beginning of the season, people watch brand-new shows, so the ratings on a regular show can tremble a little. When new shows prove not to be as appetizing as what's already on, ratings go back to their usual pattern. But the ratings can go in the toilet for five or six weeks at the start and, if you're new on the show, you put it on your own shoulders. So, actually, the only worries I had were essentially invented by me and ignoring the fact that these people are all consummate pros and wouldn't put you through any awfulness. It was easy.

"There was a lot of joking on the set. We saved up one morning a whole bunch of pancakes left over from the mess, and the minute Alan had finished talking, we landed about eight of these hard, cold things on him. Ah, it was wonderful.

"Do you know the story about my dressing room? I came back from Thanksgiving in Year Nine and some of the actors had contacted the paint department and, as a joke, they painted my room orange and purple. When I walked in the next morning, not knowing this had been done, I turned on the light and got a retina burn. For two hours in front of the camera, I couldn't quite tell who I was focusing on. I had the room repainted—with Farrell's mustache.

"People find ways to grow closer to one another because of the danger of their work. It is very hard. You lay yourself on the line every time the camera rolls. That includes a kind of pressure that makes you rely on other people and makes you find strength in yourself to let other people rely on you. It is a wonderful weaving. You weave relationships with a fabric that is strong enough to withstand the psychological, and emotional, and time pressures of doing the show. That happened to us. M*A*S*H at its best dealt with such breadth and accuracy of observation about life, not just in a war but in any kind of stress . . . that our feelings became much more closely allied.

"Also, we were such different characters. No one of us did something that any of the others did. We all covered completely different areas of the human network. None of us encroached on the other's turf, so that at once we were defined and allowed to draw close because there was more trust. The bottom line of why the show succeeded so well was that it never talked down to anybody. We were never limited in subject matter by the network or the studio. We didn't treat people like dolts.

"Winchester is all around us. I don't think he had to do with family background or old money or education. He was trying to protect the ways he perceived himself as being weak by choosing slightly grand things to achieve. I'm not suggesting that Winchester is two-dimensional. I'm saying that underneath, he was not insecure or frightened but always had the sense he wasn't quite good enough to be a member of the family he was attached to. Even though there was a great deal of social assurance to him and, I suppose, snobbery, I found him at his best to be at once valuable and ridiculous and finally likable. It just costs you a little more to find him—to get through the bullshit he spreads in your way. He had disguises of perpetual security and assurance, and he hated it when people got to him. He spent as much time covering his tracks as he did keeping his persona intact. The show was secure enough to allow him to alter subtly in the end. It seems to me that he finally began to live where he was instead of living twelve thousand miles away. The relationships he found himself depending on were more real at the end than he allowed them to be originally.

"M*A*S*H was not an unfunny show by any means, but the reason it's funny is that it comes out of characters, people who are thoroughly defined as human beings. They react to an essentially stupid environment, one filled with an awful lot of blood . . . and the pain of having to save people that other people are working to blow off the face of the earth. It makes you much stronger inside yourself. You use your own human resources better and you tend not to compromise, but you tend to accept other forms of behavior from people as their way of staying sane and, I think, the pain is visible under the humor. We never made a joke at the expense of human pride or sensitivity."

David Ogden Stiers

Year Ten (1981–82)

THAD MUMFORD and DAN WILCOX,
Producers/Writers

"When Dan and I started to work for the show, we felt a certain amount of intimidation, given the history of the program and the public's love of it. I figured the show had been on for seven years and that most of the great ideas had probably already been done, and we might end up with nothing but cobwebs.

"One of the problems M*A*S*H had was that we were locked in time. Unlike other series, we couldn't move a neighbor in next door to create new situations and new stories. We were locked in the Korean War with a certain amount of flexibility, but not a whole lot. We tried to be faithful to the history of the war and, in so doing, we were sort of limited to what we could embellish. You can't change history. M*A*S*H was a way to show that war is hell, and you show that war is hell by showing people in an insane situation acting crazy to try to maintain their sanity. We always kept that in the back of our minds. It's sort of a one-line précis of what we were writing. That gave us a clear line and a character motivation. One of the reasons Larry Gelbart claims he left the show was because he felt he couldn't say "war is hell" any more in a fresh way.

"We ended up doing different stories in a sense because they weren't as strident about how awful war was, although war was still always the omnipresent villain—it was always there in an unspoken way.

"And then after *Comrades in Arms*, things were different for Margaret and Hawkeye, together and apart. Loretta felt she couldn't be as antagonistic toward Hawkeye as she had been. We had to adapt to that change. Alan became a staunch feminist. The old Hawkeye was an overly chauvinistic skirt-chaser. Over the years, as Alda changed, it became more difficult to write the character. It was easier to write skirt chasing and booze jokes.

"I will say, though, that the actors didn't improvise a word."

"When Thad and I first joined the staff, we would get a great idea for a story and say, 'How about this?' and Burt would say, 'We did that in Year Three.' It was always hard to come up with stories. On the other hand, we had a bunch of stories hanging around the office that had to do with the Korean War, and we knew if we got to that point, they would be ready and waiting for us."

CHAPTER XI

Above and opposite: That's Show Biz

THAT'S SHOW BIZ

"Fast Freddie" Nichols and his gang of traveling "gypsies" were on a USO tour of South Korea when they made an unscheduled stop at the 4077. Marina Ryan, one of their singers, needed emergency surgery before her appendix burst. She was rushed into surgery just in time. Without proper medical care, a ruptured appendix can be fatal.

To show their appreciation to the MASH unit, the troupe decided to give their show in postop.

They were a smash hit. Klinger loved "Fast Freddie's" shtick; Charles got along well with one of the female musicians; Potter and the burlesque queen Brandy became friends. Margaret even loosened up enough to go on stage and sing a chorus of "Molly Malone."

The next morning, the troupe bid their adieus as they headed off to the 121 Evac, only to be stopped by Klinger, who got a speedy call from G-2 announcing that roads would be closed because a major offensive was about to take place. The entertainers were grounded at the MASH.

"Mr. Nichols, let me put it this way," Potter said. "In show folks lingo, there's people out there knockin' 'em dead. So unless you want your next review to be in the obituaries, sit tight."

"We've got to stay on schedule," "Fast Freddie" sputtered, "or my club date in Hoboken is gonna be right down the latrine."

"I've been to Hoboken," said Potter. "You're better off here."

"Do you think the enemy is attacking because they saw his show?" Hawkeye asked.

When the wounded arrived, the USO team helped in triage. To free up another bed, Hawkeye authorized Marina's release. She wanted to stay with him.

"When you got here, you were very sick. I literally swept you off your feet. All you see is a miracle man in a white suit. You don't even know me."

"Let me stay."

"We're the wrong blood type," he said kindly.

They all shipped out the next morning.

IDENTITY CRISIS

Father Mulcahy was making small talk with Corporal Josh Levin. "You're Jewish, aren't you? Well, I thought you'd like to know I do a wide range of services here. Are you orthodox, conservative, or reform?

"Uh...orthodox," said Levin.

Mulcahy admitted he didn't know much about orthodoxy, but it turned out that Levin knew less. He begged for the father to hear his confession. The startled priest thought he was just indulging the boy.

"Bless me, Father, for I have sinned. Josh Levin was one of my buddies who got killed. He was going home in two weeks. I took his dog tags and discharge orders. My name is Gerald Mullen."

They spent days discussing the problem. Father Mulcahy asked to speak of the matter outside of confession. He tried to convince Mullen what a mistake he was making to live the rest of his life as Levin, but said he trusted him to make the right decision—one he could live with his entire life.

Mullen turned in Levin's dog tags and went back to Charlie company, a new man.

RUMOR AT THE TOP

Logistics and Support sent Major Nathaniel Burnham to the 4077 at the behest of General Bertram Eugene Torgeson, one of Potter's least favorite people.

"He and I came out of the cavalry together. Went to medical school together. Four years later, I was a doctor, and he was just four years older. He washed out. His IQ was lower than his boot size."

Hawkeye and B.J. used their higher IQs to figure out that a new MASH was being set up and that Potter would be taken away from the 4077 to head it. They banded together to make him look just a little incompetent. Meanwhile, Charles did everything he could to make himself look better—so he would be appointed to replace Potter.

Burnham was so impressed by Charles that he asked the major to join the new MASH—which would be located *closer* to the front. Charles declined.

"We'd never split up the 4077," Burnham confessed. "It's hard enough in this Army to find anything that works. When you do, you don't mess with it. Pulling someone out of here would be like breaking up the Yankees."

GIVE 'EM HELL, HAWKEYE

Dear Harry,

I know as president you're busy stopping the buck and all, so I'll be brief. I am a doctor and a Democrat—loyal Democrat—now living in Korea or, as I call it, hell. I'd like to be home before winter, when hell freezes over.

I'm sure you're aware that the peace talks are a year old and we're all a year older. I've given it a lot of thought and, call me a crackpot, but I think I've got a solution to this problem. Stop the war.

Harry, do you know what this country looks like? Picture Swiss cheese with cities. Believe me, putting slipcovers on the land mines won't help. If you end this fiasco right now, I pledge to purchase all your daughter's records. Don't bother to deliver them. I'd love to pick them up on my way home.

Sincerely,
Hawkeye Pierce, MD
Medical Democrat

WHEELERS AND DEALERS

Mail didn't always bring the best news. Like the time Peg wrote to say she had taken a job as a waitress at Papanek's Coffee Shop to help pay off the second mortgage. B.J. was beside himself with hurt pride.

"By now I was supposed to be in practice, with the second mortgage a memory. It's due in six months, and I let her down." He took to playing poker and pinball to make extra money.

"You can't pay off the mortgage with nickels," said Hawkeye, infuriated at his friend's bad humor. "Dammit, bad news from home doesn't give you the right to become Public Enemy Number One."

Margaret was even more angry at B.J.'s behavior and attitude. "How dare you think your brand of suffering is worse than anybody else's? If the worst thing that's happened to you is that your pretty little wife is gonna help pay the bills for a while, don't come to me for sympathy!"

B.J. calmed down and apologized. He even made a personal contribution to the next week's poker game—Peg sent a box of mints to replace the usual pretzels. When they ran out, she'd probably send toothpicks.

COMMUNICATION BREAKDOWN

Charles received a week's worth of newspapers in his usual first-class package from home, while everyone else had to go paperless because fourth-class mail was not being put through. He grudgingly agreed to share, *after* he read each day's news.

But the real communication breakdown in the compound occurred between one of Hawkeye's patients—a wounded North Korean—and a South Korean MP who came to claim him.

"That patient is in more danger than you know," the South Korean said. "His kidneys . . . they are not strong. When he was a small boy, he was very sick."

"How do you know?" asked the doctor.

"He is my brother," the South Korean whispered. "My father knew war was coming. He sent me to live in south. He did not know which side would win or lose, so he put one son on either side so one would be on side of victory to carry family name. If I am seen talking to him, others may think I am spy."

Hawkeye was overwhelmed. "A brother's biggest problem should be wondering who Dad likes best, not this."

To give the brothers some time together, Hawkeye ordered a blood transfusion for the wounded man. He typed and matched the brother's blood then wheeled the two into preop.

"Talk to your brother," Hawkeye explained. "Tell him he's fine . . . and anything else you want to tell him."

SNAP JUDGMENT/SNAPPIER JUDGMENT

A rash of petty thievery broke out in the 4077 and per-

Communication Breakdown

sonal treasures were not safe unless locked away. When the father of a grateful patient sent a Polaroid camera to Hawkeye in appreciation for the work done on his son, the camera soon became more trouble than the patient had been. When it was stolen, Hawkeye filled in a stolen goods report, which Klinger forgot to send in. Wanting to help, he went to "Little Chicago"—a mobile black market that offered the best of the Far East. Sure enough, there was the camera. Klinger bought it back for Hawkeye, but an investigating MP decided that Klinger was the thief. The deeper the investigation went, the worse it looked for Klinger. Finally, he was brought up on charges. Neither Hawkeye nor B.J. were allowed to represent him because they were witnesses for the prosecution, so Charles volunteered to be Klinger's Perry Mason.

He turned into Klinger's Waterloo, as well.

"I intend to show that my client is totally innocent of the malicious and unfounded charges against him, Mr. President," began Charles, grandly.

"Truman is president, and you're out of order. It's not your turn. The prosecution speaks first," the judge said.

And speak he did. Even Klinger's best traits were soon held against him. Hawkeye and B.J. felt compelled to do something before Klinger was sent to the stockade. Realizing that the thefts always occurred during OR, they faked a PA announcement and then waited with baited camera for the thief to go after Charles's valuable tape recorder, which they left out as part of the trap. They caught the man, took his pictures to court, and won Corporal Maxwell Q. Klinger his freedom—just as he was about to be sentenced to twenty years at hard labor.

"Two of my least favorite words."

Above: 'Twas the Day After Christmas
Left: Give 'Em Hell, Hawkeye

Above: Wheelers and Dealers

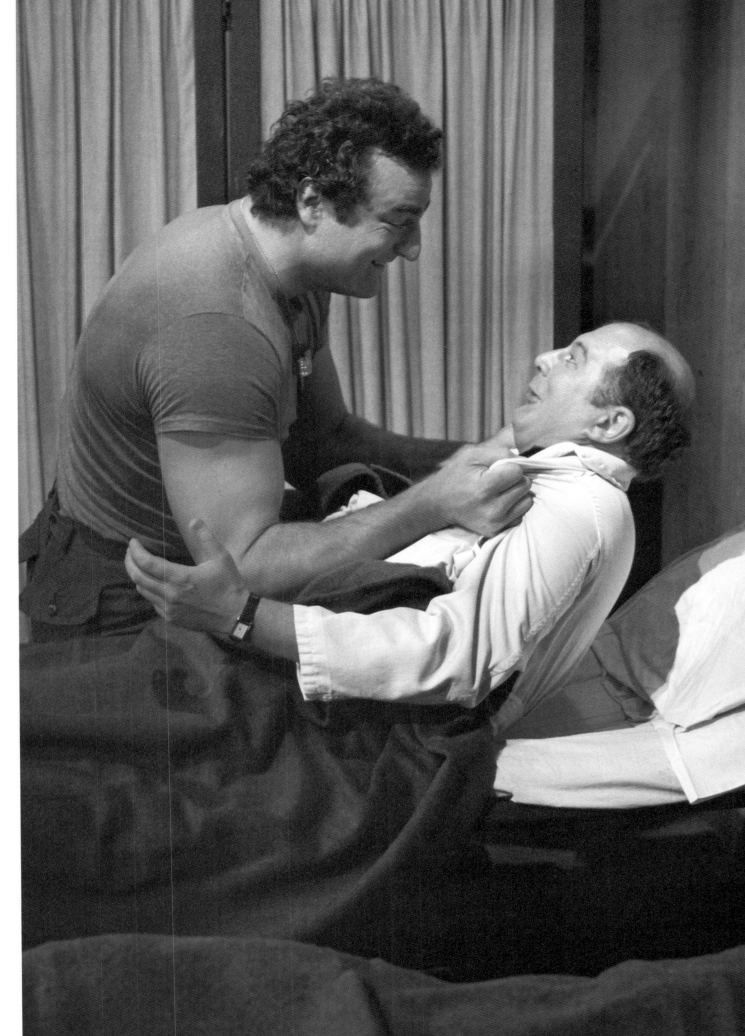

*Promotion
Commotion*

'TWAS THE DAY AFTER CHRISTMAS

Boxing Day is the British holiday that falls the day after Christmas. One of the ways it was celebrated by British troops in the field was that officers and noncoms exchanged jobs for a day. This grew out of the English custom of masters and servants trading places for the day. Colonel Potter thought that it would help morale at the 4077 if the tradition was adopted. So he became the company clerk while Klinger took over as CO.

"It's the only British tradition that's harder to swallow than mutton," sneered Charles.

"Sounds like Backwards Day in Hannibal...one year, a twelve-year-old boy got to be mayor for the day. He caught on real quick. By lunchtime, he was collecting play money for a nine-year-old on the building commission."

The switcheroo at the 4077 lasted for most of the day, until incoming wounded forced the doctors to revert to their own roles.

"You know, Beej," said Hawkeye, "that's what this country is all about. I'm about to perform critical surgery, and only an hour ago I was another nameless orderly scrubbing the floors."

FOLLIES OF THE LIVING— CONCERNS OF THE DEAD

Private James Weston died at the 4077 MASH early in 1953. His body was duly tagged and reported to Graves Registration, but his ghost lingered on, at least as seen by Klinger, who was delirious with a high fever.

"Look at this...he's giving me last rites...they're gonna stick me in a bag...stick me in a truck and that'll be it...can't anyone do anything about it? I don't feel dead...there's got to be a mistake...when they put me in the chopper, my company commander said I was gonna be all right...he wouldn't lie to me. I was in a lot of pain before. But look at me. I'm walking around here...I can talk...I think there's been a big mistake...I guess I'm really dead...it's over...but don't lose your sense of humor...it's not so bad. But I'm worried about my folks. I'd really appreciate it if you'd let them know it's all right. Do you hear what I'm saying? It's not that bad."

Twenty-four hours later, Klinger woke up in postop.

"Hi, Captain," he said to B.J. "What happened to that kid, Weston?"

"Who?" B.J. asked.

THE BIRTHDAY GIRLS

Margaret got R&R in Tokyo for her birthday and was all set to celebrate with a friend—a nice dinner, tickets to the Kabuki theater, and all the refinements of civilization. Klinger volunteered to take her to the airport at Kimpo.

"Where does that road go?" Margaret screeched at her driver.

"To Kimpo, like a barrel goes to the bottom of Niagara Falls. That road is full of rocks and potholes and..."

"If it's faster, take it." Margaret commanded.

Klinger took it, until the road took them, and their Jeep. Klinger pronounced it DOA—dead on its axles. Margaret stormed and fumed. "I wanted this year to be different, something that was special for me, to be with a person, somebody I chose, doing things I want to do. Is that too much to ask for one stinking day of the year? So look at me, sitting on the side of the road without so much as a birthday hat."

"There's a newspaper in the Jeep," Klinger volunteered. "I'll make you a birthday hat."

"I *hate* birthday hats!"

Klinger nonetheless shared his Scotch and offered Margaret a bran muffin with a match stuck in it as a candle. Margaret finally accepted them with the grace of a proper birthday girl.

"There are so many things I was sure I'd have in my life by now. Every birthday reminds me of what's still not there. This just turned out to be another day in the middle of nowhere."

BLOOD AND GUTS

Clayton Kibbee, the big-time war correspondent, came to the 4077 with a few pints of blood donated by some of his readers. He wanted to do an on-the-spot follow-up story of what happened to those very same six pints of blood. The first pint went to save the life of a careless GI who was taking a wild spin on a motorcycle. By the time Kibbee finished retelling the story for his readers, it was red, white, and blue — but not too true. Hawkeye was furious.

"Kibbee's writing an adventure tale that makes Korea sound like a Boy Scout jamboree. If he had his way, every subscription to *Boy's Life* would have a ninety-day trial draft card."

The next pint went into a man who took some shrapnel while fishing with hand grenades. He and his buddy lacked rods and reels, so they threw grenades into a pond, waited for them to explode, and the fish to float to the surface.

"Dateline Korea: 'GI injured in amphibious assault, fights off entire school of frogmen,' " Hawkeye quipped.

Disappointed in the lack of action his blood was getting, Kibbee took off for the front. He managed to crash the motorcycle he was using and needed the rest of the blood himself.

Potter read about it in Kibbee's column the next week. "As for the last two pints of blood, there's no big finale, no heroes. They helped an old soldier who'd had visions of glory but finally got it through his thick head how tragic and inhumane war can be. Maybe he'll know better next time."

A HOLY MESS

When Private Nick Gillis discovered that not only had his wife been unfaithful but that she had given birth to someone else's child, he went AWOL—and a little bit nuts. At first, he asked to talk to Father Mulcahy, but after services in the Mess Tent, he asked for sanctuary as well. That led Mulcahy—and the Army in the Far East—to explore the question of when a Mess Tent was a Mess Tent and when it was a church and, therefore, capable of representing sanctuary.

"Colonel," said Mulcahy, "I don't feel bound by military law in this matter but by sacred principles. The only person I'd answer to is the Command Chaplain at I-Corps. Until I hear from him to the contrary, Private Gillis will remain in sanctuary here."

When I-Corps ruled against sanctuary, Father Mulcahy suggested to Gillis that he return to his unit. Gillis grabbed a rifle and pointed it at Potter and the MPs who came to get him.

"How dare you?" asked Mulcahy. "You take refuge in this house of the Lord when it serves your purpose. Then when it's no longer convenient, you desecrate it by pointing a deadly weapon at another human being. Private, a faith of convenience is a hollow faith. Give me the gun."

Then Mulcahy lunged toward the man and pulled the rifle away. Private Gillis collapsed in his arms, in tears.

"I'm sorry, Father."

"I know," Mulcahy said gently.

THE TOOTH SHALL SET YOU FREE

Major Lawrence Weems was the worst kind of bigot. The sneaky kind. He seemed so concerned for his men when he stopped by the 4077 to see how the wounded were doing. Everyone was so impressed with him—everyone except his wounded. They knew they had been sent into high-risk situations.

One of his men was a Corporal Matthew Dorsey. Dorsey was a black man. He was not wounded severely enough to be sent home, but he pressured Hawkeye to fudge the papers a little, explaining that he was needed at home. When the corporal recovered, he told a different story about his home life. So different that Hawkeye became suspicious. Klinger got to work on the phone and came up with some answers.

"Only eleven percent of Weems's unit are Negroes, but they've suffered forty-six percent of the casualties."

"There were better odds in *Uncle Tom's Cabin*," remarked Hawkeye disdainfully.

Colonel Potter took over the situation to smoke out Weems's duplicity.

"Just because Truman desegregated the troops doesn't mean I like it," he said in casual conversation, dangling the bait.

"This Army hasn't been the same," Weems agreed. "Nobody tells me who I have to eat, sleep, and fight with."

Blood and Guts

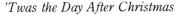

'Twas the Day After Christmas

Left:
Sons and Bowlers

Opposite:
The Tooth Shall
Set You Free

Opposite:
Blood Brothers

Promotion Commotion

"So you send 'em out for high-risk duty?" Hawkeye asked.

"That way they get more points and get rotated home faster," Weems explained with enthusiasm, "or they get wounded. We didn't ask for them to be here in the first place, right?"

When the conversation ended, they brought Weems to The Swamp for a drink, and to meet Major Quentin Rockingham, Assistant Deputy Chief of Staff for Personnel at I-Corps.

"I think you've stated your case with great eloquence," Rockingham said. "I'm sure the court-martial board will find it equally impressive."

PRESSURE POINTS

When Hawkeye had to reopen one of Colonel Potter's patients, the Old Man thought he was losing his touch. That happens to surgeons, especially as they pass the age of sixty. Potter was so shaken, he sent for Sidney Freedman.

"Who's the top secret patient you wanted me to see?"

"You're looking at him."

It took the sixty-two-year-old surgeon a while to get it all out, but finally Potter confessed his fears.

"Of course, you're afraid," Sidney assured him. "But you can't let the fear make your decision for you. I can't tell if you've lost your touch. Someday you will. Everybody does eventually. But whether that someday is today, you're the only one who can answer."

Incoming wounded interrupted further discussion, and Potter was off to OR. He took a deep breath then prepared to scrub.

"Okay, boys and girls. Let's get to work."

Potter was back to rough and ready.

WHERE THERE'S A WILL, THERE'S A WAR

B.J. went to Seoul for a haircut and a manicure. When the aid station called in for a surgeon, Hawkeye took his place. Heavy fighting brought the phone lines down, so when word came along that a surgeon had been killed at the aid station, everyone at the 4077 thought it was Hawkeye.

Actually, the reason he had to go in was to replace a dead man, but no one at the 4077 knew that at the time. Hawkeye wasn't having the time of his life, though. In fact, he expected to be dead soon.

"I, Benjamin Franklin Pierce, being of sound mind and endangered body, hereby decree this to be my Last Will and Testament. I bequeath to my father all my worldly possessions with the exception of the following: To Charles Emerson Winchester, though we may have wounded your pride, you never lost your dignity. I therefore bequeath to you the most dignified thing I own—my bathrobe. Purple is the color of royalty. To Father Francis Mulcahy, I leave five cents. You are a man of God, and I know worldly possessions mean little to you, Father. So I leave you a nickel along with something I value more highly than anything I own—my everlasting respect. To you, Margaret Houlihan, I leave my treasured Groucho nose and glasses. Perhaps they'll remind you of how much I enjoyed that silly side you show all too infrequently. To Sherman Potter, who's a lot like my dad, I leave *The Last of the Mohicans*, my dad's favorite book. I'd like you to have the copy he gave me. To Maxwell Q. Klinger, I leave the shirt off my back, not just any shirt, but my beloved Hawaiian shirt. To Erin Hunnicutt, I leave you a list of all the young men your daddy took care of while he was in Korea. Many of them have him to thank for being alive today. I want you to understand why he had to be away from you those first years of your life. I hope I have the chance to give you this list in person. But around here, you never know.

Benjamin Franklin Pierce

A corpsman interrupted Hawkeye as he was signing his name. "Good news for you, doc. I-Corps just called. They'll take you back to your unit now."

PROMOTION COMMOTION

Hawkeye, B.J., and Charles all sat on the promotion board, which was no secret to the enlisted men—especially those who were up for promotions. People suddenly got so nice it was disgusting. Except for Elmo Hitalski. "Nice" wasn't in his vocabulary. He just promised Charles a knuckle sandwich if he didn't get promoted.

Hitalski was not easy to promote. He did not get along well with others. In fact, he had a list of social problems. There was no way he would get another stripe.

Klinger, on the other hand, was also up for promotion and came out a sergeant. Hitalski came out with nothing. When he started to bust up the compound, Charles decided to deal with him. He gave the man Klinger's new stripe and explained that it came with a transfer.

"There's no new openings for sergeants in any units out here," hedged B.J. "So you're going back to the States."

The man left and Sergeant Klinger was on the phone to do his duty to God, country, and the scam.

"Hello, Kimpo? I want to report a man who's AWOL, dangerous, and impersonating a sergeant. Elmo Hitalski. He just busted up our Officers Club and threatened to do the same to a medical officer. He's carrying forged travel papers, and he's going to attempt to board the five o'clock flight to Toyko."

That was one way to get rid of trouble.

HEROES

Gentleman Joe Cavanaugh, the former middleweight champion, stopped by the 4077 on his tour of Korea and quickly proved to just about everyone that he was no gentleman. Then he had the poor taste to get sick and go into a coma—while the press stood around watching.

"We want to know a little about the doctor who's in the Champ's corner at the biggest fight of all," said one of the reporters, anxious to get some kind of story before the Champ bit the dust. "Where'd you go to medical school?"

"Absorbine Junior College," quipped Hawkeye.

Charles and B.J. were a bit offended by the attention Hawkeye got and the way he seemed to rise to it. Charles put it succinctly, "Everyone in this camp is sick to death of watching you throw yourself at those vultures."

"I agree with Charles," said B.J. Hawkeye just stared at him in disbelief. He might have said something nasty or even thrown a punch, but the PA announced incoming wounded.

B.J. drew a patient whose heart was "wiggling like a bunch of worms." To save the patient, he decided to try an experiment with electroshock that he had read about in a medical journal. Although it had only been tried with dogs, the patient was a goner anyway, so Potter gave the go-ahead.

"Klinger! We've got a little science project to work on and it's due right away!"

They rigged a light bulb, a socket, and an electrical switch with two wires that led to electrodes. They were attached under the patient. Then Klinger flipped on the juice. The patient's chest jumped twice and then his heart began its regular beat.

"You did it!" Hawkeye whooped with joy. Then he ran for the reporters to give them one helluva story.

No one cared.

SONS AND BOWLERS

After being soundly defeated in numerous sporting events by the Marines, Potter decided to put together a MASH bowling team. Potter, Klinger, and Hawkeye would be part of the team, but they lacked one member. Although Margaret claimed she was pretty good, no one would pay any attention to her because she had bungled the softball game the week before. Then Klinger discovered that the Marines had added a pro to their squad— Marty Ubancic, the Trenton Tornado. Before entering the service, he had placed third in the US Open Bowling Championships.

There was only one way the doctors could pull this one off—the same way they won that famous football game against the 325th Evac. With medical expertise. They gave the pro a tablet of methylene blue and waited for the necessary results.

"Thanks for the pick-me-up," said a grateful Ubancic.

"Hey!" Klinger said. "Whose side are you guys on anyway?"

"Believe me, Klinger, it does nothing for pep. It turns the urine blue."

The doctors then convinced Ubancic that he had a neurological problem that would be jeopardized with strain. When his CO insisted he bowl, Marty threw such light

That Darn Kid

balls that most of them went into the gutter. Margaret joined the team to replace Hawkeye—who was on the phone talking to his dad in a hospital in Portland, Maine—and had the pleasure of knocking the pins off the Marines. It seems that Marty had taught Margaret everything he knew on their date the night before.

PICTURE THIS

Potter decided to paint a portrait of the MASH gang for Mildred's birthday present, but infighting among the Swampmen made it impossible to pose the group together. Things got so bad that Hawkeye was grateful when Igor told him about a little hut behind Rosie's Bar that could be rented if things got too hot in The Swamp.

"I don't know," Hawkeye said. "Moving out of The Swamp seems a little drastic. I was thinking more along the lines of a murder/suicide thing."

Nonetheless, Hawkeye left The Swamp and took over the hut. Within twenty-four hours, things got worse. Hawkeye was lonely. B.J. was driving Charles crazy. Only Potter was happy. He figured out a way to paint the

Sons and Bowlers

portrait with two people posing at a time since he couldn't get them into a group.

"I'm sure the Last Supper wasn't this difficult to paint," said Mulcahy, "but then, the apostles were more civilized."

"I just hope I'm getting what this painting is really all about. The camaraderie, the affection we have for each other. Oh, I'm getting the bodies all right. I just wonder if I'm getting the souls. Maybe I bit off more than I can chew."

Old-fashioned teamwork, and some affection as well, sent various members of the group to the others with fictions that were meant to heal their split. Margaret told Hawkeye he had to come back because B.J.'s daughter had a kidney problem and B.J. had no one to share the problem with. Mulcahy told Charles to invite Hawkeye back to The Swamp because the chief surgeon had confessed to him his loneliness.

When Hawkeye moved back in, each person took credit for the fix, thus starting off another round of fighting. Potter unveiled his picture in an atmosphere of irony—the "still life" version on the wall was all smiles and good cheer.

THAT DARN KID

Klinger bought the goat from a departing farmer who had to sell his possessions in order to flee to the safety of the south. Good old Klinger. He saw dollar signs in his daydreams as he thought about all the fresh milk and cheese the goat would produce. Goat milk sold for a dollar a glass at the 4077.

Incoming wounded forced everyone into the OR. Hawkeye, as paymaster, had just begun to pay out salaries when the choppers arrived. He gave the remaining payroll to Klinger, who stored both the loot and the goat in his office. When surgery was over, the money was gone and the goat was still munching.

HQ did not believe that a goat had eaten the payroll, so they sent someone to investigate.

"A goat—just when you think you've heard them all," Major Van Zandt said to Hawkeye. "You signed for the money and the money isn't here. I don't care if you stole it or lost it, you owe the Army $22,000."

To convince Van Zandt that the goat really did eat the money, Hawkeye and Klinger "accidentally" allowed the goat to eat all of the major's reports. Van Zandt entered the tent just in time to see the last of the papers going down her gullet. He knelt by the goat and tried to pull shreds of paper from her mouth.

"You guys set me up," he wailed. "It's not going to work. Pierce, I'm going to make sure you get everything you've got coming to you."

"Great. You and I can play gin in the stockade."

"Well," Potter said, "you boys are the only ones who can get each other off the hook. If the goat had a previous record as a paper-eater by an authorized investigator and corroborated by a CO, then you'll both go free."

Hawkeye and Van Zandt shook on it.

YEAR TEN (1981–82)

NAME: SWIT, LORETTA
CHARACTER: HOULIHAN, MARGARET ("HOT LIPS")
RANK: MAJOR, USANC
SERIAL NUMBER: RA31619185

"Hot Lips changed a lot in eleven years. Initially, Margaret Houlihan behaved as though a man were the only thing that could complete her life, and she didn't see what richness her life contained. She gained a lot of self-esteem through the years, and she came to realize that what she did, what she offered, was valuable. To oversimplify it, I took each traumatic change that happened in her life and kept it. I didn't discard anything. I didn't go on into the next episode as if it were a different character in a different play. She was a character in constant flux. She never stopped developing.

"I mean, certain things had to remain the same. She had to remain one of the antagonists because that was the structure of the show. In the second season, we saw for the first time that she was unhappy with Frank and wanted more from her life. Then around the third or fourth year, in an episode called *The Nurses*, Hot Lips gave the nurses a speech telling them how lonely she was because she was in charge and that's the way it was, so she couldn't really have any friends. Her marriage and her divorce changed her. Her affair with Hawkeye in *Comrades in Arms* changed both characters, so that they were never really rivals again.

"Sometimes I would get letters from nurses saying how grateful they were that a nurse was finally being portrayed as a person, a caring human being. As far as the audience is concerned, I think it identifies with at least one or two or maybe all of us. We have become people to them and never caricatures. We're very real to them.

"I don't like it when people act like Margaret was the only character who went through big changes over the years. Yes, she came a long way. She had the most changes to make. When we started, she was a one-joke character. No actress could have played her that way. Around the second or third year, I decided to try playing her as a real person, in an intelligent fashion, even if it meant hurting the jokes. The first season, it was a struggle to find her character, she was so one-dimensional. Breaking up with Frank Burns mellowed her considerably, and the failure of her marriage made her self-reliant. She became more meticulous about choosing her company, and she became friendlier with people, for example, Hawkeye or B.J., with whom she used to be antagonistic. She could laugh more easily. She always used to be the brunt of a joke; then she enjoyed the jokes, was even part of them.

"The press and the public have fallen in love with all the changes Margaret made. They never stop to see that all the other characters changed a lot, too. Margaret's changes reflected a change in sexual stereotyping that I think was important and terrific, but I'm pleased with the incredible changes in Colonel Potter. He was a real Army type who became one of the boys. He turned into a father for me rather than a disciplinarian. Klinger stopped wearing a dress, for God's sake; Radar was a child-boy who left Korea a grown-up and mature person—and that was very exciting.

"Everyone glommed onto Margaret's changes and said, 'She's wonderful,' but what made this show work was that everyone evolved, everyone changed. Over the years, they changed the formula. Hawkeye stopped being a womanizer; B.J. changed. While he remained a totally devoted husband, he did have an affair with one of the nurses and had to explore a lot of things inside himself.

"We all worked on the 'what if' quotient. What if Hot Lips and Hawkeye did this and that; what if Klinger and Hot Lips got stuck together, what if.... There was always this smoldering thing going on. You wanted to know if Hawkeye and Hot Lips were left alone, would they tear each others' throats out or would they make love. He admired her qualities, and she was a very attractive woman. You couldn't conduct an eleven-year run without taking the opportunity to explore those possibilities...and don't forget that passionate good-bye kiss.

"We were all apprehensive after Year Four when Larry Gelbart left. We missed him throughout the rest of the show. I mean, there's nothing wrong with that. We had super people after him, but we were entitled to miss him, too. I think he loved us enough to be very secure about leaving. He left us in a position of being able to fend for ourselves. Our characters were firmly established by then. We were able to carry on.

"By the tenth year, Margaret had had the most traumatic experiences of any of the group. The most happened to her emotionally. She had that affair with Frank for all those years; then she got engaged and married and divorced and thought she was pregnant; she had the thing with Hawkeye; she went through various stages of becoming liberated. The big experiences in life are what we tried to show within our own basic situation.

"In Ten, we knew that Eleven would be the last of it. We talked about what happened to people on other shows when they ended it. We were not prepared for what happened in Year Eleven with the press, but we sat down then and discussed it so we could cope. We were bursting out—our cup runneth over. We had to leave the war; we had to leave Korea; we had to go home. There's no way to tell you what it was like. I just keep thinking about a song my friend Fred Ebb wrote, *It Was a Good Time*. All I wanted to do was sing that song, 'It was a good time/it was the best time/it was a party/just to be near you.'

"I don't think we ever repeated a joke in eleven years.

"Nobody had the attitude, 'Oh, it'll be okay.' Everyone worked until it was perfect. We treated it like something special. Always.

"Nobody was selfish. Nobody ever said, 'How am I coming out?'

"We got up each morning and went to work and did the best we could with what we had. The good time that showed up on screen was not pretense. The affection, the admiration, the respect for each other—and for the show and for the written word—were very real. We all cared about the joke and the tear."

Loretta Swit

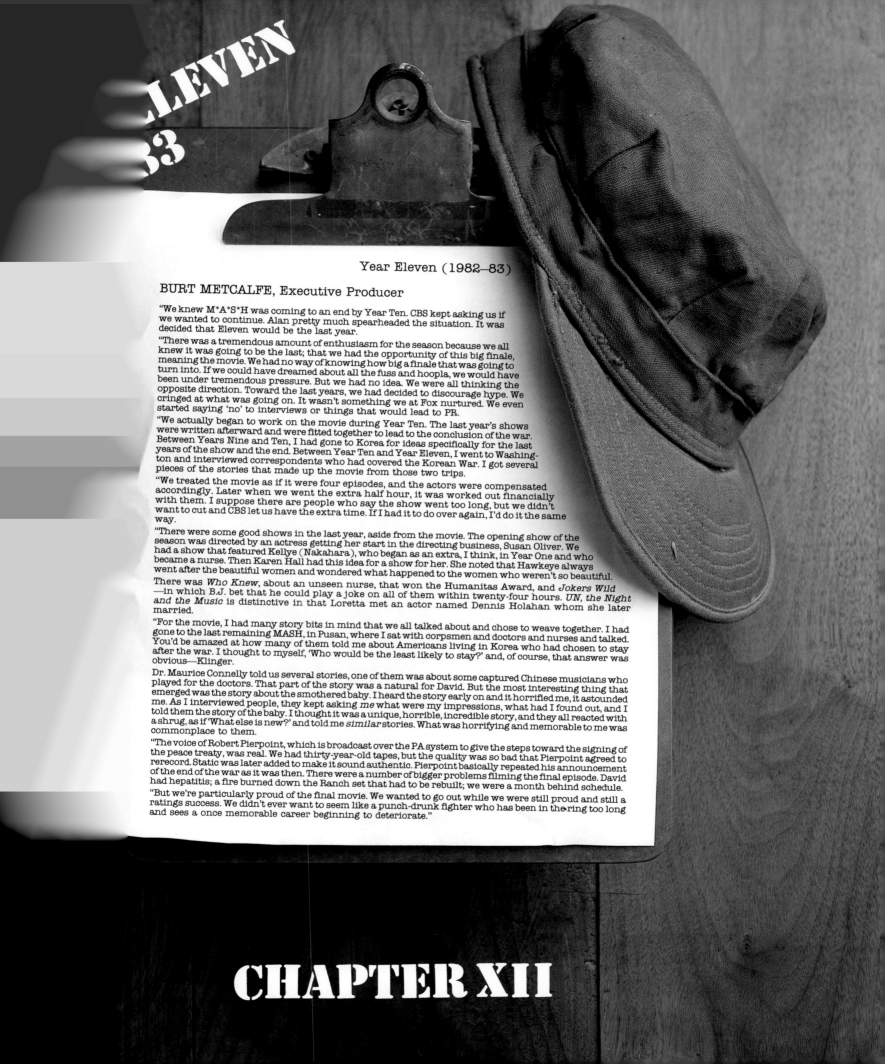

Year Eleven (1982—83)

BURT METCALFE, Executive Producer

"We knew M*A*S*H was coming to an end by Year Ten. CBS kept asking us if we wanted to continue. Alan pretty much spearheaded the situation. It was decided that Eleven would be the last year.

"There was a tremendous amount of enthusiasm for the season because we all knew it was going to be the last; that we had the opportunity of this big finale, meaning the movie. We had no way of knowing how big a finale that was going to turn into. If we could have dreamed about all the fuss and hoopla, we would have been under tremendous pressure. But we had no idea. We were all thinking the opposite direction. Toward the last years, we had decided to discourage hype. We cringed at what was going on. It wasn't something we at Fox nurtured. We even started saying 'no' to interviews or things that would lead to PR.

"We actually began to work on the movie during Year Ten. The last year's shows were written afterward and were fitted together to lead to the conclusion of the war. Between Years Nine and Ten, I had gone to Korea for ideas specifically for the last years of the show and the end. Between Year Ten and Year Eleven, I went to Washington and interviewed correspondents who had covered the Korean War. I got several pieces of the stories that made up the movie from those two trips.

"We treated the movie as if it were four episodes, and the actors were compensated accordingly. Later when we went the extra half hour, it was worked out financially with them. I suppose there are people who say the show went too long, but we didn't want to cut and CBS let us have the extra time. If I had it to do over again, I'd do it the same way.

"There were some good shows in the last year, aside from the movie. The opening show of the season was directed by an actress getting her start in the directing business, Susan Oliver. We had a show that featured Kellye (Nakahara), who began as an extra, I think, in Year One and who became a nurse. Then Karen Hall had this idea for a show for her. She noted that Hawkeye always went after the beautiful women and wondered what happened to the women who weren't so beautiful. There was *Who Knew*, about an unseen nurse, that won the Humanitas Award, and *Jokers Wild* —in which B.J. bet that he could play a joke on all of them within twenty-four hours. *UN, the Night and the Music* is distinctive in that Loretta met an actor named Dennis Holahan whom she later married.

"For the movie, I had many story bits in mind that we all talked about and chose to weave together. I had gone to the last remaining MASH, in Pusan, where I sat with corpsmen and doctors and nurses and talked. You'd be amazed at how many of them told me about Americans living in Korea who had chosen to stay after the war. I thought to myself, 'Who would be the least likely to stay?' and, of course, that answer was obvious—Klinger.

Dr. Maurice Connelly told us several stories, one of them was about some captured Chinese musicians who played for the doctors. That part of the story was a natural for David. But the most interesting thing that emerged was the story about the smothered baby. I heard the story early on and it horrified me, it astounded me. As I interviewed people, they kept asking *me* what were my impressions, what had I found out, and I told them the story of the baby. I thought it was a unique, horrible, incredible story, and they all reacted with a shrug, as if 'What else is new?' and told me *similar* stories. What was horrifying and memorable to me was commonplace to them.

"The voice of Robert Pierpoint, which is broadcast over the PA system to give the steps toward the signing of the peace treaty, was real. We had thirty-year-old tapes, but the quality was so bad that Pierpoint agreed to rerecord. Static was later added to make it sound authentic. Pierpoint basically repeated his announcement of the end of the war as it was then. There were a number of bigger problems filming the final episode. David had hepatitis; a fire burned down the Ranch set that had to be rebuilt; we were a month behind schedule.

"But we're particularly proud of the final movie. We wanted to go out while we were still proud and still a ratings success. We didn't ever want to seem like a punch-drunk fighter who has been in the ring too long and sees a once memorable career beginning to deteriorate."

CHAPTER XII

HEY, LOOK ME OVER

I-Corps had a strange sense of humor. They wanted to know how long it took to set up shop again after a bug out, so they decided to send someone to the 4077 to see how long it would take Margaret to get things running.

Margaret was almost hysterical.

She pushed the nurses harder than ever before, but no harder than she pushed herself. They worked day and night to restore order to a hospital that had fallen to chaos once the nurses retreated. The autoclave door had fallen off; medical instruments were covered in debris; dust lay in thick layers on top of the doors.

"Thanks to you doctors, I'm going to be thrown out of the Army because I don't know where my own equipment is," Margaret moaned.

When Colonel Beatrice Bucholtz—famous for her white glove inspections—arrived, Margaret was ready. Only Nurse Kellye was not on hand. She was sitting next to a dying man, holding his hand.

"Sarah? Is that you?" he called.

"It's okay," Kellye replied. "I'm here. It's Sarah."

"I'm scared, Sarah."

"Don't think about it. Think about the good stuff we'll do when you get better. We'll go on a picnic."

"That would be nice, Sarah. Bologna sandwiches with mustard on white bread. I feel better already."

Kellye learned over and kissed her patient's cheek.

Then he died.

Margaret passed inspection with flying colors, and Hawkeye realized how incredible all the nurses were.

TRICK OR TREATMENT

Any occasion to liven up the 4077 was a good occasion, so when Halloween rolled around, everyone was ready to party. B.J. made himself up as a clown, complete with false nose, baggy fatigues, and red suspenders. His big feet were perfect. Hawkeye chose to come as one of his alter egos—Superman—dressed in long johns with red boxer shorts and a handmade "S" crest on the chest. Before they even got to the party, a Marine—who had been celebrating early—became their first "trick or treater." He had a pool ball stuck in his mouth.

"Gadzooks!" said Charles, "Do you realize you have something in your mouth? I can't imagine what it could be. Oh, look! It has a little 9 painted on it. Could that be your age?"

Charles was all bedside manner when it came to dealing with drunken Marines.

"Attention, all personnel. Some party guests have arrived dressed as wounded soldiers."

One of the soldiers arrived with a toe tag. Toe tags are reserved for the dead, who are supposed to be separated from the wounded at the front. He was left lying in the compound awaiting last rites by Father Mulcahy, who was at a Halloween party at the orphanage.

Graves Registration arrived for the body and was about to take off in their ambulance when Mulcahy re-

turned. The padre climbed into the back of the truck, lowered the sheet from the body, and began the ancient words. He had just begun his prayers when he noticed a tear rolling down the cheek of the "dead" man.

"I can't believe Battalion Aid declared him dead," Mulcahy said.

"I wouldn't condemn those folks so fast," cautioned Potter. "They're moving out, all hell is breaking loose, and a man comes in with no pulse, no heartbeat, and more holes in him than a golf course. It's just the first time being dead wasn't terminal. Padre, welcome to the club. You saved a life."

FOREIGN AFFAIRS

The Army had this great technique for getting North Korean pilots to surrender their Soviet-made aircraft. They offered huge rewards to any pilot who would turn over his plane to the United States. Major Harlan Reddish, a public information officer, arrived from Tokyo to take charge of Hawkeye's newest patient—one Lieutenant Chong Wha Park—whom Reddish believed was the first such pilot to surrender.

"How does it feel to be America's newest war hero?" he asked the North Korean pilot.

When the man didn't respond, Reddish shouted his question at him. Potter had to intercede.

"He doesn't understand loud English any more than he understands quiet English. Better get someone to translate, son."

But Chong Wha was loyal to his team—North Korea. He was wounded, had landed his plane, and was taken to the 4077 for medical aid. He did not know about the $50,000 reward, nor did he care. He wanted to get back in his plane and go back to work—for *his* side of the war.

Chong Wha's interpreter, Joon-Sung, was very willing to go to America, claim the money, and become a hero. So he swapped clothing with the pilot. The pilot went to a POW camp.

"I think he'll make a great hero," B.J. remarked when the switch was completed.

"Yeah," Hawkeye agreed, "just so no one asks him to fly a plane."

THE JOKER IS WILD

When Hawkeye caught B.J. nailing his shoes to the floor, he was really miffed. He decided B.J. was jealous of his relationship with Trapper and was pulling childish pranks either to get attention or get even, since Trapper was well known as the king of the practical jokers. Not so, claimed B.J. and he bet Hawkeye that he could pull a joke that would catch Charles, Potter, Father Mulcahy, Margaret, Klinger, and even Hawkeye within twenty-four hours.

Over the next twenty-four hours, Hawkeye stayed on his toes, which did not have nails in them, and exhibited the most peculiar behavior. "I'm just staying one step ahead, Father," explained Hawkeye of his strange methods. "He's not going to get me."

It got so bad that B.J. was forced to admit that everyone else was in on the joke with him. The whole scheme had been to get Hawkeye to act paranoid while he was *waiting* for something to happen.

"It was quite fascinating to watch you turn into a basket case, not knowing where B.J. would strike next," Father Mulcahy admitted.

"So there you have it, Hawk. My greatest joke was the joke that never came!"

WHO KNEW?

"Take it from me," Hawkeye whispered as he returned to the tent late one night. "Milly Carpenter is quite a woman."

The next morning, Nurse Carpenter was found dead. She had gone for a late night stroll and stepped on a land mine. Hawkeye was asked to give the eulogy, since he had been dating her.

As he interviewed the other people in the compound, he couldn't find anyone who knew her well enough to give him information for his speech. Then Father Mulcahy turned over the woman's diary, and Hawkeye found some important lessons for himself and the others, as well.

"Milly Carpenter was twenty-seven when she died. Not many of us knew her well, and that's our loss because she was someone worth knowing. I didn't find that out myself until I read her diary. We thought she was kind of distant, unfriendly. In fact, she had a kind of awe for us for having done our jobs so well for so long. She would have told us that, but she couldn't. She was too shy to express her deepest feelings, so she wrote them in this diary.

"I'm a little like Milly myself. I cover up my feelings with jokes, and I don't tell the people I care about the most important thing I can tell them. That I do care. It's too late for Milly to change, and that's sad. Maybe we can all take a page from her diary to remind us of what we need to learn.

"To all the people here that I have sweated and endured with, you're very important to me. I hope in the future I do a better job of letting you know it. I love every one of you. Good-bye, Milly."

BOMBSHELLS

Rumors ran all over the camp on a regular basis. Above all, there was this rumor that the peace talks would amount to something. People who were bored enough, or hopeful enough, would grasp onto anything. That's how Hawkeye and Charles got into so much trouble when they casually began talking about Marilyn Monroe's impending visit to the 4077.

"Look," said Potter, smelling a rat, "I've been around long enough to know you can't believe everything you

The Joker Is Wild

hear. In World War I, we got word the war was over because Kaiser Wilhelm was entering the priesthood—he didn't."

Klinger's double-talk with I-Corps resulted in a double-talk version of an official confirmation of the Marilyn rumor, and before you could say *Some Like It Hot*, General Franklin Scherwin had heard the rumor and canceled his R&R so he, too, could be at the 4077 for the big moment.

"I wonder if General Scherwin can spell big words like 'dishonorable discharge'. . ." Hawkeye mused to Charles as the hot water got hotter.

Hawkeye saved them from the stockade by placing a long-distance call to an operator in Hollywood, who then sent a telegram.

Dear MASH 4077: Unavoidably detained in rushes. Stop. Filming schedule changed. Stop. Am unable to get away. Stop. Feel heartsick. Stop. Please give big, wet kiss to doctors. Stop. Kiss, kiss, love, love. Marilyn.

SETTLING DEBTS

Dear Hawkeye,

I've been setting aside my egg money every month. One day I checked the bankbook and, lo and behold, I had enough to buy the whole henhouse. I am enclosing the mortgage and would like you and everyone who's close to Sherman to give him a surprise mortgage-burning party. I'm sorry I can't be there with you to celebrate, but tell Sherman that while you're burning the mortgage, I'll burn the free calendar the bank sent us.

Yours very truly,
Mildred Potter

Hey, Look Me Over

Foreign Affairs

Bombshells

Who Knew?

Friends and Enemies

THE MOON IS NOT BLUE

After General Rothaker outlawed booze at the 4077, moviegoing became the prime source of entertainment. *Sahara* was getting dusty, so Hawkeye and B.J. decided to get some decent movies sent their way. When they heard that a new movie starring David Niven, *The Moon Is Blue,* had been banned in Boston, it became their prime objective. They went to Seoul to see Special Services.

"I'm Hunnicutt and this is Pierce," said B.J. "We're doctors, and your movies are making us sick."

"You want *The Moon Is Blue?* You've got to be kidding. That's the hottest property in the whole Far East. Now, beat it, babes! You bother me."

But Klinger's connections brought in the film. He happened to know the distributor in Tokyo and also knew that the distributor had a secret. "So I called him up and rattled the skeleton in the closet. Next thing I knew, he was sending us his best, *The Moon Is Blue.* It'll be in the mail in the morning in Seoul."

But Special Services in Seoul got the movie and wouldn't send it to the 4077. Hawkeye even had the labels switched with *State Fair.* To no avail. The movie said *State Fair* when it arrived, and to Hawkeye and Klinger's horror—*State Fair* it was.

You can't kid a kidder.

RUN FOR THE MONEY

It was another one of Klinger's crazy, get-rich-quick schemes. He read on the roster the name of an Olympic runner, who had been assigned to the 4077. Klinger suggested that they welcome the world-class, hundred-yard-dash man by challenging the 8063 MASH in a race. Naturally, no one else knew who the new recruit was, so Klinger expected to clean up.

There was just one hitch. When the man showed up for duty it turned out to be the father, not the speedy son. Klinger had overlooked the fact that his ace was a "junior." Dad was in no shape to run a race. He could barely carry his own duffel bag.

Father Mulcahy stepped in, but no amount of training—or prayer, for that matter—could make a world-class runner out of him. Mulcahy was so slow that the spectators felt sorry for him. The head of the 8063 was heard remarking to Colonel Potter, "Your priest is so slow, I think maybe his beads are weighing him down!"

However, just as with the tortoise and the hare, the race had a surprising conclusion. Suddenly, the 8063rd's contender ran out of gas and Father Mulcahy shot by him, coming in for a fast finish. Then he stopped short.

"I will cross this line only on one condition," he shouted to the crazed crowd. "All the winnings must be donated to the orphanage."

Angrily, the crowd agreed and Mulcahy finished first. His worthy opponent struggled over the finish line but still managed to give the padre a valiant wink.

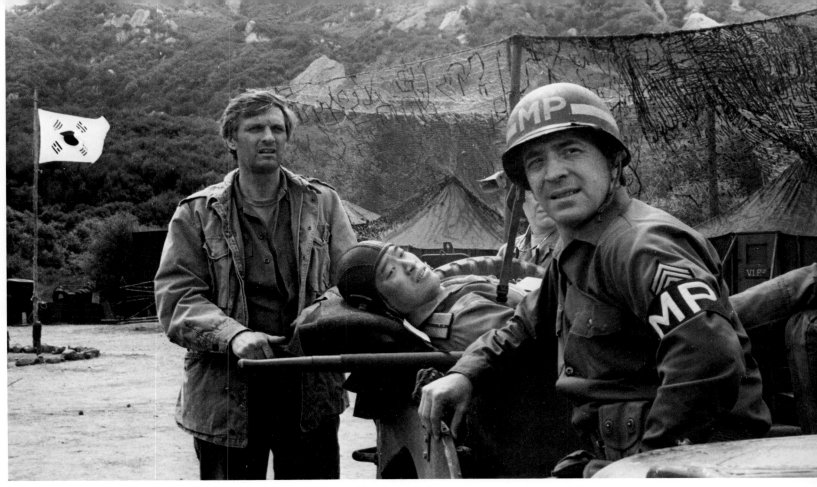

Foreign Affairs

"I suspect there's some cahootinizing going on," Colonel Potter said.

"Well," Father Mulcahy confessed, "he agreed to throw the race on behalf of the orphans. Thank God."

FRIENDS AND ENEMIES

Triage was in progress when Hawkeye spotted a seriously wounded soldier wearing the I-Corps insignia.

"What's a kid from I-Corps doing at the front? The only wounds those guys are supposed to get are paper cuts."

Beside the boy, on another litter, lay his CO—Colonel Woody Cooke, who was wounded in the leg. Cooke was an old friend of Sherm Potter's, and the two spent their spare time catching up on their lives.

The way Woody told his story, he was just an old Army pro going up to the front to straighten out a snafu with a fuel supply line. The way the rest of his wounded men told the story to Hawkeye and B.J., Cooke had ordered his men to hold an untenable position. Although their commander had told the men to keep clear of the ridge, when Cooke came up, and as he outranked the existing CO, he gave the men a direct order to hold the ridge.

"Why wasn't this reported to I-Corps," Potter asked the soldier, who repeated his story.

"What's the use?" the boy asked. "It'd just get whitewashed along the way by somebody who was a friend of Colonel Cooke's."

"Why didn't you report it here?"

Run for the Money

Run for the Money

As Time Goes By

Hey, Look Me Over

"For the same reason, sir." The boy looked away, but Potter got the message.

The next day, Potter tried to talk it over with his friend, but the man got up and left. A sad and sorry Potter made out his report.

UN, THE NIGHT AND THE MUSIC

Three international diplomats stopped by the 4077 on an inspection tour, each with a different sort of lesson to teach the MASH staff. One of them had a special effect on Major Houlihan.

Per Johannsen was a handsome, Swedish civilian delegate who got a warm welcome from Margaret. So warm, in fact, that he had to explain to her about his war wound.

"When I first came to Korea a year and a half ago, I was involved in an unfortunate accident. A Jeep in which I was riding drove over a land mine. I was wounded. Nerve damage has left me impotent. Believe me, I have often longed for the affection of a woman. This is the first time since I was hurt that I've let myself get so close to a woman. I'm sorry."

Margaret rose to the occasion. "You don't have to apologize. I'm the one who should be sorry for putting you in this awkward position."

"Then why don't we just say goodnight?"

"I'd really rather not. I'd like to stay a while . . . and talk."

"I just realized that shortly my roommate will be returning to the tent."

"No problem. Why don't we just continue the conversation in my tent. I have no roommates."

They walked off into the evening together, arms around each others' waists. Margaret had come a long way.

STRANGE BEDFELLOWS

Potter was thrilled when I-Corps gave a clearance to his son-in-law, Bob Wilson, to visit the 4077. He was in the Orient checking out some corporate business and, while in the neighborhood, just dropped by to visit the war. The two men sat up with the rest of the doctors for drinks and memories until Bob went off to the VIP tent and his father-in-law returned to his office, where he took a very strange call.

It seemed that the Imperial Hotel in Tokyo had discovered Mrs. Robert Wilson's silk nightgown in the room and wanted to know where to forward it.

"Mrs. Wilson can get a new nightgown," Potter said sadly into the phone, while he pondered the information he had received.

He called his daughter at home to make sure things were okay with her marriage and then approached the subject with Bob. He told him a little tale about his own bout with temptation to make his point quite clear.

"Nothing like this has ever happened before," Bob said, "if that makes it better. I love Evy and Stuart, and I

never meant to hurt them, or you either. I'd give anything if it didn't happen."

SAY NO MORE

Margaret gave herself a home perm and was on her way to the curls of her dreams when incoming wounded forced her into OR with the solution still on her locks. Hours of surgery with a wet head left her with a sore throat and a bad case of the flu. So bad, in fact, that she had to cancel her trip to Tokyo, where she was going to hear a lecture by Dr. Steven Chesler, the top authority on emergency care.

"The last I heard," Charles said in his usual manner, "the only things needed for lectures were ears."

"No," whispered Margaret, "Heard he was coming . . . wrote him how much looking forward to lecture . . . wrote me saying how impressed with my triage idea . . . hoped to meet me after. Me!"

When Chesler called Margaret at the 4077, her laryngitis was so bad she had to ask Charles to take the call for her. Chesler's plans had changed. He had to cancel his lecture and wanted Margaret to meet him in Seoul for a discussion at the hospital.

But her condition did not improve, and she had to cancel out. "He expects nurse . . . not frog," she whispered dismally.

The next day, the frog got a surprise visit from her prince. Dr. Chesler arrived at the 4077. Charles grinned like a Cheshire cat.

"Why are you here?" hissed Margaret.

"I couldn't refuse your invitation," the doctor said.

GIVE AND TAKE

Two patients on opposite sides of the war found themselves next to each other in the recovery room.

"I shot him," the American soldier said with some pride as he motioned to the North Korean soldier beside him. "We were ambushed. A bullet grazed my head and knocked me out. Next thing I knew, something was pulling at my feet. That bastard, he must have thought I was dead and was trying to steal my boots. Before he knew I was awake, I grabbed his rifle and let him have it."

"Congratulations," said B.J., sarcastically.

"What do you want us to do with him?" Hawkeye asked. "Have him stuffed and hung over the mantelpiece?"

Curiously enough, the men struck up a tentative friendship after Klinger gave the North Korean a candy bar and the North Korean gave it to the man who shot him. When the man died, no one was more upset than the American, who had been his enemy but had become his friend.

"My boots. All he wanted was my lousy boots. His feet were freezing. I'd have done the same thing. He was just a guy like me, and I shot him. I killed him. For a pair of boots. How can I ever look at a pair of shoes again without thinking of him?"

AS TIME GOES BY

Charles read about a time capsule buried in the cornerstone of a new Los Angeles skyscraper and thought it was so ludicrous he had to tell everyone about it. Margaret didn't think it was so funny. In fact, she liked the idea and decided to make her own time capsule to bury in Ouijongbu.

"We could put something in the ground to remind people we were here," she suggested to her cohorts.

"I thought that's what land mines were for," Hawkeye deadpanned.

Nonetheless, Hawkeye decided to help, and the two gathered together whatever meaningful odds and ends they could find: a broken fan belt from a chopper to symbolize the wounded and the manner in which they arrived; Radar's teddy bear to stand for all the soldiers who came over as boys and went home as men; a fishing fly that had belonged to Henry Blake to remind them of all those loved ones who did not return home; a bottle of Charles's cognac; Father Mulcahy's boxing gloves. "In the future, if countries feel the need to go to war, they can use these to settle it."

Above and right: As Time Goes By

GOODBYE, FAREWELL AND AMEN

Dwight David Eisenhower took office as president of the United States in January, 1953. One of his primary concerns was to end the war in Korea. He advised negotiators that terms that had been unacceptable to Truman would be acceptable to him.

In March, 1953, large prisoner exchanges began to take place, signaling that the two years of negotiations at Panmunjom had become a little more serious. At the beginning of June, the UN and the Communists reached agreement on one of the stickiest remaining issues of debate—the repatriation of prisoners of war. On July 12, the United States and the Republic of Korea announced that they, too, had reached agreement, thus paving the way to the final truce.

At 10 A.M. on July 27, 1953, men from each country that had fought in the Korean War signed the armistice. At 10:12 A.M., the job was finished. The war officially ended at 10 P.M. that night.

American troops knew the end was approaching by late spring. They hoped to be home by July 4 for a *real* Independence Day. The final weeks—and then days— were the most tense. So many North Koreans surrendered that UN troops did not know how to feed, clothe, or shelter them. Few wanted to be repatriated to a Communist regime. Fighting grew more fierce as the end drew near. More than ten thousand UN troops were killed while the final squabbling dragged on. Some of the most savage acts of the war were committed in the last weeks of fighting.

*   *   *   *

Dear Dad,

For the first time, I understand what a nervous disorder is because it seems I've got one. I guess I'll be seeing you soon since I doubt they'll let a surgeon operate whose cheese has slipped off his cracker.

Sorry I haven't written you for awhile, but I've been on R&R at this wonderful resort—The Seoul Old Soldiers Never Die They Just Giggle Academy. We're planning on having a bridge tournament here as soon as we can find someone with a full deck.

On the 4th of July, Colonel Potter decided to let several members of the 4077 take the day off for an old-fashioned celebration. They went to the beach at Inchon. Inchon was west of Ouijongbu, and most of the fighting was in Kum Song, to the northeast. It was a nice summer day and the beach trip seemed just the thing to break the tension.

On the way back to the MASH unit, the bus stopped to pick up some refugees. About a half a mile later, it stopped again, this time to pick up some wounded GIs.

"We gotta get this bus into the bushes," one of the GIs said. "There's an enemy patrol coming down the road. Everyone get quiet. Nobody make a sound until they've passed us."

The bus was hidden. Inside, everyone grew nervous.

Each person sat on the edge of his seat, quietly breathing the tense air; terrified that each breath might be his last. Suddenly, a refugee baby began to wail.

"Shhhh," Hawkeye hissed.

The child's mother was in despair. She could not quiet the baby. If its sounds attracted the North Koreans, everyone could be killed.

Soundlessly, the woman smothered her child.

*   *   *   *

Dear Dad,

I am doing better now. You remember Sidney Freedman? He's been here all week pulling shrapnel from my memory. I think the worst is over now. Remember when I was a kid, you told me that if my head wasn't attached to my shoulders, I'd lose it? That's what happened when I saw that woman kill her baby. A baby, Dad. A baby. But Sidney says that confronting the memory is half the battle. So I'm going back to the 4077. Sort of like the criminal returning to the scene of the crime. I asked them to send me to a foxhole in Crabapple Cove, but there aren't many foxes there—only lobster. So write me care of the war, Dad. Any place I hang my scalpel is home.

*   *   *   *

Pierce's hysterical breakdown was conquered once Sidney forced him to admit that he had actually seen the woman smother her child and not a chicken—as Hawkeye's tormented memory had "chosen" to remember it. Repressing the real memory had triggered his collapse. Tentatively, he returned to the 4077. He felt unsure of himself when he got there, worse when he discovered that B.J. had gone home without even saying good-bye.

"Is it the war that stinks or just me?" Hawkeye asked Margaret. "My best friend went home without so much as a damn note. Trapper did the same thing."

*   *   *   *

But B.J. never quite made it home. When heavy fighting made it impossible for his replacement to get to the 4077, Potter put in an urgent call to I-Crops for *any* surgeon they could lay hands on. B.J. was brought back.

"I got as far as Guam," he explained. "I'm sitting in this crummy Officers Club and a guy says, 'Are you Hunnicutt, the surgeon?' and I said, 'No, I'm Hunnicutt, the chaplain,' so he said, 'Well, chaplain, you better start praying for a miracle because you're going back to Korea to do surgery. . . . Sorry I didn't leave you a note, Hawk, but I didn't have time."

"That's okay," Hawkeye replied tartly. "I didn't even know you were gone. I thought you were in the bathroom."

Just as the end of the war was announced on the PA system, more wounded were brought in.

"Does this look like peace to you?" Margaret asked bitterly as she surveyed the scene.

In the OR, the doctors began to talk about what they would eat when they got home. It seems that all short-timers begin to think of food. B.J. wanted a big glass of ice cold milk; Hawkeye wanted a piece of chocolate cake; Potter wanted fresh corn on the cob.

Opposite (above and below) and overleaf: Scenes from *Goodbye, Farewell and Amen*

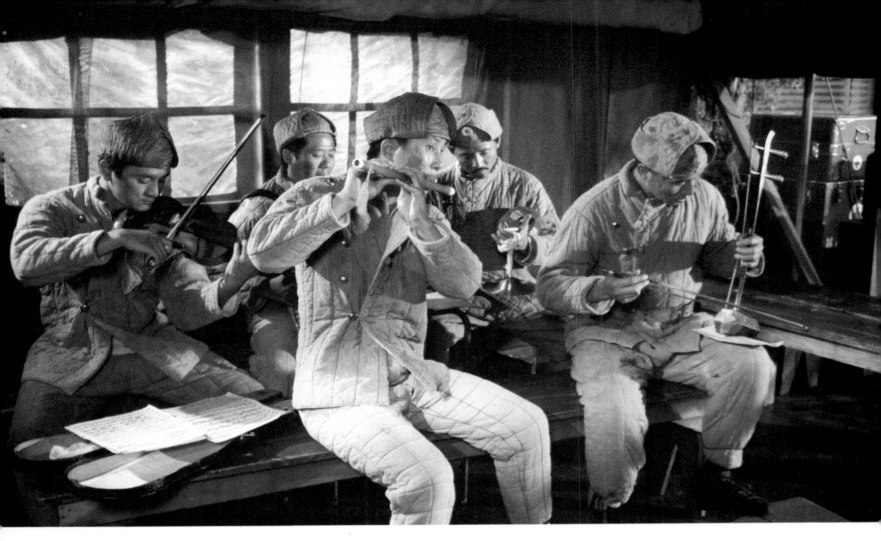

Above and opposite: Goodbye, Farewell and Amen

While Hawkeye had been away at the psychiatric hospital the 4077 itself had come under enemy fire. A tank had blundered into the compound like a wounded water buffalo and began drawing shells; Father Mulcahy ran out to release the POWs so they could escape the explosions and was knocked flat himself. It turned out to be only a mild concussion but Mulcahy found that he'd lost some of his hearing. He swore B.J. to secrecy so that he wouldn't be sent home, leaving his orphans.

Charles spent much of his time worrying whether he'd get the appointment he wanted as Chief of Thoracic Surgery at Mercy Hospital in Boston. To take his mind off things he taught Mozart's Quintet for Clarinet and Strings to a group of Chinese soldier-musicians who had surrendered to him one day when he was on his way to the latrine. In their fashion, they learned to play it quite well but when they were shipped out Charles returned to the surgery as his only diversion.

*   *   *   *

Surgery was interrupted by an announcement on the PA system requesting a surgeon for triage. Charles took off his rubber gloves and went outside. Wounded were being tagged in the traditional manner.

"What else do we have?" he asked the corpsman.

"This POW, sir. Part of his chest is blown off. He was in the back of the truck when it got hit."

Charles moved to the patient's litter. He checked the man's carotid artery first—then saw his face. It was one of his Chinese musicians—his eyes glassy and unfocused. Charles recoiled with horror.

"What happened to the others?" he asked numbly.

"He's the only one who made it this far," the corpsman reported.

It was, indeed, the end of the war for Charles Emerson Winchester III. "I've just discovered I'll be head of Thoracic Surgery at Boston Mercy Hospital. My life will go on as expected. For me, music had always been a refuge from this miserable experience. Now it will always be a reminder."

Yet there was a happy moment in the final melancholy. Klinger announced that he and Soon-Lee would marry. Soon-Lee was a Korean girl who had been brought to the 4077 a few months earlier when she was found holding a carbine and was accused of murder. She had been proved innocent and stayed on at the 4077 working as a translator. Now that they were getting married, Soon-Lee refused to go to Toledo until she found her family—dead or alive.

So Max Klinger, the most unlikely man in the world to stay in Korea, chose of his own free will to stay. Father Mulcahy married them; Soon-Lee wore Klinger's old wedding dress; Klinger wore the tuxedo that Hawkeye's father had sent over at the beginning of the war.

"Gee, two weddings," commented B.J. "One here and one in Toledo; one where you eat rice and one where you throw it."

"John Francis Patrick Mulcahy," the padre said. "Remember that name if you name any children after me."

Klinger and Soon-Lee left their "family" wedding in what Sergeant Rizzo described as a limousine. It was

the best he could do under the circumstances—an ox cart with a "Just Married" sign trailing a string of Klinger's old high heels.

The next day, corpsmen began to pack up the canvas for the last time, and the members of the 4077 began to ship out. The remaining wounded were trucked to the 8063 MASH. Father Mulcahy rode up front.

Margaret and Charles were going to share a Jeep to the 8063, but Margaret loaded it down with so much baggage that Charles didn't have any room.

"You stay with your belongings, Margaret," he suggested. "Sergeant Rizzo will find me another mode. I wonder, though, if you have room in all those things for one more item?" Then he gave her his treasured copy of Elizabeth Barrett Browning's *Sonnets from the Portuguese*, and kissed her hand before he boarded his own ride out—a garbage truck.

Potter decided to take Sophie for one last trot and arranged for his Jeep to pick him up at the orphanage, where he was leaving his horse.

"Well, boys," he said to Pierce and Hunnicutt, "it would be hard to call what we've been through fun, but I'm sure glad we went through it together. You always managed to give me a good laugh right when I needed it most. Never will I forget the time you dumped Winchester's drawers in the OR. 'Course, I had to pretend I was mad at you, but inside, I was laughing to beat all hell."

"We've been thinking about a little something to give you before you left," B.J. said.

"It's not much," said Hawkeye, "but it comes from the heart."

And the two men stood at attention and saluted their departing CO.

Then Hawkeye's chopper arrived. It was his turn to say goodbye.

"Look, Beej, I know it's tough for you to say good-bye, so I'll say it. Maybe we will see each other again. In any case, I want you to know how much you've meant to me."

The men hugged. B.J. drove off on his motorcycle. Hawkeye's "Huey" lifted off the chopper pad for its ascent over the Korean hills. As he looked down at the deserted 4077, Hawkeye smiled.

B.J. had left him a final message spelled out in stones;
GOOD-BYE

EPILOGUE

Nice war we had. Of course, every war has its cute things. World War II had nice songs. The War of the Roses had nice flowers. We've got booms, they had blooms. Actually, every war has its 'ooms. You've got doom, gloom, everybody ends in a tomb, the planes go zoom, and they bomb your room.

Benjamin Franklin Pierce, MD

The Korean 'Police Action'
June 25, 1950 to July 27, 1953
U.S. troops killed: 33,629
Wounded: 103,284
Captured or missing: 5,178
Communist dead: 1,347,000
Korean civilians killed: 400,000
Korean orphans: 100,000
Korean homeless: 3,000,000

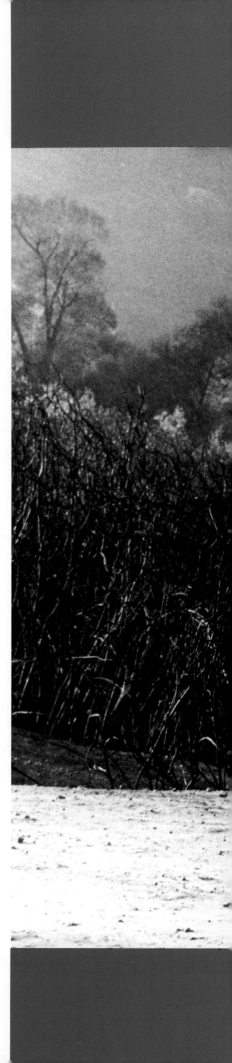

Goodbye, Farewell and Amen

Writers and Directors

Year One

M*A*S*H—THE PILOT
Written by Larry Gelbart
Directed by Gene Reynolds

HENRY, PLEASE COME HOME
Written by Laurence Marks
Directed by William Wiard

TO MARKET, TO MARKET
Written by Burt Styler
Directed by Michael O'Herlihy

GERM WARFARE
Written by Larry Gelbart
Directed by Terry Becker

THE MOOSE
Written by Laurence Marks
Directed by Hy Averback

I HATE A MYSTERY
Written by Hal Dressner
Directed by Hy Averbeck

CHIEF SURGEON WHO?
Written by Larry Gelbart
Directed by E.W. Swackhamer

REQUIEM FOR A LIGHTWEIGHT
Written by Bob Klane
Directed by Hy Averback

COWBOY
Written by Bob Klane
Directed by Don Weis

YANKEE DOODLE DOCTOR
Written by Laurence Marks
Directed by Lee Philips

BANANAS, CRACKERS AND NUTS
Written by Burt Styler
Directed by Bruce Bilson

EDWINA
Written by Hal Dresner
Directed by James Sheldon

DEAR DAD
Written by Larry Gelbart
Directed by Gene Reynolds

LOVE STORY
Written by Laurence Marks
Directed by Earl Bellamy

TUTTLE
Written by Bruce Shelly and David Ketchum
Directed by William Wiard

THE RINGBANGER
Written by Jerry Mayer
Directed by Jackie Cooper

DEAR DAD...AGAIN
Written by Sheldon Keller and Larry Gelbart
Directed by Jackie Cooper

SOMETIMES YOU HEAR THE BULLET
Written by Carl Kleinschmitt
Directed by William Wiard

THE LONG JOHN FLAP
Written by Alan Alda
Directed by William Wiard

MAJOR FRED C. DOBBS
Written by Sid Dorfman
Directed by Don Weis

STICKY WICKET
Written by Laurence Marks and Larry Gelbart; story by Richard Baer
Directed by Don Weis

THE ARMY-NAVY GAME
Written by Sid Dorfman; story by McLean Stevenson
Directed by Gene Reynolds

CEASE-FIRE
Written by Laurence Marks and Larry Gelbart; story by Larry Gelbart
Directed by Earl Bellamy

SHOWTIME
Written by Robert Klane and Larry Gelbart; story by Larry Gelbart
Directed by Jackie Cooper

Year Two

DIVIDED WE STAND
Written by Larry Gelbart
Directed by Jackie Cooper

RADAR'S REPORT
Written by Laurence Marks; story by Sheldon Keller
Directed by Jackie Cooper

5 O'CLOCK CHARLIE
Written by Larry Gelbart and Laurence Marks; story by Keith Walker
Directed by Norman Tokar

FOR THE GOOD OF THE OUTFIT
Written by Jerry Mayer
Directed by Jackie Cooper

DR. PIERCE AND MR. HYDE
Written by Alan Alda and Robert Klane
Directed by Jackie Cooper

L. I. P. (LOCAL INDIGENOUS PERSONNEL)
Written by Carl Kleinschmitt
Directed by William Wiard

KIM
Written by Marc Mandel, Larry Gelbart, and Laurence Marks
Directed by William Wiard

THE TRIAL OF HENRY BLAKE
Written by McLean Stevenson, Larry Gelbart, and Laurence Marks
Directed by Don Weis

DEAR DAD...THREE
Written by Larry Gelbart and Laurence Marks
Directed by Don Weis

THE SNIPER
Written by Richard M. Powell
Directed by Jackie Cooper

CARRY ON, HAWKEYE
Written by Bernard Dilbert, Larry Gelbart, and Laurence Marks; story by Bernard Dilbert
Directed by Jackie Cooper

THE INCUBATOR
Written by Larry Gelbart and Laurence Marks
Directed by Jackie Cooper

DEAL ME OUT
Written by Larry Gelbart and Laurence Marks
Directed by Gene Reynolds

HOT LIPS AND EMPTY ARMS
Written by Linda Bloodworth and Mary Kay Place
Directed by Jackie Cooper

OFFICERS ONLY
Written by Ed Jurist
Directed by Jackie Cooper

HENRY IN LOVE
Written by Larry Gelbart and Laurence Marks
Directed by Don Weis

FOR WANT OF A BOOT
Written by Sheldon Keller
Directed by Don Weis

OPERATION NOSELIFT
Written by Erik Tarloff; story by Paul Richards and Erik Tarloff
Directed by Hy Averback

THE CHOSON PEOPLE
Written by Laurence Marks, Sheldon Keller, and Larry Gelbart; story by Gerry Renert and Jeff Wilhelm
Directed by Jackie Cooper

AS YOU WERE
Written by Larry Gelbart and Laurence Marks; story by Gene Reynolds
Directed by Hy Averback

CRISIS
Written by Larry Gelbart and Laurence Marks
Directed by Don Weis

GEORGE
Written by John Regier and Gary Markowitz
Directed by Gene Reynolds

MAIL CALL
Written by Larry Gelbart and Laurence Marks
Directed by Alan Alda

A SMATTERING OF INTELLIGENCE
Written by Larry Gelbart and Laurence Marks
Directed by Larry Gelbart

Year Three

RAINBOW BRIDGE
Written by Larry Gelbart and Laurence Marks
Directed by Hy Averback

LIFE WITH FATHER
Written by Everett Greenbaum and Jim Fritzell
Directed by Hy Averback

SPRINGTIME
Written by Linda Bloodworth and Mary Kay Place
Directed by Don Weis

IRON GUTS KELLY
Written by Larry Gelbart and Sid Dorfman
Directed by Don Weis

PAYDAY
Written by John Regier and Gary Markowitz
Directed by Hy Averback

O.R.
Written by Larry Gelbart and Laurence Marks
Directed by Gene Reynolds

OFFICER OF THE DAY
Written by Laurence Marks
Directed by Hy Averback

THE GENERAL FLIPPED AT DAWN
Written by Jim Fritzell and Everett Greenbaum
Directed by Larry Gelbart

THERE IS NOTHING LIKE A NURSE
Written by Larry Gelbart
Directed by Hy Averback

PRIVATE CHARLES LAMB
Written by Larry Gelbart and Sid Dorfman
Directed by Hy Averback

A FULL RICH DAY
Written by John D. Hess
Directed by Gene Reynolds

CHECK-UP
Written by Laurence Marks
Directed by Don Weis

BIG MAC
Written by Laurence Marks
Directed by Don Weis

ALCOHOLICS UNANIMOUS
Written by Everett Greenbaum and Jim Fritzell
Directed by Hy Averback

HOUSE ARREST
Written by Jim Fritzell and Everett Greenbaum
Directed by Hy Averback

ADAM'S RIB
Written by Laurence Marks
Directed by Gene Reynolds

MAD DOGS AND SERVICEMEN
Written by Linda Bloodworth and Mary Kay Place
Directed by Hy Averback

THE CONSULTANT
Written by Larry Gelbart and Robert Klane
Directed by Gene Reynolds

WHITE GOLD
Written by Larry Gelbart and Simon Muntner
Directed by Hy Averback

BOMBED
Written by Jim Fritzell and Everett Greenbaum
Directed by Hy Averback

LOVE AND MARRIAGE
Written by Arthur Julian
Directed by Lee Philips

AID STATION
Written by Larry Gelbart and Simon Muntner
Directed by William Jurgensen

BULLETIN BOARD
Written by Larry Gelbart
Directed by Alan Alda

ABYSSINIA, HENRY
Written by Everett Greenbaum and Jim Fritzell
Directed by Larry Gelbart

Year Four

WELCOME TO KOREA
Written by Everett Greenbaum, Jim Fritzell, and Larry Gelbart
Directed by Gene Reynolds

CHANGE OF COMMAND
Written by Jim Fritzell and Everett Greenbaum
Directed by Gene Reynolds

IT HAPPENED ONE NIGHT
Written by Larry Gelbart and Simon Muntner; story by Gene Reynolds
Directed by Gene Reynolds

OF MOOSE AND MEN
Written by Jay Folb
Directed by John Erman

DEAR MILDRED
Written by Everett Greenbaum and Jim Fritzell
Directed by Alan Alda

THE LATE CAPTAIN PIERCE
Written by Glen Charles and Les Charles
Directed by Alan Alda

SMILIN' JACK
Written by Larry Gelbart and Simon Muntner
Directed by Charles S. Dubin

DEAR PEGGY
Written by Jim Fritzell and Everett Greenbaum
Directed by Burt Metcalfe

HEY, DOC
Written by Rich Mittleman
Directed by William Jurgensen

THE KIDS
Written by Jim Fritzell and Everett Greenbaum
Directed by Alan Alda

THE BUS
Written by John D. Hess
Directed by Gene Reynolds

QUO VADIS, CAPTAIN CHANDLER
Written by Burt Prelutsky
Directed by Larry Gelbart

SOLDIER OF THE MONTH
Written by Linda Bloodworth
Directed by Gene Reynolds

DEAR MA
Written by Everett Greenbaum and Jim Fritzell
Directed by Alan Alda

DELUGE
Written by Larry Gelbart and Simon Muntner
Directed by William Jurgensen

THE GUN
Written by Larry Gelbart and Gene Reynolds
Directed by Burt Metcalfe

MAIL CALL AGAIN
Written by Jim Fritzell and Everett Greenbaum
Directed by George Tyne

THE PRICE OF TOMATO JUICE
Written by Larry Gelbart and Gene Reynolds
Directed by Gene Reynolds

HAWKEYE
Written by Larry Gelbart and Simon Muntner
Directed by Larry Gelbart

SOME 38TH PARALLELS
Written by John Regier and Gary Markowitz
Directed by Burt Metcalfe

DER TAG
Written by Everett Greenbaum and Jim Fritzell
Directed by Gene Reynolds

THE NOVOCAINE MUTINY
Written by Burt Prelutsky
Directed by Harry Morgan

THE MORE I SEE YOU
Written by Larry Gelbart and Gene Reynolds
Directed by Gene Reynolds

THE INTERVIEW
Written by Larry Gelbart
Directed by Larry Gelbart

Year Five

BUG OUT (1 Hour Show)
Written by Jim Fritzell and Everett Greenbaum
Directed by Gene Reynolds

MARGARET'S ENGAGEMENT
Written by Gary Markowitz
Directed by Alan Alda

OUT OF SIGHT, OUT OF MIND
Written by Ken Levine and David Isaacs
Directed by Gene Reynolds

LT. RADAR O'REILLY
Written by Everett Greenbaum and Jim Fritzell
Directed by Alan Rafkin

THE NURSES
Written by Linda Bloodworth
Directed by Joan Darling

HAWK'S NIGHTMARE
Written by Burt Prelutsky
Directed by Burt Metcalfe

THE GENERAL'S PRACTITIONER
Written by Burt Prelutsky
Directed by Alan Rafkin

THE ABDUCTION OF MARGARET HOULIHAN
Written by Allan Katz and Don Reo; story by Gene Reynolds
Directed by Gene Reynolds

DEAR SIGMUND
Written by Alan Alda
Directed by Alan Alda

THE COLONEL'S HORSE
Written by Jim Fritzell and Everett Greenbaum
Directed by Burt Metcalfe

MULCAHY'S WAR
Written by Richard Cogan
Directed by George Tyne

HAWKEYE GET YOUR GUN
Written by Jay Folb; story by Gene Reynolds and Jay Folb
Directed by William Jurgensen

THE KOREAN SURGEON
Written by Bill Idelson
Directed by Gene Reynolds

EXORCISM
Written by Jay Folb; story by Gene Reynolds and Jay Folb
Directed by Alan Alda

END RUN
Written by John D. Hess
Directed by Harry Morgan

PING PONG
Written by Sid Dorfman
Directed by William Jurgensen

THE MOST UNFORGETTABLE CHARACTERS
Written by Ken Levine and David Isaacs
Directed by Burt Metcalfe

38 ACROSS
Written by Jim Fritzell and Everett Greenbaum
Directed by Burt Metcalfe

HANKY PANKY
Written by Gene Reynolds
Directed by Gene Reynolds

HEPATITIS
Written by Alan Alda
Directed by Alan Alda

MOVIE TONIGHT
Written by Gene Reynolds, Don Reo, Allan Katz, and Jay Folb
Directed by Burt Metcalfe

SOUVENIRS
Written by Burt Prelutsky; story by Burt Prelutsky and Reinhold Weege
Directed by Joshua Shelley

POST OP
Written by Ken Levine and David Isaacs; story by Gene Reynolds and Jay Folb
Directed by Gene Reynolds

MARGARET'S MARRIAGE
Written by Everett Greenbaum and Jim Fritzell
Directed by Gene Reynolds

Year Six

FADE OUT—FADE IN (1 Hour Show)
Written by Jim Fritzell and Everett Greenbaum
Directed by Hy Averback

FALLEN IDOL
Written by Alan Alda
Directed by Alan Alda

LAST LAUGH
Written by Everett Greenbaum and Jim Fritzell
Directed by Don Weis

IMAGES
Written by Burt Prelutsky
Directed by Burt Metcalfe

WAR OF NERVES
Written by Alan Alda
Directed by Alan Alda

THE WINCHESTER TAPES
Written by Everett Greenbaum and Jim Fritzell
Directed by Burt Metcalfe

THE LIGHT THAT FAILED
Written by Burt Prelutsky
Directed by Charles S. Dubin

TEA AND EMPATHY
Written by Bill Idelson
Directed by Don Weis

THE GRIM REAPER
Written by Burt Prelutsky
Directed by George Tyne

THE MASH OLYMPICS
Written by Ken Levine and David Isaacs
Directed by Don Weis

IN LOVE AND WAR
Written by Alan Alda
Directed by Alan Alda

CHANGE DAY
Written by Laurence Marks
Directed by Don Weis

PATIENT 4077
Written by Ken Levine and David Isaacs
Directed by Harry Morgan

THE SMELL OF MUSIC
Written by Jim Fritzell and Everett Greenbaum
Directed by Stuart Miller

COMRADES IN ARMS (Two Parts)
Written by Alan Alda
Directed by: 1st Part—Burt Metcalfe; 2nd Part—Alan Alda

THE MERCHANT OF KOREA
Written by Ken Levine and David Isaacs
Directed by William Jurgensen

WHAT'S UP, DOC?
Written by Larry Balmagia
Directed by George Tyne

POTTER'S RETIREMENT
Written by Laurence Marks
Directed by William Jurgensen

MAIL CALL THREE
Written by Everett Greenbaum and
Jim Fritzell
Directed by Charles S. Dubin

YOUR HIT PARADE
Written by Ronny Graham
Directed by George Tyne

TEMPORARY DUTY
Written by Larry Balmagia
Directed by Burt Metcalfe

DR. WINCHESTER AND MR. HYDE
Written by Ken Levine, David Isaacs,
and Ronny Graham
Directed by Charles S. Dubin

MAJOR TOPPER
Written by Allyn Freeman
Directed by Charles S. Dubin

Year Seven

COMMANDER PIERCE
Written by Ronny Graham
Directed by Burt Metcalfe

PEACE ON US
Written by Ken Levine and David Isaacs
Directed by George Tyne

B.J. PAPA SAN
Written by Larry Balmagia
Directed by James Sheldon

BABY, IT'S COLD OUTSIDE
Written by Gary David Goldberg
Directed by George Tyne

THE BILLFOLD SYNDROME
Written by Ken Levine and David Isaacs
Directed by Alan Alda

LIL
Written by Sheldon Bull
Directed by Burt Metcalfe

THEY CALL THE WIND KOREA
Written by Ken Levine and David Isaacs
Directed by Charles S. Dubin

OUR FINEST HOUR
(1 Hour Show; Black & White)
Written by Ken Levine and David Isaacs,
Larry Balmagia, and Ronny Graham
Directed by Burt Metcalfe

NONE LIKE IT HOT
Written by Ken Levine, David Isaacs,
and Johnny Bonaduce
Directed by Tony Mordente

OUT OF GAS
Written by Tom Reeder
Directed by Mel Damski

MAJOR EGO
Written by Larry Balmagia
Directed by Alan Alda

DEAR COMRADE
Written by Tom Reeder
Directed by Charles S. Dubin

AN EYE FOR A TOOTH
Written by Ronny Graham
Directed by Charles S. Dubin

POINT OF VIEW
Written by Ken Levine and David Isaacs
Directed by Charles S. Dubin

PREVENTATIVE MEDICINE
Written by Tom Reeder
Directed by Tony Mordente

DEAR SIS
Written by Alan Alda
Directed by Alan Alda

THE PRICE
Written by Erik Tarloff
Directed by Charles S. Dubin

HOT LIPS IS BACK IN TOWN
Written by Larry Balmagia and
Bernard Dilbert
Directed by Charles S. Dubin

INGA
Written by Alan Alda
Directed by Alan Alda

THE YOUNG AND THE RESTLESS
Written by Mitch Markowitz
Directed by William Jurgensen

RALLY ROUND THE FLAGG, BOYS
Written by Mitch Markowitz
Directed by Harry Morgan

AIN'T LOVE GRAND
Written by Ken Levine and David Isaacs
Directed by Mike Farrell

C*A*V*E
Written by Larry Balmagia and Ronny
Graham
Directed by William Jurgensen

A NIGHT AT ROSIE'S
Written by Ken Levine and David Isaacs
Directed by Burt Metcalfe

THE PARTY
Written by Burt Metcalfe and Alan Alda
Directed by Burt Metcalfe

Year Eight

TOO MANY COOKS
Written by Dennis Koenig
Directed by Charles S. Dubin

ARE YOU NOW, MARGARET
Written by Thad Mumford and Dan Wilcox
Directed by Charles S. Dubin

GUERILLA MY DREAMS
Written by Bob Colleary
Directed by Alan Alda

PRIVATE FINANCE
Written by Dennis Koenig
Directed by Charles S. Dubin

MR. AND MRS. WHO
Written by Ronny Graham
Directed by Burt Metcalfe

GOOD-BYE RADAR (Part 1)
Written by Ken Levine and David Isaacs
Directed by Charles S. Dubin

GOOD-BYE RADAR (Part 2)
Written by Ken Levine and David Isaacs
Directed by Charles S. Dubin

PERIOD OF ADJUSTMENT
Written by Jim Mulligan and John
Rappaport
Directed by Charles S. Dubin

THE YALU BRICK ROAD
Written by Mike Farrell
Directed by Charles S. Dubin

NURSE DOCTOR
Written by Sy Rosen, Thad Mumford and
Dan Wilcox; story by Sy Rosen
Directed by Charles S. Dubin

LIFE TIME
Written by Alan Alda and Walter D.
Dishell, MD
Directed by Alan Alda

DREAMS
Written by Alan Alda; story by Alan Alda
and James Jay Rubinfier
Directed by Alan Alda

DEAR UNCLE ABDUL
Written by John Rappaport and Jim
Mulligan
Directed by William Jurgensen

CAPTAINS OUTRAGEOUS
Written by Thad Mumford and Dan Wilcox
Directed by Burt Metcalfe

STARS AND STRIPE
Written by Dennis Koenig
Directed by Harry Morgan

HEAL THYSELF
Written by Dennis Koenig; story by Dennis
Koenig and Gene Reynolds
Directed by Mike Farrell

YESSIR, THAT'S OUR BABY
Written by Jim Mulligan
Directed by Alan Alda

BOTTLE FATIGUE
Written by Thad Mumford and Dan Wilcox
Directed by Burt Metcalfe

MORALE VICTORY
Written by John Rappaport
Directed by Charles S. Dubin

OLD SOLDIERS
Written by Dennis Koenig
Directed by Charles S. Dubin

LEND A HAND
Written by Alan Alda
Directed by Alan Alda

GOODBYE, CRUEL WORLD
Written by Thad Mumford and Dan Wilcox
Directed by Charles S. Dubin

APRIL FOOLS
Written by Dennis Koenig
Directed by Charles S. Dubin

WAR CO-RESPONDENT
Written by Mike Farrell
Directed by Mike Farrell

BACK PAY
Written by Thad Mumford, Dan Wilcox, and
Dennis Koenig
Directed by Burt Metcalfe

Year Nine

THE BEST OF ENEMIES
Written by Sheldon Bull
Directed by Charles S. Dubin

CEMENTING RELATIONSHIPS
Written by David Pollock and Elias Davis
Directed by Charles S. Dubin

NO SWEAT
Written by John Rappaport
Directed by Burt Metcalfe

LETTERS
Written by Dennis Koenig
Directed by Charles S. Dubin

FATHER'S DAY
Written by Karen L. Hall
Directed by Alan Alda

YOUR RETENTION PLEASE
Written by Erik Tarloff
Directed by Charles S. Dubin

TAKING THE FIFTH
Written by Elias Davis and David Pollock
Directed by Charles S. Dubin

DEATH TAKES A HOLIDAY
Written by Mike Farrell
Directed by Mike Farrell

A WAR FOR ALL SEASONS
Written by Dan Wilcox and Thad Mumford
Directed by Burt Metcalfe

TELL IT TO THE MARINES
Written by Hank Bradford
Directed by Harry Morgan

DEPRESSING NEWS
Written by Dan Wilcox and Thad Mumford
Directed by Alan Alda

OPERATION FRIENDSHIP
Written by Dennis Koenig
Directed by Rena Down

NO LAUGHING MATTER
Written by Elias Davis and David Pollock
Directed by Burt Metcalfe

OH, HOW WE DANCED
Written by John Rappaport
Directed by Burt Metcalfe

BOTTOMS UP
Written by Dennis Koenig
Directed by Alan Alda

THE RED/WHITE BLUES
Written by David Pollock and Elias Davis
Directed by Gabriel Beaumont

BLESS YOU, HAWKEYE
Written by Dan Wilcox and Thad Mumford
Directed by Nell Cox

THE LIFE YOU SAVE
Written by John Rappaport and Alan Alda
Directed by Alan Alda

BLOOD BROTHERS
Written by Elias Davis and David Pollock
Directed by Harry Morgan

THE FORESIGHT SAGA
Written by David Pollock and Elias Davis
Directed by Charles S. Dubin

Year Ten

THAT'S SHOW BIZ—PART 1
Written by Elias Davis and David Pollock
Directed by Charles S. Dubin

THAT'S SHOW BIZ—PART 2
Written by Elias Davis and David Pollock
Directed by Charles S. Dubin

IDENTITY CRISIS
Written by Dan Wilcox and Thad Mumford
Directed by David Ogden Stiers

RUMOR AT THE TOP
Written by David Pollock and Elias Davis
Directed by Charles S. Dubin

GIVE 'EM HELL, HAWKEYE
Written by Dennis Koenig
Directed by Charles S. Dubin

WHEELERS AND DEALERS
Written by Dan Wilcox and Thad Mumford
Directed by Charles S. Dubin

COMMUNICATION BREAKDOWN
Written by Karen L. Hall
Directed by Alan Alda

SNAP JUDGMENT/SNAPPIER JUDGMENT—
PART 1
Written by Paul Perlove
Directed by Hy Averback

SNAP JUDGMENT/SNAPPIER JUDGMENT—
PART 2
Written by Paul Perlove
Directed by Hy Averback

'TWAS THE DAY AFTER CHRISTMAS
Written by David Pollock and Elias Davis
Directed by Burt Metcalfe

FOLLIES OF THE LIVING—CONCERNS OF
THE DEAD
Written by Alan Alda
Directed by Alan Alda

THE BIRTHDAY GIRLS
Written by Karen L. Hall
Directed by Charles S. Dubin

BLOOD AND GUTS
Written by Lee H. Grant
Directed by Charles S. Dubin

A HOLY MESS
Written by Elias Davis and David Pollock
Directed by Burt Metcalfe

THE TOOTH SHALL SET YOU FREE
Written by Elias Davis and David Pollock
Directed by Charles S. Dubin

PRESSURE POINTS
Written by David Pollock
Directed by Charles S. Dubin

WHERE THERE'S A WILL, THERE'S A WAR
Written by Elias Davis and David Pollock
Directed by Alan Alda

PROMOTION COMMOTION
Written by Dennis Koenig
Directed by Charles S. Dubin

HEROES
Written by Thad Mumford and Dan Wilcox
Directed by Nell Cox

SONS AND BOWLERS
Written by Elias Davis and David Pollock
Directed by Hy Averback

PICTURE THIS
Written by Karen L. Hall
Directed by Burt Metcalfe

THAT DARN KID
Written by Karen L. Hall
Directed by David Ogden Stiers

Year Eleven

HEY, LOOK ME OVER
Written by Alan Alda
Directed by Susan Oliver

TRICK OR TREATMENT
Written by Dennis Koenig
Directed by Charles S. Dubin

FOREIGN AFFAIRS
Written by David Pollock and Elias Davis
Directed by Charles S. Dubin

THE JOKER IS WILD
Written by John Rappaport and Dennis
Koenig
Directed by Burt Metcalfe

WHO KNEW?
Written by David Pollock and Elias Davis
Directed by Harry Morgan

BOMBSHELLS
Written by Dan Wilcox and Thad Mumford
Directed by Charles S. Dubin

SETTLING DEBTS
Written by Dan Wilcox and Thad Mumford
Directed by Mike Switzer

THE MOON IS NOT BLUE
Written by Larry Balmagia
Directed by Charles S. Dubin

RUN FOR THE MONEY
Written by Mike Farrell, David Pollock, and
Elias Davis
Directed by Nell Cox

FRIENDS AND ENEMIES
Written by Karen L. Hall
Directed by Jamie Farr

UN, THE NIGHT AND THE MUSIC
Written by David Pollock and Elias Davis
Directed by Harry Morgan

STRANGE BEDFELLOWS
Written by Mike Farrell
Directed by Karen L. Hall

SAY NO MORE
Written by John Rappaport
Directed by Charles S. Dubin

GIVE AND TAKE
Written by Dennis Koenig
Directed by Charles S. Dubin

AS TIME GOES BY
Written by Dan Wilcox and Thad Mumford
Directed by Burt Metcalfe

The Final 2½-Hour Special

GOODBYE, FAREWELL AND AMEN
Written by Alan Alda, Burt Metcalfe, John
Rappaport, Thad Mumford, Dan Wilcox,
David Pollock, Elias Davis, and Karen Hall
Directed by Alan Alda

Awards and Nominations   •DENOTES WINNERS

1973

Academy of Television Arts and Sciences—Emmy Awards
OUTSTANDING COMEDY SERIES
—Gene Reynolds, Producer

OUTSTANDING NEW SERIES
—Gene Reynolds, Producer

OUTSTANDING CONTINUING PERFORMANCE BY AN ACTOR IN A LEADING ROLE IN A COMEDY SERIES—Alan Alda

OUTSTANDING PERFORMANCE BY AN ACTOR IN A SUPPORTING ROLE IN COMEDY —Gary Burghoff

OUTSTANDING PERFORMANCE BY AN ACTOR IN A SUPPORTING ROLE IN COMEDY —McLean Stevenson

OUTSTANDING DIRECTORIAL ACHIEVEMENT IN COMEDY—Gene Reynolds, M*A*S*H Pilot

OUTSTANDING WRITING ACHIEVEMENT IN COMEDY—Larry Gelbart, M*A*S*H Pilot

OUTSTANDING ACHIEVEMENT IN FILM EDITING FOR ENTERTAINMENT PROGRAMMING
—Stanford Tischler and Fred W. Berger

Hollywood Foreign Press Association—Golden Globe Awards
BEST COMEDY SHOW—M*A*S*H

BEST ACTOR IN A COMEDY OR MUSICAL —Alan Alda

Directors' Guild Awards
• GENE REYNOLDS—M*A*S*H Pilot

Writers' Guild Awards
• Teleplay by LARRY GELBART, "Chief Surgeon Who?"

American Cinema Editors —Eddie Awards
• FRED W. BERGER—"Bananas, Crackers & Nuts"

STANFORD TISCHLER—M*A*S*H Pilot

1974

Academy of Television Arts and Sciences—Emmy Awards
• OUTSTANDING COMEDY SERIES
—Gene Reynolds and Larry Gelbart, Producers

• OUTSTANDING LEAD ACTOR IN A COMEDY SERIES—Alan Alda

• ACTOR OF THE YEAR—SERIES—Alan Alda

OUTSTANDING SUPPORTING ACTOR IN COMEDY—Gary Burghoff

OUTSTANDING SUPPORTING ACTOR IN COMEDY—McLean Stevenson

OUTSTANDING SUPPORTING ACTRESS IN COMEDY—Loretta Swit

• OUTSTANDING DIRECTING IN COMEDY —Jackie Cooper, "Carry On, Hawkeye"

OUTSTANDING DIRECTING IN COMEDY —Gene Reynolds, "Deal Me Out"

OUTSTANDING WRITING IN COMEDY —Linda Bloodworth and Mary Kay Place, "Hot Lips and Empty Arms"

OUTSTANDING WRITING IN COMEDY —McLean Stevenson, "The Trial of Henry Blake"

OUTSTANDING FILM EDITING FOR ENTERTAINMENT PROGRAMMING —Stanford Tischler and Fred W. Berger

Hollywood Foreign Press Association—Golden Globe Awards
BEST ACTOR IN A COMEDY OR MUSICAL —Alan Alda

BEST SUPPORTING ACTRESS IN A TELEVISION SHOW—Loretta Swit

Directors' Guild Awards
GENE REYNOLDS—"Deal Me Out"

Writers' Guild Awards
Teleplay by BERNARD DELBERT, LARRY GELBART, and LAURENCE MARKS; Story by BERNARD DELBERT, "Carry On, Hawkeye"

Teleplay by LARRY GELBART and LAURENCE MARKS, "The Incubator"

Teleplay by LAURENCE MARKS; Story by SHELDON KELLER, "Radar's Report"

Teleplay by CARL KLEINSCHMITT, "Sometimes You Hear the Bullet"

Teleplay by BRUCE SHELLY and DAVID KETCHUM, "Tuttle"

American Cinema Editors —Eddie Awards
• FRED W. BERGER and STANFORD TISCHLER, "The Trial of Henry Blake"

1975

Academy of Television Arts and Sciences—Emmy Awards
OUTSTANDING COMEDY SERIES
—Gene Reynolds and Larry Gelbart, Producers

OUTSTANDING LEAD ACTOR IN A COMEDY SERIES—Alan Alda

OUTSTANDING CONTINUING PERFORMANCE BY A SUPPORTING ACTOR IN A COMEDY SERIES—Gary Burghoff

OUTSTANDING CONTINUING PERFORMANCE BY A SUPPORTING ACTOR IN A COMEDY SERIES—McLean Stevenson

OUTSTANDING SINGLE PERFORMANCE BY A SUPPORTING ACTOR IN A COMEDY OR DRAMA SERIES—Harry Morgan, "The General Flipped at Dawn"

OUTSTANDING CONTINUING PERFORMANCE BY A SUPPORTING ACTRESS IN A COMEDY SERIES—Loretta Swit

• OUTSTANDING DIRECTING IN A COMEDY SERIES—Gene Reynolds, "O.R."

OUTSTANDING DIRECTING IN A COMEDY SERIES—Hy Averback, "Alcoholics Unanimous"

OUTSTANDING DIRECTING IN A COMEDY SERIES—Alan Alda, "Bulletin Board"

OUTSTANDING ACHIEVEMENT IN CINEMATOGRAPHY FOR ENTERTAINMENT PROGRAMMING FOR A SERIES —William Jurgensen, "Bombed"

OUTSTANDING FILM EDITING FOR ENTERTAINMENT PROGRAMMING FOR A SERIES —Stanford Tischler and Fred W. Berger, "The General Flipped at Dawn"

People's Choice Awards
• FAVORITE MALE TELEVISION PERFORMER —Alan Alda (Tie with Telly Savalas)

Hollywood Foreign Press Association—Golden Globe Awards
• BEST ACTOR IN A COMEDY OR MUSICAL —Alan Alda

Directors' Guild Awards
HY AVERBACK, "Alcoholics Unanimous"

Writers' Guild Awards
• Teleplay by LARRY GELBART and LAURENCE MARKS, "O.R."

Teleplay by SID DORFMAN, "Private Charles Lamb"

American Cinema Editors —Eddie Awards
• FRED W. BERGER and STANFORD TISCHLER, "A Full Rich Day"

1976

Academy of Television Arts and Sciences—Emmy Awards
OUTSTANDING COMEDY SERIES
—Gene Reynolds and Larry Gelbart

OUTSTANDING LEAD ACTOR IN A COMEDY SERIES—Alan Alda

OUTSTANDING CONTINUING PERFORMANCE BY A SUPPORTING ACTOR IN A COMEDY SERIES—Gary Burghoff

OUTSTANDING CONTINUING PERFORMANCE BY A SUPPORTING ACTOR IN A COMEDY SERIES—Harry Morgan

OUTSTANDING CONTINUING PERFORMANCE BY A SUPPORTING ACTRESS IN A COMEDY SERIES—Loretta Swit

• OUTSTANDING DIRECTING IN A COMEDY SERIES —Gene Reynolds, "Welcome to Korea"

OUTSTANDING DIRECTING IN A COMEDY SERIES—Alan Alda, "The Kids"

OUTSTANDING WRITING IN A COMEDY SERIES —Larry Gelbart and Gene Reynolds

OUTSTANDING WRITING IN A COMEDY SERIES —Larry Gelbart and Simon Muntner, "Hawkeye"

OUTSTANDING ACHIEVEMENT IN CINEMATOGRAPHY FOR ENTERTAINMENT PROGRAMMING FOR A SERIES —William Jurgensen, "Hawkeye"

• OUTSTANDING FILM EDITING FOR ENTERTAINMENT PROGRAMMING FOR A SERIES —Stanford Tischler and Fred W. Berger, "Welcome to Korea"

People's Choice Awards
FAVORITE TELEVISION COMEDY PROGRAM —M*A*S*H

FAVORITE MALE TELEVISION PERFORMER —Alan Alda

Hollywood Foreign Press Association—Golden Globe Awards
• BEST ACTOR IN A COMEDY OR MUSICAL —Alan Alda

Directors' Guild Awards
HY AVERBACK, "Bombed"

Writers' Guild Awards
Teleplay by LAURENCE MARKS, "Big Mac"

• Teleplay by EVERETT GREENBAUM and JIM FRITZELL and LARRY GELBART, "Welcome to Korea"

American Cinema Editors —Eddie Awards
• FRED W. BERGER and STANFORD TISCHLER— "Welcome to Korea"

The George Foster Peabody Awards
• FOR BROADCAST EXCELLENCE—M*A*S*H

1977

Academy of Television Arts and Sciences—Emmy Awards
OUTSTANDING COMEDY SERIES
—Gene Reynolds, Executive Producer; Allan Katz, Don Reo, and Burt Metcalfe, Producers

OUTSTANDING LEAD ACTOR IN A COMEDY SERIES—Alan Alda

• OUTSTANDING CONTINUING PERFORMANCE BY A SUPPORTING ACTOR IN A COMEDY SERIES—Gary Burghoff

OUTSTANDING CONTINUING PERFORMANCE BY A SUPPORTING ACTOR IN A COMEDY SERIES—Harry Morgan

OUTSTANDING CONTINUING PERFORMANCE BY A SUPPORTING ACTRESS IN A COMEDY SERIES—Loretta Swit

• OUTSTANDING DIRECTING IN A COMEDY SERIES—Alan Alda, "Dear Sigmund"

OUTSTANDING DIRECTING IN A COMEDY SERIES—Joan Darling, "The Nurses"

OUTSTANDING DIRECTING IN A COMEDY SERIES—Alan Rafkin, "Lt. Radar O'Reilly"

OUTSTANDING WRITING IN A COMEDY SERIES —Alan Alda, "Dear Sigmund"

OUTSTANDING CINEMATOGRAPHY IN ENTERTAINMENT PROGRAMMING FOR A SERIES—William Jurgensen, "Dear Sigmund"

OUTSTANDING FILM EDITING IN A COMEDY SERIES—Samuel E. Beetley and Stanford Tischler, "Dear Sigmund"

People's Choice Awards
FAVORITE TELEVISION COMEDY PROGRAM —M*A*S*H

FAVORITE MALE TELEVISION PERFORMER —Alan Alda

Hollywood Foreign Press Association—Golden Globe Awards
BEST TELEVISION SERIES COMEDY OR MUSICAL—M*A*S*H

BEST ACTOR IN A COMEDY OR MUSICAL —Alan Alda

Directors' Guild Awards
• ALAN ALDA, "Dear Sigmund"

Writers' Guild Awards
• Teleplay by ALAN ALDA, "Dear Sigmund"

Teleplay by JAY FOLB; Story by GENE REYNOLDS and JAY FOLB, "Hawkeye Get Your Gun"

American Cinema Editors —Eddie Awards
STANFORD TISCHLER and SAMUEL E. BEETLEY, "Dear Sigmund"

1978.

Academy of Television Arts and Sciences—Emmy Awards
OUTSTANDING COMEDY SERIES
—Burt Metcalfe, Producer

OUTSTANDING LEAD ACTOR IN A COMEDY SERIES—Alan Alda

OUTSTANDING CONTINUING PERFORMANCE BY A SUPPORTING ACTOR IN A COMEDY SERIES—Gary Burghoff

OUTSTANDING CONTINUING PERFORMANCE BY A SUPPORTING ACTOR IN A COMEDY SERIES—Harry Morgan

OUTSTANDING CONTINUING PERFORMANCE BY A SUPPORTING ACTRESS IN A COMEDY SERIES—Loretta Swit

OUTSTANDING DIRECTING IN A COMEDY SERIES—Burt Metcalfe and Alan Alda, "Comrades in Arms—Part I"

OUTSTANDING WRITING IN A COMEDY SERIES —Alan Alda, "Fallen Idol"

OUTSTANDING FILM EDITING IN A COMEDY SERIES—Stanford Tischler and Larry L. Mills, "Fade Out—Fade In"

People's Choice Awards
- FAVORITE TELEVISION COMEDY PROGRAM
—M*A*S*H

FAVORITE MALE TELEVISION PERFORMER
—Alan Alda

Directors' Guild Awards
ALAN ALDA and BURT METCALFE,
"Comrades in Arms"

Writers' Guild Awards
Teleplay by JAMES FRITZELL and EVERETT
GREENBAUM, "Fade Out—Fade In"

American Cinema Editors
—Eddie Awards
- STANFORD TISCHLER and LARRY L. MILLS,
"Fade Out—Fade In"

1979

Academy of Television Arts and Sciences—Emmy Awards
OUTSTANDING COMEDY SERIES
—Burt Metcalfe, Executive Producer

OUTSTANDING LEAD ACTOR IN A COMEDY
SERIES—Alan Alda

OUTSTANDING SUPPORTING ACTOR IN A
COMEDY OR COMEDY-VARIETY OR MUSIC
SERIES—Gary Burghoff

OUTSTANDING SUPPORTING ACTOR IN A
COMEDY OR COMEDY-VARIETY OR MUSIC
SERIES—Harry Morgan

OUTSTANDING SUPPORTING ACTRESS IN A
COMEDY OR COMEDY-VARIETY OR MUSIC
SERIES—Loretta Swit

OUTSTANDING DIRECTING IN A COMEDY OR
COMEDY-VARIETY OR MUSIC SERIES
—Charles S. Dubin, "Point of View"

OUTSTANDING DIRECTING IN A COMEDY OR
COMEDY-VARIETY OR MUSIC SERIES
—Alan Alda, "Inga"

- OUTSTANDING WRITING IN A COMEDY OR
COMEDY-VARIETY OR MUSIC SERIES
—Alan Alda, "Inga"

OUTSTANDING WRITING IN A COMEDY OR
COMEDY-VARIETY OR MUSIC SERIES
—Ken Levine and David Isaacs, "Point of
View"

OUTSTANDING FILM EDITING FOR A SERIES
—Stanford Tischler and Larry L. Mills,
"The Billfold Syndrome"

People's Choice Awards
- FAVORITE TELEVISION COMEDY PROGRAM
—M*A*S*H
- FAVORITE MALE TELEVISION PERFORMER
—Alan Alda

Directors' Guild Awards
CHARLES S. DUBIN, "Point of View"

Writers' Guild Awards
- Teleplay by GARY DAVID GOLDBERG, "Baby,
It's Cold Outside"

Teleplay by KEN LEVINE and DAVID ISAACS,
"Point of View"

American Cinema Editors
—Eddie Awards
STANFORD TISCHLER and LARRY L. MILLS,
"The Billfold Syndrome"

1980

Academy of Television Arts and Sciences—Emmy Awards
OUTSTANDING COMEDY SERIES
—Burt Metcalfe, Executive Producer

OUTSTANDING LEAD ACTOR IN A COMEDY
SERIES—Alan Alda

- OUTSTANDING SUPPORTING ACTOR IN A
COMEDY OR VARIETY OR MUSIC SERIES
—Harry Morgan

OUTSTANDING SUPPORTING ACTOR IN A
COMEDY OR VARIETY OR MUSIC SERIES
—Mike Farrell

- OUTSTANDING SUPPORTING ACTRESS IN A
COMEDY OR VARIETY OR MUSIC SERIES
—Loretta Swit

OUTSTANDING DIRECTING IN A COMEDY
SERIES—Alan Alda, "Dreams"

OUTSTANDING DIRECTING IN A COMEDY
SERIES—Charles S. Dubin,
"Period of Adjustment"

OUTSTANDING DIRECTING IN A COMEDY
SERIES
—Burt Metcalfe, "Bottle Fatigue"

OUTSTANDING DIRECTING IN A COMEDY
SERIES
—Harry Morgan, "Stars and Stripe"

OUTSTANDING WRITING IN A COMEDY SERIES
—David Isaacs and Ken Levine, "Good-
bye Radar," Part 2

OUTSTANDING ACHIEVEMENT IN FILM
EDITING FOR A SERIES
—Larry L. Mills and Stanford Tischler,
"The Yalu Brick Road"

People's Choice Awards
- FAVORITE TELEVISION COMEDY PROGRAM
—M*A*S*H
- FAVORITE MALE TELEVISION PERFORMER
—Alan Alda
- FAVORITE ALL AROUND MALE ENTERTAINER
—Alan Alda

Hollywood Foreign Press Association—Golden Globe Awards
- BEST ACTOR IN A COMEDY OR MUSICAL
—Alan Alda

Directors' Guild Awards
- CHARLES S. DUBIN, "Period of Adjustment"

Writers' Guild Awards
- Teleplay by THAD MUMFORD and DAN
WILCOX, "Are You Now, Margaret"

Teleplay by JOHN RAPPAPORT and JIM
MULLIGAN, "Period of Adjustment"

Teleplay by MITCH MAROWITZ, "The Young
and the Restless"

Teleplay by KEN LEVINE and DAVID ISAACS,
"Good-bye Radar," Parts 1 and 2

American Cinema Editors
—Eddie Awards
- STANFORD TISCHLER and LARRY L. MILLS,
"The Yalu Brick Road"

1981—82

Academy of Television Arts and Sciences—Emmy Awards
OUTSTANDING COMEDY SERIES
—Burt Metcalfe, Producer

- OUTSTANDING LEAD ACTOR IN A COMEDY
SERIES—Alan Alda

- OUTSTANDING SUPPORTING ACTRESS IN A
COMEDY SERIES—Loretta Swit

OUTSTANDING SUPPORTING ACTOR IN A
COMEDY SERIES—Harry Morgan

OUTSTANDING SUPPORTING ACTOR IN A
COMEDY SERIES—David Ogden Stiers

OUTSTANDING DIRECTING IN A COMEDY
SERIES—Alan Alda,
"Where There's a Will, There's a War"

OUTSTANDING DIRECTING IN A COMEDY
SERIES
—Hy Averback, "Sons and Bowlers"

OUTSTANDING DIRECTING IN A COMEDY
SERIES
—Charles S. Dubin, "Pressure Points"

OUTSTANDING DIRECTING IN A COMEDY
SERIES
—Burt Metcalfe, "Picture This"

OUTSTANDING WRITING IN A COMEDY SERIES
—Alan Alda, "Follies of the Living—
Concerns of the Dead"

People's Choice Awards
- FAVORITE TELEVISION COMEDY PROGRAM
—M*A*S*H
- FAVORITE MALE TELEVISION PERFORMER
—Alan Alda

Hollywood Foreign Press Association—Golden Globe Awards
- BEST TELEVISION SERIES COMEDY OR
MUSICAL—M*A*S*H (1981)

Directors' Guild Awards
- ALAN ALDA, "The Life You Save"
HARRY MORGAN, "Blood Brothers"

Writers' Guild Awards
Teleplay by THAD MUMFORD and DAN
WILCOX, "A War for All Seasons"

Teleplay by JOHN RAPPAPORT, "No Sweat"

Teleplay by THAD MUMFORD and DAN
WILCOX, "Bless You, Hawkeye"

1982—83

Academy of Television Arts and Sciences—Emmy Awards
OUTSTANDING COMEDY SERIES
—Burt Metcalfe, Executive Producer

OUTSTANDING LEAD ACTOR IN A COMEDY
SERIES—Alan Alda

OUTSTANDING SUPPORTING ACTOR IN A
COMEDY, VARIETY, OR DRAMATIC SERIES
—Harry Morgan

OUTSTANDING SUPPORTING ACTRESS IN A
COMEDY, VARIETY, OR DRAMATIC SERIES
—Loretta Swit

OUTSTANDING DIRECTING IN A COMEDY
SERIES—Alan Alda

OUTSTANDING FILM EDITING FOR A COMEDY
SERIES—Stanford Tischler and Larry L. Mills

M*A*S*H* Products

ADI, Inc.
Book bags/pencil cases/soft lunch kits

ALLANDO ASSOCIATES
Knapsacks/pens/Radar's Teddy Bear/
jewelry/lighters/canvas chairs

AMERICAN POSTCARD COMPANY
Postcards/fans

AMAV INDUSTRIES LTD
Color-in activity sets (Canada)

AUSTRALIAN UNITED FOODS
Ice cream (Australia)

BACHMAN INDUSTRIES
H-O gauge train set

BENSONS TRADING CO. PTY LTD
Show bags/hats (Australia)

B & W CHARACTER
Hats/rainwear (Australia)

BEN COOPER
Costumes

BETTER T-SHIRT
T-shirts/clothing (Canada)

BIBB COMPANY
Sheets/pillowcases/curtains/bedspreads

BLM
Newsletter

BOBBS MERRILL
Softcover trade paperback scrapbook

BRADLEY TIME DIVISION
Children's and adults' watches

BUTTON UP COMPANY
Metal buttons

CADACO
Dart board game

CANNAY
Clothing (United Kingdom)

CHARLESTON HOSIERY
Children's hosiery

CRONER TRADING PTY LTD
Show bags/games (Australia)

D.D. BEAN
Hats/posters

D. DECKER
Play tents/playhouse/costumes/medical
kit (United Kingdom)

PAPERSELLERS LTD
Greeting cards/gift wrap/party items/
note pads (Canada)

DON RUSS
Bubble gum trading cards

EMPIRE OF CAROLINA
Ride-on toys

FLEXIPRINT
T-shirt transfers (Australia)

GEORGE FENMORE ASSOCIATES
M*A*S*H at the Smithsonian Souvenir
Program

GAME IMPORTS
Synthetic sports bags and backpacks

HARVESTON PTY
Vehicles/play sets (Australia)

HARRY N. ABRAMS, INC.
Hardcover book/calendar

IDEAS WORKSHOPS
Hats/dog tags/T-shirts/badges
(Australia)

IMPORTS, INC.
Key chains/buttons/umbrellas/patches/
hats/mugs

JA-RU, INC.
Rack toys

JONAL GARMENTS
Clothing (New Zealand)

KEDD ENTERPRISES, INC.
Buttons (Canada)

KELLWOOD (ALP)
Slumber and sleeping bags

KIDCO
Die-cast toy vehicles

LIBBEY GLASS DIVISION
Premium/promotional glassware

MIKO T-SHIRTS
T-shirts (Canada)

MILTON BRADLEY
Jigsaw puzzles/games

MUSEUM EDITIONS LTD.
Limited edition print

NOVEL GREETING CARDS
Greeting cards

OLD NEW ENGLAND MINT
Limited edition belt buckles

MICHAEL ALAN DESIGNS
Mass market posters/limited edition
posters/preframed posters

NEW AMERICAN LIBRARY
Official M*A*S*H Paperback Trivia
Book

PERFECTFIT
T-shirts/tops/Sloppy Joes (Australia)

PLYMOUTH, INC.
Back-to-school stationery products

QUINN, BREIN & MCCARTHY
Multi-city Touring Mall Show

ROACH
T-shirt transfers

ROMAN CERAMICS
M*A*S*H vodka/Scotch/gin/whiskey/
M*A*S*H beer

ROYAL ORLEANS
Collector plates/ceramic postcards/
M*A*S*H barware

**SALES CORPORATION OF
AMERICA**
Clothing/hats/T-shirts/tops/pants/
jackets

SAUGUS ENTERPRISES
M*A*S*H motor pool display

SEW HOY & SONS LTD
T-shirts/tops/ladies sleepwear

SHS INDUSTRIES
Ladies sleepwear (Australia)

SPORTS PROMOTION
Premium promotional poster

STOR & LITER ACTION TRADING
Bumper stickers/T-shirts/towels/
ceramic mugs (Sweden)

TERRIMONDO
Towels/bath sheets

TONKA TOYS
Large plastic Jeep

TRI-PLAS
Premium promotional plastic glassware

TRI-STAR INTERNATIONAL
Plastic vehicles/play sets/action
figures/canteens/flashlights/dog tags

VIEW-MASTER
View-Master reels

WATERBURY
Ladies nightwear

WORMSER
Boys pajamas

XEROX EDUCATIONAL
Poster magazine (in-school)

Reprinted 1987

ISBN 0 86287 080 1

Illustrations © 1984 Twentieth Century-Fox Film Corporation,
except pages 20, 24, 25, 239 (photographs by Dane A. Penland,
courtesy National Museum of American History, Smithsonian
Institution) and chapter-opening pages (photograph by Tom
Puzzutelli)

Published by Columbus Books Limited, 19-23 Ludgate Hill,
London EC4M 7PD, England. All rights reserved. No part of the
contents of this book may be reproduced without the written
permission of the publishers.

Printed and bound in Japan